Tiff *Gear*

Tiff *Gear*

The autobiography of Tiff Needell

Haynes Publishing

First published in April 2011

A catalogue record for this book is available from the British Library

ISBN 978 0 85733 089 5

Library of Congress catalog card no 2010939712

Published by Haynes Publishing,
Sparkford, Yeovil, Somerset BA22 7JJ, UK
Tel: 01963 442030 Fax: 01963 440001
Int. tel: +44 1963 442030 Int. fax: +44 1963 440001
E-mail: sales@haynes.co.uk
Website: www.haynes.co.uk

Haynes North America Inc.,
861 Lawrence Drive, Newbury Park, California 91320, USA

Printed in the USA by Odcombe Press LP,
1299 Bridgestone Parkway, La Vergne, TN 37086

Contents

DEDICATION

TO PATSY, whose enduring love and support helped me through all the ups and downs while I chased my dreams. Without her I would never have got where I am today nor become the father of our three lovely boys, Jack, Harry and George.

FOREWORD

BY JEREMY CLARKSON

WHEN TIFF called to ask if I'd write a foreword for his pamphlet, I was absolutely delighted. Because I thought he'd died in 1987.

Tiff began his racing career in Rome, challenging big names such as Ben Hur and Charlton Heston in front of a baying crowd of senators and emperors. Having excelled in the Colosseum, many were surprised to find he switched to boat racing and even more surprised when John Logie Baird invented the television and asked Tiff to be one of the first people to appear on it.

Eventually, Tiff was invited to appear on the BBC's motoring show called 'Top Gear' and, a month later, I could not believe it when the producers called me, wondering if I'd like to join him. What would the great man be like, I wondered. Would he be tall, short, angry, aloof? In fact he was drunk.

This is one of the least known things about Tiff. Yes, he can drive. When he's behind the wheel, it's poetry. But what he's best at, actually, is drinking. We have had many nights out over the last 20 or so years and he's always the first to climb on a table, and the last to go to bed.

It is incredible, then, that despite his great age, and his reckless lifestyle, Tiff still has the body, hair and face of a 14-year-old. Actually 'incredible' is the wrong word. I meant to say 'annoying'.

Tiff, though, is a great mate, and a good man, and his story is more than just the story of a two-bit racing driver who never quite made the grade. It's the story of someone we should all try to be like.

CHAPTER 1

THE GRAND PRIX CAREER

The two-minute board had been raised. The Team Ensign mechanics had started the engine and left me alone on the grid. I was about to become a bona fide Grand Prix driver and yet my mind felt blank. It was as if I wasn't really there – I mean, how could I be? Surely dreams never actually come true.

Only one thing came to my mind, the haunting bass line from Fleetwood Mac's 'The Chain', which had been adopted as the BBC's Grand Prix signature tune. Somehow I felt I must be watching this on the television but I wasn't, I was there on the grid at Zolder, ready for the start of the 1980 Belgian Grand Prix...

It was round five of the Formula One World Championship. The previous race had been at Long Beach on the west coast of the United States and I'd been at home in bed, listening to the commentary on the radio late in the evening, when Clay Regazzoni had had a massive accident in the single Ensign entry. It was obvious that he was seriously injured which, I am afraid, meant only one thing to me – there would be a drive going at the next race.

There were no such things as reserve drivers in those days and the race drivers did whatever testing was needed; teams being in a position to afford the luxury of being able to pay someone to do the donkeywork was still a fair way off. So, when seats became available for whatever reason, you either waited for the phone to ring or, if you were like me, you got out there and started knocking on doors.

For poor Regazzoni it was the end of his career. Braking hard at the end of the main straight, the brake pedal had broken and he'd plunged straight into an abandoned car and then the tyre wall. The impact folded the car around him and broke his back. Safety was another thing that was very different in those days.

It was a shattering blow for Team Ensign boss Mo Nunn who'd been struggling to run his single entry on the Grand Prix grids since 1973. A car dealer from the Walsall area of the Midlands, he'd been a successful driver himself before turning his hand to building his own single-seater racing cars. It had looked like 1980 was going to be his best year yet. He had headline sponsorship from the British Leyland parts subsidiary Unipart and former Ferrari and Williams Grand Prix winner Regazzoni as his driver. The team had picked up a few fifths and sixths in the past but the previous season had been a disaster, with the lone Ensign failing even to qualify for nine of the 15 Grands Prix, so it was vital that they bounced back with a successful season.

The Long Beach crash had hit the team hard. It wasn't like a driver leaving for another team – Clay had been hugely popular, but now they were forced to look for someone else. My problem was deciding how soon to make that call. Jumping in too early would be seen as insensitive, but leave it too late and you ran the risk of being thought not keen enough. Nowadays every young driver seems to have a manager to push their name forwards, but back then it was just me.

I decided not to ask Mo directly but approach Unipart instead. I'd raced for them in Formula Three so knew them quite well and they told me that I was already on the list. As so often in this sport, it was down to the usual 'don't call us, we'll call you' scenario. I'd spent the best part of the previous winter in just such limbo, on a very short list of two for a top Formula Two drive – and the decision hadn't gone in my favour. Every time you get so close to a major break and miss out it's a devastating experience, but you just have to pick yourself up and battle on.

With nothing to do other than wait for Unipart to call I took myself off to the third round of the European Formula Two Championship at the Nürburgring in Germany in my trusty – and slightly rusty – seven-year-old Ford Capri. There was still the chance of a drive going and it's always good to be seen; it would also help take my mind off *that* call. While I've always tried to look on the optimistic side of life, at the same time I've always tried to prepare myself for disappointment – and there's always plenty of it in motor racing – so I'd pretty much persuaded myself that it wasn't going to happen. And then it did. A Ford Capri has never travelled so quickly from the Nürburgring to Calais!

Mo Nunn was at his Chasetown factory near Walsall on the Sunday when I arrived for a seat fitting. I did my best not to be too demanding as I tried to fold myself into the tight confines of the aluminium monocoque chassis. Team morale was at a real low and I didn't want to add to their problems. At six foot one inch with size 11 feet I was always a bit on the tall side for a racing driver – I'd even had to cut the toes off my driving boots to squeeze them into the tight confines of some footwells. My knees would be jammed up under the dashboard and my elbows wedged down on to my rib cage, so every little inch of space that could be gained was invaluable.

Two days later and I was to get just half a day testing at Donington before the team would head to Belgium. This was the time of the very first 'ground-effect' Grand Prix cars, where the dark art of accelerating the airflow under the cars to create a negative pressure was still being unravelled – the 'effect' being that the cars were literally sucked into the ground. Added to the pressure from the wings, these cars had immense downforce, way more than anything I'd ever driven before, so I knew it was going to be a big step up – and with just one Formula Two race in Japan under my belt so far that year I'd actually had precious little time in any racing car at all.

After two years with the Unipart Formula Three team, the previous season had been one of bits and pieces. I'd got a scholarship to drive four races in the British F1 Championship – a series for year-old Grand Prix cars – and picked up a couple of one-off Formula Two drives, but the big push had been for the 1980 drive that I didn't get.

The test day came and went in a blur. It was an incredible experience, plunging down Donington's daunting Craner Curves at over 170mph, forcing myself simply to believe the grip would be there. I was worried by the way the steering got heavier and heavier as the speed increased – there was no power steering in those days. By the end of the day my neck muscles ached from the strain of coping with cornering loads they'd never handled before. Back then I used to run and play squash to keep generally fit, but there were few specialist trainers. The feeling was that the best way to get race fit was simply to drive the car, although I had adapted a rugby skullcap so that I could lie on my side on a table and do 'neck-ups' with a 5kg weight hanging off the side of the table. That probably did more harm than good!

I was on the verge of becoming a Grand Prix driver. The test seemed to have gone okay, but with just one car there was nothing with which to compare my times. The Ensign was far from the fastest car in the field – Regazzoni had been a lowly 23rd on the grid in Long Beach so my first challenge was just to qualify for the race. There were no guaranteed places on the grid, with 27 cars entered and only the fastest 24 getting a start.

At least I knew the Zolder track, having finished second there on my Formula One debut a year earlier in the British F1 Championship. I was also used to the power, because the Ensign used the same hugely popular three-litre Ford Cosworth DFV that powered no fewer than 21 of the Zolder entries. It was just the big step up in cornering speeds – and the pressure of being 'on trial' for a place at the very pinnacle of a sport I'd been obsessed with for as long as I could remember.

There were two one-hour qualifying sessions on Friday and Saturday afternoons, with both days having a 90-minute untimed practice session in the morning. It sounds like a lot of time but it seemed to fly by. Settle in... check the car... build up the pace... check the tyre temperatures and pressures... do a five-lap run... try different suspension settings... another five-lap run... try different wing settings... another five-lap run... chequered flag, the session's over.

Somehow, by the end of Friday's qualifying, I was provisionally 'on the grid'. I was 23rd fastest, the same as Clay in Long Beach, and one spot ahead of my schooldays' hero, Emerson Fittipaldi, who I'd out-qualified by over half a second. But would that be enough? There was still the Saturday session to come... and then Saturday dawned beautifully dark and rainy. Of course I felt I could go faster and move up a place or two, but on the other hand if it rained then Saturday's qualifying times would be much slower and I would be guaranteed a place in the race.

The team wouldn't even let me go out in the untimed session – they were worried their rookie might stick it in the fence – but, come the afternoon, with the track still wet and a place on the grid now guaranteed, some wet-weather running was obviously a good idea should race day dawn the same. With less grip but more 'feel' in the steering, the car became much more alive in my hands. While the ground effect tended to hold the car on one line, now I was much more able to get the car to do what I wanted. Yes, I had a couple of spins exploring the outer limits and the times wouldn't alter the grid, but by the end of that session I was 12th fastest on the day.

So the great day dawned and I took my place on the last row of the grid for the Belgian Grand Prix. Alongside me was double World Champion Emerson Fittipaldi, on the row in front future World Champion Keke Rosberg and just ahead of him future quadruple World Champion Alain Prost – so it was a pretty classy bottom six. John Watson, the only other British driver on the grid, was also there, in 20th spot, so there was the potential for plenty of patriotic coverage of the back of the field from the one and only Murray Walker.

The green flag waved and, with Fleetwood Mac still flowing through my mind, we set off in formation on the traditional weaving, tyre-warming lap. I wasn't too worried about the start itself as I was used to the DFV's characteristics. For me it remains the greatest Grand Prix engine ever created and it was a joy to drive. Although it was easy to stall at low revs, when it would cough and splutter, once you got over 7,000 revs, it came 'on cam' and the power would chime in, in one beautifully smooth surge, all the way to its 11,500rpm limit.

'Red light'… hold a steady 9,000 and ease the clutch up to its biting point. 'Green light'… slip the clutch ever so slightly before dumping it completely as you hammer the throttle to the floor… flick up through the five-speed gearbox with the tiny lever to the right of the steering wheel and plunge downhill towards the first corner. Nothing, but absolutely nothing, gives a bigger adrenaline rush than this – the opening corner of your first Grand Prix.

I stayed ahead of Emerson for four glorious laps before conceding the place. By lap 12 we were up to 18th and 19th, with Watson, having pitted, now behind me and four cars already on the retirement list. Unfortunately I was to be the next. Without warning the engine suddenly lost power exiting the chicane behind the pits and emitted the dreaded death rattle… there was nothing I could do other than switch everything off and coast to the side of the road.

It had been a weekend racked with emotion. Nine years after I'd had the incredible luck to win a racing car in a magazine competition I'd worked my way up to the peak of a huge mountain. What had started out as a schoolboy's fantasy had turned into reality: Tiff Needell was a Grand Prix driver. The problem was that I was only there on probation.

I'd spent the weekend no longer as a driver hanging around trying to hustle drives and bump into team managers who might champion my cause but as someone who was there because he'd earned his place the hard way. I had no management team, or even a manager, and no private backers to help open doors. It was the most satisfying moment of my career but all the time I knew it might not last. All I could do was make the most of my opportunity, but with Monte Carlo as the next Grand Prix that wasn't going to be the easiest of tasks, especially as the tight street circuit meant that only the fastest 20 cars in the field would be allowed to start the race.

I did get another day of testing with Ensign at the short Snetterton Circuit in Norfolk – supposedly to give me a bit more feel for the confines of Monaco – but the big problem remained that I was in a one-car team so there was no-one to be directly compared to, no rival to act as my barometer. It felt like we were making progress but we wouldn't know until we got there.

To drive the Monaco Grand Prix circuit in any car is an amazing experience, but to do it in a Formula One car is simply mind-blowing. You exit the first corner at Saint Devote with the cambered contour of the road daring your rear wheel to kiss the steel barriers before you flick past them and launch yourself uphill towards Casino Square. It feels like you're going for lift-off in a space shuttle. The road meanders slightly this way and that as it climbs the hill, but with a wall of Armco barrier on each side you can only see a hundred yards or so ahead – it looks like you are heading into a dead end, yet it's flat out all the way.

At the top there is a blind crest and in those days you needed to brake just before it or you would, quite literally, be cashing in your chips at the casino. You hug the inside round the long left that fires you straight into the Square. Directly in front of the entrance to the Hôtel de Paris you must flick the car to the right and fire it over another crest with an almost inevitable flash of opposite lock and another shave of the barriers before plunging sharply downhill.

The Station Hairpin demands first gear, and every little bit of lock a Formula One car has, just to get round. Then it's second… and third… and second… and out to the water's edge at Portier with another likely kiss of steel. Third, fourth, fifth… flat out through the right-handed curve in the street-lit tunnel.

It was the first time I'd ever really felt a car and my body leaving my brain behind. In the first practice session so much was going on in the short two-mile lap that I was still thinking about what had happened in the previous corner as I was arriving at the next. As the laps went by so my brain began gradually to catch up with my body. It was like having blurred vision that gradually came into focus.

By the end of that first untimed session – uniquely held on the Thursday in Monaco – I still wasn't quite there. To make matters worse it started to rain just as the first qualifying session was about to start in the afternoon. With 27 cars on track fighting for just 20 places the circuit had never been busier. Reigning World Champion Jody Scheckter had even led a protest on behalf of the more experienced drivers to have a pre-qualifying session for the lower half of the grid, but the French authorities would have none of it. Fortunately for me I'd had that wet-weather experience in Belgium, but Monaco leaves no margin at all for error and this wasn't a no-pressure test session; if conditions worsened for Saturday this would be the session that formed the grid.

But once again I found the conditions were actually in my favour. I hadn't been able to set a time in the morning that would have been good enough to qualify in that frantic blur of opening action, but now I was right on top of the car, the drop in speed bringing everything fully into focus. It was the greatest experience I'd had behind the wheel of any racing car. By the end of the session I was in – provisionally 19th on the grid for the Monte Carlo Grand Prix.

Friday was a day off, and it dragged by as if it were a week. I rain danced, thunder and lightning danced, and prayed to every cloud in the sky to make Saturday a washout. The only good thing about the wait was that it gave time for my right hand to begin to heal – with around 40 gear changes a lap I'd suffered the Monaco new boy's traditional embarrassment of blisters on my palm! And of course Saturday dawned bright and dry and, to make matters worse, in the morning session I walloped the massive kerb in the fast chicane that fired you back from the exit of the tunnel on to the harbour front. It was like a narrow gap in the central reservation of a motorway and you simply had to slot the car through at some 120mph with no room at all for any error – nowadays it's a stop-and-go chicane with a car park to escape into if you get it wrong.

Back in the pits I discovered I'd damaged the suspension pick-up point on the chassis so I would have to switch to the spare car, which hadn't been run all weekend and had a completely different set-up. With brand-new brakes all round I had to bed them in first – a process which in those days meant gradually building up the heat over a series of laps, then getting them hotter than they would ever get in the race and then cooling them back down for a couple of laps. Well, of course I rushed the job and tried to go too fast too soon and ended up down the escape road at Saint Devote. The one-hour session that would form the grid was rapidly passing by and I'd yet to set a representative time…

Back to the pits for my final set of new tyres – which would be at their best for just three or four laps – and the pressure was on. Clear laps round Monaco were at a premium. Well aware that if I held up the likes of Scheckter I'd be in for a new boy's ear bashing, I had to worry not only about the track ahead but also the cars behind.

After one-and-a-half laps bringing the tyres up to temperature I had no-one in sight until I came across a cruising Carlos Reutemann in the middle of the swimming-pool complex, towards the end of the lap. With nine Grand Prix wins already to his name the Argentine racer was in his first year with Williams and one of the favourites for the title that year. He was a man to be respected.

I moved to go past – and he moved to block me! Okay, he was going for it on the next lap, so I'd go with him. By the time we got back to the swimming pool he was well ahead but my lap had still been a good one… until dear Carlos suddenly slowed around the swimming pool and blocked my path once more. Another lap… and he did it again! I learned later that Carlos didn't like 'so-so' laps on his time sheets as he always sought perfection, but right now his little game was destroying my own chances of simply making the race. What was a complete no-no for the novices was obviously fair game for the big boys.

On the fourth lap we once again got a clear run and this time as I entered the swimming-pool section Carlos was nowhere to be seen, but as *he* headed for a time that would put him on the outside of the front row and lead to his first win for Williams, *I* headed backwards into the Armco barrier. With the tyres now past their best and me probably over driving to compensate, I'd spun the bloody thing at the end of the swimming pool. What niggles me most nowadays is that that is another of the areas which is now an acre of open tarmac with some bits of kerb stuck in the middle to 'suggest' where the cars should go: make a mistake there now and there's no penalty.

As it was, I headed back to the pits with the wing hanging off the back and that was it. I hadn't even done one representative lap time and I languished in 26th spot, 1.5 seconds short of qualifying. John Watson failed to qualify as well, so there were no British drivers on the grid for the 1980 Monaco Grand Prix – and I would never have the chance again.

CHAPTER 2

THE BEGINNING

'It's Thursday night. It's "Top of the Pops" ' – the 'must-see' viewing for an audience that would reach 15 million in its heyday – but mainly watched by me for the weekly gyrations of its Pan's People dancers. However, tonight was different. Olivia Newton-John was singing 'If Not For You' in her seductive one-piece velvet cat suit – and I liked Olivia Newton-John... a lot!

Then the phone rang. It was Thursday! Who would call at such a time? I was alone in the room and the only telephone in the house was on the table behind me, attached to the wall, as they all used to be in those days. Reluctantly I dragged myself out of the armchair while keeping my eyes firmly on the television.

'Hello?'

'Is that Tiff Needell?'

'Yes.'

'Well, I'm Simon Taylor, the editor of *Autosport* magazine, and you're a very lucky young man. You've won the—'

The voice continued to talk into my ear, Olivia Newton-John was still singing 'If Not For You', but my mind had gone blank. The competition... the *Autosport* competition that I'd entered three months earlier... the competition to win a Lotus 69F Formula Ford... to win a racing car that was so beyond my reach that it was like winning the football pools. I think I said some words. I remember mentions of a 'presentation' and 'photos', but little was sinking in. I'd won it. I'd actually won it! I'd won the only thing I wanted in life. I was going to have the chance to do something I'd dreamed of for as long as I could remember. I was going to get that chance in a million to be a racing driver.

I'd spent years clinging to the fences of Goodwood, Brands Hatch and Silverstone, watching my heroes flash past. I'd covered my bedroom walls with their photos, and while my friends went from pop stars to pin-ups mine remained firmly reserved for racing cars.

Formula Ford was the new training ground for aspiring young Grand Prix stars, a budget formula that fed into the established path from Formula Three to Formula Two and then, for the very few, the ultimate of Formula One. This was an era when karting was thought of more as a bit of fun than a serious motorsport training ground.

As a 15 year old I'd been at Brands Hatch, clinging to the fence at Druids Corner for the very first Formula Ford race on 2 July 1967, and I'd seen my dream take a real shape. This was to be my way in – if only I could find the money. Formula Ford began with a £1,000 price tag – which you can multiply by 25 to put it into modern money – so it wasn't cheap, but it made for a very level playing field and the cars were easy to maintain and run.

The winner of that first race was Ray Allen, driving a car run by the Brands Hatch-based racing drivers' school, Motor Racing Stables. So having saved up some money cleaning cars, mowing lawns, caddying at the St George's Hill Golf Club and being a Christmas postman, the first thing I did when I left school in the summer of 1969 was to borrow Mum's Morris 1000 and head straight there. Earlier that year I'd entered an *Autosport* competition to win a Lotus 61 Formula Ford, but that would be too much of a dream come true, wouldn't it? No, I'd have to do it the hard way, show the racing school how brilliant I was, and surely they'd find me a car to race.

That 'Initial Trial' at Brands consisted of an evaluation in a Ford Cortina 1600E with an instructor sitting alongside and then five laps in one of the school's ageing Lotus 51 Formula Fords. Back then the Cortina was one of the hottest saloons of its day – and certainly a big step up from a Morris 1000. I'd never even seen a rev counter before and constantly exceeded the limit I'd been set, but little did I care. I was actually driving round Brands Hatch and, despite having watched from almost every vantage point, it seemed very different from behind the wheel with the rise and fall of the circuit limiting the view.

With the importance of the 'rev limit' drilled into my brain, I was now allowed to head for the garage of the Formula Fords. With no engine rev limiters the only way the school could control the pupils was by setting strict limits. The chief instructor was the wonderful Tony Lanfranchi, who used his broad northern accent to impress just how easily he could 'hear' if we were breaking the rules – and a 'telltale' marker on the rev counter was there to prove if he was right or wrong when we finished.

Beginners would start on 4,500rpm and could then progress through the school in 500-rev steps to the 6,000 maximum… but none of this was really going through my mind as I sank myself into a single-seater racing car for the first time. No seat belts, no seat adjustment, a cushion if required, but at just over six feet I slid into the fibreglass seat as if it were made for me. The euphoria of the moment is hard to describe. Nervous… apprehensive… terrified of stalling it and making a fool of myself. The pedals were so close together I could hit them all at once; the gear lever was just a little stick to the right of the steering wheel, but the view ahead was mesmerising. I could almost reach out and touch the front wheels.

I was wearing my own open-face motorcycle helmet with a pair of goggles and my head was sitting well above the little Perspex wrap-around windscreen. No gloves, no overalls, just a T-shirt, sweater and jeans – simple days! The laps rushed by with my emotions leaping from carefree exhilaration to a self-conscious paranoia that all eyes were upon me – especially Tony Lanfranchi's. As I peeled into the pit lane a smile broke out on my face that would be there for weeks. Just how good was that? The instant response of the steering, the front wheels bobbing up and down in front of me, the rush of adrenaline surging through my veins. If I'd wanted to be a racing driver before, I was now completely addicted to the idea. I'd had my first fix of the most intoxicating drug and I was hooked.

Of course the instructors saw 'a great deal of promise' and encouraged me to return as often as I could – but the £10 for every ten laps wasn't an easy thing to earn and awaiting my arrival that September was the City University in London and a five-year sandwich degree course in Civil Engineering – the back-up plan that to everyone except me was the path that my life was surely bound to follow.

I'd been fortunate to gain sponsorship from George Wimpey & Co. Ltd who would pay me for work experience in the summer months while the winter was spent commuting from the family flat in Weybridge to university with a full grant to spend – thanks, or no thanks, to a means test that recognised my lovely father's complete lack of ability to earn the fortune that my own ambitions so desperately needed. With my season ticket from Weybridge to the Angel Islington paid for, the sacrifices began. Sadly, the debauched life of the typical university student was not to be for me. I was hooked on an expensive drug and I needed regular fixes. There was no spare money at home but there was plenty of food so I would go for weeks without even eating lunch, occasionally rewarding myself with a Mars Bar at Waterloo station on my way home.

By now Mum's Morris 1000 was going through rear tyres at a rather frightening rate as I demonstrated my driving prowess to my friends. I was actually stopped by the police on one wet day to be asked if I 'normally drove round roundabouts sideways'. The trademark style for which I would become famous had already emerged. I'm not quite sure how either the Morris 1000 or I survived those early days, but I guess the great thing was that while it handled brilliantly in terms of balance and style it ran out of grip at very low speeds, so impacts with the scenery were fairly soft.

In my last term at school I was caught out by a massive downpour while hurtling some poor girl home down a fancy private road. Floating on water, I was never going to make the next bend – and the front garden I was heading for was protected by neatly spaced rocks. With not enough room to get between them, I just about managed to make sure I only hit one of them, smashing over it like a vaulting gymnast before executing a neat handbrake turn on the front lawn and escaping via the driveway. A kiss and a cuddle were definitely out of the question – and it was probably for the best as I swiftly headed home to check damage that included a leaking sump and a hole punched in the floor in front of the rear seats. Mum wasn't going to be happy. With a drip tray installed under the engine and chewing gum stemming the flow I went to bed working on a plan.

With my A-level exams over I was home from my Ottershaw boarding school for the weekend, but luckily the school and its workshop weren't far away. The temporary fix with the chewing gum had kept most of the oil in the sump but welding equipment was needed. The sump wasn't too much of a problem, but the bulging hole behind the driver's seat would take a bit of explaining. After much hammering, swearing and welding the job was finished, and the only time my indiscretion was nearly discovered was when Mum was cleaning out the car and couldn't seem to remember the rear carpets being glued to the floor...

My first summer job was as a site engineer on a housing estate in Witham, Essex. As the engineer in charge of laying out all the roads, sewers and foundations it was quite a responsible job for a daydreaming 18 year old, but it was one I thoroughly enjoyed – even if, to me at least, it was only a means to an end.

Having progressed through the Brands Hatch school to the 6,000-rev class, I was now eligible to enter their school races. These were very amateur events, with just four cars on the grid contesting four heats and a final, yet they were sponsored by the *Daily Mail* as their 'Stars of Tomorrow Championship' so there was publicity to be gained.

All I had to do now was save the money to do those races and, looking back on how I survived the summer of 1970, my budget sounds like something out of a 'Monty Python' sketch. They ran one race a month and the entry fee was £30, but my monthly take-home pay as a trainee civil engineer was only £45. Having found a room to rent for £10 a month this meant that I had just £5 left to live on... for a whole month. With no car, I would hitchhike back down the A12 to London and then get the train home – hopefully without being asked if I had a ticket. Home brought the comfort of clean clothes and free food plus the use of the Morris 1000 to get to Brands for the races.

The virtual disappearance of hitchhiking as a form of free travel in our modern trustless world is a great loss to so many young people and a sad reflection on how society has changed from the post-war 'help your neighbour' feeling to the modern 'aggressive' society that sometimes makes the weak prisoners in their own homes. Such is progress.

Up against seasoned school racers I managed to clock up four heat wins and a couple of seconds in the finals to finish fourth in the championship, but the quote in the *Daily Mail* that I was 'regarded by the instructors at Motor Racing Stables as a very bright hope for the future' was all that I needed. Surely now I could bump into that millionaire – or preferably millionairess – who would be so impressed they would have to sponsor me?

Another long winter of structural engineering, fluid mechanics and geology at university slowly passed by. More saving, more sacrifices, no millionaires and another year of school races seemed the only option – but then Olivia Newton-John sang 'If Not For You'...

When my Mum came into the room to enquire who had called she must have thought I looked ill.

'Are you in trouble? Was that the police?' A certain amount of communication with officers of the law wishing to debate some of my early driving experiences had convinced her that I would be arrested any day. She'd lived through it all before with my Dad, who once paid a speeding fine with a bag full of farthings.

Woken from my trance I managed to start talking in a quiet monotone. 'I've won that *Autosport* competition. I've won a Formula Ford Lotus 69F.' I think I said it several times, somehow trying to convince myself that it actually was true. Mum's Mum – whose house we now lived in – was quickly on the case.

'Is it a competition where you can take the money or the prize?'

It was a common thing in competitions back then to offer a lump sum of cash instead of the headline award, and Nana obviously thought that that would be a better option – there wasn't, and of course it wouldn't have been.

By now I was warming to the reality of it all. I had won it, I really had. Friends had to be called, the Flint Gate pub had to be visited... several pints later it was pointed out to me that the date that this result was to be announced would be 1 April. Was I really sure that it had been the real Simon Taylor? Despite the hangover I couldn't get on the phone quick enough the following day.

'I'm sorry, Mr Taylor, but I didn't quite take in all you were saying yesterday and I would be most grateful if you could just run it by me one more time.'

The only photograph I could send him was a classic photo-booth passport snap – and when he talked of presenting me with the car and its trailer in a week's time the reality of the practicalities involved began to dawn on me. For starters, to tow a trailer you need a car – and a car with a tow bar.

By now I did have my first car: a Morris 1000 Traveller. I'd bought the estate version because my big brother had had one and, as he was a bit of a hero brother, what was right for him was right for me. Unfortunately I didn't have his engineering know-how and I'd bought mine on a whim, in the dark, for an extortionate £75 and woken up the next day to discover I'd splashed out on a rust bucket with mouldy woodwork. There was no way I could attach a tow bar to it in a week, but fortunately brother Michael, who was living in London, had a car which boasted one, so the grand presentation at a Lotus dealer in London was fixed for the following week.

Next problem… where was I going to put it? We might have moved from a rented flat to my grandmother's three-storey semi in Weybridge but we still didn't have a garage. More phoning of friends finally found one as a temporary loan, but I was fast waking up to the fact that life was about to get very complicated.

For the moment, though, I was simply floating on a cloud. The car was more beautiful than I could ever have imagined. Bearing *Autosport*'s red and white colours with supporting sponsors' logos all hand painted in white it could have been a Grand Prix Ferrari it looked so good. As Michael headed for Weybridge I simply couldn't stop looking behind at *my* Lotus 69F bouncing along behind us on the trailer.

Michael had left school at the age of 16 and headed to Derby for a mechanical apprenticeship with Rolls-Royce. Anything that went wrong he could take apart and fix, whereas I was brilliant at pulling things apart – and then phoning for help! Of course now, with no money to hire anyone, I had to become an overnight racing mechanic.

Ironically, I had actually won the competition by appearing to have a great deal of mechanical sympathy. It was the type of competition that was very popular at that time. Ten items would be listed relating to the prize and what you had to do was put them in order of importance – none of this picking the obvious answer from three choices and simply dialling a number. For the Lotus, the items were all about preparing a car for a race. You could do as many entries as you wanted at two shillings per go – decimalisation wasn't due for another month yet – and I had poured over the options for hours. Was 'suitability and degree of wear of tyres for conditions' more important than 'suspension statically set correctly'? In the end I invested in 40 different combinations for the grand total of £4 – a £50 gamble in modern money – but then there was the dreaded slogan that would act as a tie-breaker: 'State in not more than 15 words why you think motor racing is a worthwhile sport.'

More hours and more screwed-up pieces of paper had headed for the basket before I settled on words that, in the end, would make all the difference. Presented with the same ten items the judging panel, consisting of three professionals from the world of motorsport, had come up with the same combination as one of my lines – but so had a certain Ian Moore from Trowbridge...

The Lotus went to the best slogan, and because of it I was actually about to find out whether, as I'd suggested, 'the close competition, the intense concentration, the satisfaction of success, this makes motor racing worthwhile' was true or not.

CHAPTER 3

THE CHILD OF THE FIFTIES

Timothy Richard Needell arrived in this world at 12.30am on 29 October 1951 at the Emsworth Nursing Home near Havant in Hampshire, now the site of a large housing estate – as are all three of the schools I would eventually attend. When my three-year-old brother Michael could only manage to utter something along the lines of 'Timffamamy' the Tiff tag was there to stay. All right, I'll admit it now: it actually started out as 'Tiffy', but when I headed off to boarding school at the age of 12 I decided it might be a good time to drop the 'y'.

I was almost born with a silver spoon in my mouth as my father's full name was Anthony Fairey Needell, a name that might bring many a chuckle in a modern-day school, but it was one that actually reflected a proud heritage as he was the nephew of Sir Richard Fairey. Sir Richard was a self-made man who'd founded his own aircraft factory that would produce models like the Fairey Swordfish, which played a crucial part in the sinking of the *Bismarck*, and the Fairey Delta, which claimed the world air speed record for Britain. However, none of the Fairey wealth would ever be transferred to his sister Anne who'd married Philip Needell, a bank clerk with a passion for painting. He'd served in the navy during the First World War – during which his only son was born – returned to banking and then taken early retirement to eke out a living as a roaming artist rather than an entrepreneurial millionaire.

Young Anthony – better known as Tony – did, however, develop his uncle's quest for speed and engineering, not with planes but with boats. Having qualified as a naval architect, he became part of the design team at Fairmile Marine while living in Weybridge, Surrey, within earshot of the Brooklands racetrack. Throughout the 1930s he would marvel at the great heroes of the sport wrestling their mighty machines round the banked circuit and dream of joining them – but the best he could afford was competing in the occasional auto-test in his mother's little Fiat.

The Second World War called a halt to racing at Brooklands and turned the track into an aircraft factory, while Tony turned his hand to designing fast motor launches and torpedo boats for Fairmile – and guarding the Weybridge Post Office as part of his Home Guard duties, frustrated at not being allowed to join the war as his job was deemed to be a 'Reserved Occupation'. Fourteen of those motor launches would be used to carry commandos on the famous World War II St Nazaire raid which was brilliantly re-created in a BBC documentary by some bloke called Jeremy Clarkson – not that I've ever forgiven him for describing my Dad's boats as 'useless'! Indeed they were far from useless to the likes of my Dad and his young team labouring over the design details back home as, without ever being questioned, they managed to include a little tap in the fuel line of the boats which served absolutely no real purpose at all – except to siphon off the odd gallon or two of the strictly rationed petrol for 'personal' use.

After the war, with the Brooklands racetrack closed for ever, Dad turned to the newly opened Goodwood Circuit to get his speed thrills, entering the first Members' Meeting there in 1949 driving a Ford V8 Coupé in a handicap event. But, in very dangerous times, he gave up the sport because he and his young wife Diana had started a family of their own when their first son Michael was born in November 1948.

But Dad still had a great passion for the sport so, almost as soon as I could walk, I found myself being whisked off to Goodwood to spectate. Early memories are still dominated by those heady days. How well I remember the first time I crawled up the huge grass bank on the exit of the chicane to be completely smitten by the sight, sound and smell of the monstrous beasts roaring past with their heroic pilots struggling to keep them under control. From that moment on all I ever wanted to be was a racing driver.

By now Dad had set himself up as a freelance naval architect designing pleasure boats and undertaking work for a variety of boatyards, some of which, for no reason that I know, were in Holland. But, wherever they were, we never really saw much of him as he began working seven days a week, a commitment which lasted all his life. He really loved his job but seemed to have little idea of how to make any real money. He'd rented Flat 5, Oatlands Mere for his young family in part of a huge old mansion in Oatlands Village, half-way between Walton-on-Thames and Weybridge in Surrey. Set in acres of land, with a lake at the bottom of a huge hill, it was a brilliant place to grow up – but perhaps not as financially rewarding as if Dad had taken out a mortgage to buy a little bit of Weybridge for himself. He didn't want to be tied down by things like mortgages – and of course he wasn't to know that Weybridge would soon turn into the most valuable property market outside London – so there we stayed, paying rent for the best part of 20 years (whenever Dad could afford it) while houses shot up all around us and their value rocketed. Of course, whenever I say I grew up in Weybridge everyone immediately thinks I come from a rich family, but they couldn't be further from the truth.

The years have flown by, but I still find it hard to believe the world that I grew up in. Part of the post-war 'Baby Boomer' generation, I was born into a country that – for the first two months of my life, at least – had a king ruling it and food rationing that would last a good two years more. I can even remember milk being delivered by a horse-drawn float!

More 'Monty Python' rings in my brain – 'we were poor but we were happy' – and somehow that is how I remember it. For much of the time we had no television, no washing machine and certainly no central heating – indeed precious few of the items we now seem to regard as basic necessities. At times we didn't even have a car. A coal fire kept the living room warm and an electric bar heated the kitchen, while bedroom warmth was simply governed by an extra blanket or two or three – and a hot water bottle, of course. I seem to remember that we had snow most winters and the lake would sometimes freeze over to offer a perfect playground. Even the River Thames froze in 1963 and the 'best' climate scientists of the day were warning us of the impending doom of another ice age. Now, of course, the self-proclaimed 'best' climate scientists of the day warn us of meltdown, so it's understandable why I'm a bit sceptical about all this man-made doom and gloom. If you ask me, Mother Nature is one step ahead of us and always will be.

Mum worked as a needlework teacher in a Catholic finishing school in Oatlands Village – yes, it's a housing estate now! The students were all from overseas and had to speak English all the time and got very confused by Mrs Needell teaching needlework. She would spend most of her earnings putting Michael and me through private education in the hope that we'd pass the 11-plus and get grammar school places. Dad would occasionally be on a good fee, but then one of the Dutch boatyards would go bankrupt, owing him a sizeable sum of money.

About the same time a concrete mixer ran into his ageing Lancia and he simply didn't have the money to fix it – and he would never own another car. When needs must he would rent cars to use on jobs, but it was left to Mum to provide any family transport and we began a succession of 1930s Austin Sevens which could be picked up for the grand sum of £10 and 'disposed of' when they broke down. Motoring was still a great adventure in those days, and on those very special trips to Goodwood we would have to stop at the garage at the foot of the South Downs and top up with water just to make sure we got over them. Eventually we moved up to an Austin A35 and then the dark green, four-door Morris 1000 that would be my first drive.

The Roberts family lived in Flat 3 and their second son, Patrick, was born a couple of months before me. From the moment our prams were parked side by side we started throwing toys at each other and have been firm friends ever since. If we weren't playing soldiers in the woods, we were swapping shilling war comics or reading *Lion*, *Tiger* and *Eagle*. When it rained we would play board games for hours on end – Monopoly, Careers, Cluedo, Risk – and then, of course, there was Scalextric. It was the most exciting Christmas ever when we unwrapped this huge box to discover that original set with the metal cars – a Ferrari and a Maserati. When the 'new' Scalextric was launched Michael had the Aston Martin and I had the Lister Jaguar, and our track layout gradually grew in size. The flat might have been cold, but it had big rooms with tall ceilings and Dad had picked up an old, full-sized snooker table with no cloth but a good slate – the perfect platform.

Patrick and I were both Cubs and Boy Scouts and enjoyed great adventures at summer camps anywhere from the New Forest to the Brecon Beacons. I always remember how important our uniform was in those days, ironing the scarf and rolling it perfectly to make the pattern match. We took pride in our appearance. I think it's an indictment of today's society that such disciplines seem to have been dropped – all part of the dreaded modern curse of 'dumbing down' to supposedly attract a wider audience.

The big event was the family summer holiday where, for the best part of ten years, we headed for exactly the same seaside bungalow at East Wittering on the South Coast of England. A trip to the Costa this or Costa that on the Spanish Mediterranean was like the idea of a modern-day family having a holiday in the Maldives – something reserved for the very rich. Apart from the odd day here or there Dad, of course, was always too busy to come, but we were joined by our two cousins Penny and Paul, Auntie Pops and grandparents Nana and Pa – eight of us, with all the luggage needed for two weeks crammed into two small cars for the great trek over the South Downs.

The destination was 'Halcyon', right on the sea front with just a footpath between the front garden and the beach: a bungalow built like a child's dream from two railway carriages! In those days old or surplus railway carriages were often sold off cheaply to ordinary folk and turned into instant accommodation. Many such cottages were built, and a few still survive to this day. Some were just a single carriage set parallel to the beach but others, like ours, consisted of two carriages set 20 feet apart with a roof covering both to create a large room in the middle, a kitchen at the back and a conservatory in the front. From the inside you would get into your bedroom by opening a real train door and, for the kids, there would be bunk beds on either side, just like the real thing. The windows were pulled up on their leather straps and the bathroom had the original frosted glass windows with 'Toilet' etched into it. Brilliant!

Whatever the weather we'd swim every day, sometimes with great rolling waves to dive through or to surf on with our little plywood boards. There was miles of sand to play on and to make huge castles to be defended from the incoming tide. Pa would check the papers for the daily sailings from Portsmouth and we would watch the great liners depart from the Solent, out past the Isle of Wight and over the horizon to far-flung places, taking it in turns to peer through the telescope. We could want for nothing more. In the evenings we would all sit around the big dining table in the central room and play marathon sessions of the card game 'Canasta' or engage in rowdy shouting matches with 'Contraband' and 'Pit' which would usually end in tears – and of course there was no television.

Sadly the original 'Halcyon' is no more, but the name remains on a completely new bungalow built on the same site. Even now I would happily go back if it wasn't for our unreliable weather and the chilly sea – we didn't see those as 'hardships' at the time, of course, because we knew nothing else.

As we entered the swinging sixties the Needell family began to venture further afield, even if initially we only went as far as the Isle of Wight. Dad had got himself involved in powerboat racing. Starting as an entrant – having designed a small runabout and found a customer who wanted to race it – he soon moved on to become a race organiser in charge of scrutineering the boats and writing new rules as the sport expanded. Of course, being my Dad, all of this was unpaid and gradually took up more and more of his time, but at least it became a family affair with Mum taking on lap scoring and timing duties and me becoming a fan of a new form of petrol-powered sport. The London Motor Boat Racing Club ran meetings on a large gravel pit near Iver Heath in Buckinghamshire where we became regular visitors. (It is now just a small pond beside the M25!) Occasionally we would head to Chasewater near Birmingham or the Cotswold Club near Fairford, but bigger things were on the horizon.

Sir Max Aitken, owner of the *Daily Express*, was a keen sailor and, having visited Miami and caught sight of the Miami–Nassau powerboat race, he was determined to bring a similar spectacle to European waters. With a house in Cowes on the Isle of Wight – the traditional home of sailing – his starting point was obvious and he selected Torquay for the finishing line as he set about creating his race. There had been no real offshore powerboat racing in Europe since the early '30s so, when Aitken began organising his dream, he was pointed in the direction of Tony Needell to write the rule book for him. As Dad's inshore racing had begun with production-based boats, so did his plan for this inaugural offshore race. He wanted genuine manufacturers to prove themselves against each other – and that included running the boats with a working toilet and a full complement of knives, forks and plates.

So nine-year-old Tiffy headed 'overseas' for the first time – well, a Red Funnel ferry across the Solent to Cowes, at least – and began to mix with the rich and famous contesting the first Cowes to Torquay powerboat race in August 1961. A total of 27 boats took the start and, after a gruelling 7 hours and 17 minutes of rough seas in a force 5 wind, racing driver Tommy Sopwith crossed the finish line to win, having averaged just 21.4 knots.

That first year Mum and I tried to beat the racers to Torquay in the Morris 1000 – taking the ferry after they'd started – but we arrived just after the first three finishers. Next year, though, I was old enough to join the rest of the organisers on a Royal Navy destroyer that shadowed the race. Then, on two momentous occasions, I had the privilege of joining Dad on the open bridge of HMS *Brave Borderer* – a motor torpedo boat that started the race and followed the leaders all the way. Apart from not getting in the way, my only 'health and safety' briefing consisted of the simple advice to duck when the Captain ducked – or expect a face full of the English Channel.

By 1968 the boats were getting to Torquay so quickly that they made them race back to Cowes as well, so my great adventures with the Royal Navy came to an end. By now, though, offshore racing was spreading to more glamorous locations – and so were the Needell family's travel plans.

As races cropped up all over Europe so did the demand for Dad's services as a rule maker and scrutineer. By now he was on all sorts of committees – eventually becoming vice-president of the Union Internationale Motonautique – and spending more and more of his time fighting battles with anyone who didn't agree with his vision of the sport's future. Initially, dates always seemed to clash with school attendance and all I would get would be postcards from far-flung destinations like Spain, Italy and Cyprus, places that to me were only names in geography classes. But finally my big opportunity came, in the summer of 1968: a trip to the South of France! Unfortunately the mode of travel wasn't to be quite as glamorous as the destination.

Dad had been loaned a Ford Thames Dormobile camper van – not so much to sleep in, but to act as a sort of mobile race control at British events – and it was decided that this was to be our ticket to the Med. Part of the reason was that the Needell family had now grown by one, with the surprise arrival of Christopher in the summer of 1967 – nine months after my parents had taken a trip to Paris for the Six Hour race on the Seine and spent a relaxing evening out on the town...

By now Dad was 51 and Mum 44 so a third child hadn't exactly been something they were planning on having, but in more ways than the obvious it gave the whole family a new lease of life. Michael had already flown the nest and, with Dad always so busy, I became big brother and all-round helper – especially when the beautiful new arrival developed colic. If you've never witnessed a baby suffering from this ailment then I'll try and paint the picture. Sweet gorgeous little thing sleeping peacefully suddenly screws up face, raises fists and feet skywards and begins to scream – and scream and scream. Bouts can last for 30 minutes or more and no amount of kindness can interrupt it. If Christopher had been Mum's first child she would never have had another! It's sometimes known as three-month colic, but he was over a year old as we boarded the Dormobile for the long trek south and he was still suffering, so we knew it was going to be a long trip.

Michael did most of the driving, with Dad adding plenty of advice when he felt it necessary, and of course it took us longer than expected

– so long that the last few hours over the foothills of the Alps, en route for the seaside town of Bandol, are forever etched in my memory. Driving into the dark, a massive storm descended on us, with horizontal rain lashing at the almost vertical windscreen... a screen that was wiped by a bizarre vacuum-powered system, a system that sees the blades almost crawl to a stop under full power and then flap madly on deceleration. Michael needed full power to get up the hills, but then Dad started telling him to slow down because he couldn't see – and then Christopher's little face screwed into a ball...

For what seemed like an eternity, everyone was screaming at everyone else. Mum ended up lying on the floor with Christopher, doing her best to appease the unappeasable, and Michael was doing something similar with Dad debating the speed of our progress and the almost complete lack of forward vision. How we ever made it I'll never know, but when we returned the following year we did so in the Morris 1000, with me as one of the drivers – and without either Mum or Christopher.

Mind you, the dramas weren't over that first time as, awaking to my first sight of the exotic waters of the Mediterranean, I ran headlong across the beach at full speed and plunged into the enticing blue water – and a seabed covered in sea urchins. With spines in my feet, knees and elbows it wasn't quite the paradise I'd been expecting. Day one was spent at the doctor's for painful spine extraction. I'd never even heard of these nasty little creatures whose prickly spikes embed into your body and then snap off – bits were still coming out two years later!

The return to Bandol was part of my very own 'summer of '69'. Quite why Bryan Adams decided to remind me of some of the 'best days of my life' with his epic song I don't know – after all he was only nine at the time – but it always brings back great memories for me. Of course I didn't actually get 'my first real six-string' but I'd left school, had my first proper drive in a racing car, hit the Mediterranean for the first time, seen the Rolling Stones in Hyde Park and stood about three feet from Paul Kossoff as Free blasted out 'All Right Now'. After years of compulsory 'short, back and sides' my hair now sat on my shoulders and the best band in the world were The Doors... 'that summer seemed to last forever'!

After spending our formative years at Staplands Primary School and Wallop Preparatory School (thanks to Mum's sacrifices), neither Michael nor I ever got to the grammar school she had hoped for, not because we failed the 11-plus but because we passed interviews to an experimental new concept in state education: a state-financed boarding school run like a public school.

Ottershaw School near Woking was opened in 1948 and was originally intended for sons of the armed forces who were stationed abroad. Later, to widen the cross-section of pupils, they began to offer places to families whose fathers worked overseas – and so the door opened for the Needell boys. Fees were set on a means basis which, once again due to my father's brilliant talent at avoiding anything that actually made a profit, meant we had what amounted to a public school education for free.

Despite the fact that it was 1964 when I packed my trunk and headed to Ottershaw, the 'free love' spirit of the swinging sixties had yet to filter its way through the system and it was a strict regime that welcomed me to my new school. 'Leave Outs' to go home were rationed to just four per term – and even then they were restricted to daytime release on Sundays only. Uniform was strict, discipline was strong and punishment for any minor in-house misdemeanours entailed being put on the 'Prefects' List'.

On a normal morning it was up at 7.00 to do your house duties (which rotated between cleaning corridors, staircases and study rooms to laying the breakfast table), but if you incurred the wrath of the prefects you were up at 6.00 to clean their shoes, iron their shirts or tidy their common room for the next seven mornings and *then* do your house chores. Unfortunately by the time I became a prefect my hippy friends had decided we should scrap the system, so my year at the top were the first to have to clean their own shoes.

Of course being a 'boys only' boarding school there was precious little contact with the opposite sex – well, none at all if it hadn't been for the ballroom dancing club where, for one night a week, the young ladies of Sir William Perkins School, Chertsey, arrived to help us all learn to dance. Boys lined up on one side of the main hall with the girls on the other and, when each dance was called, there would be a mad scrimmage across the floor to grab the hand of the prettiest girl. In my final year I had a bit of an edge on the opposition as I'd become a 'school driver' – just 17 and the mini-bus was mine! One of my duties was to pick up the girls for the dance, which unfortunately meant that once I'd done my racing driver impersonation they tended to arrive slightly more dishevelled than they'd started...

While being stuck in school for most of the year wasn't ideal, there were lots of good things about being at a boarding school. Sports facilities were excellent and the inter-house competitions were serious encounters. In the cross-country event everyone had to take part. It didn't matter where you finished, every place counted, and if you weren't all but collapsing from exhaustion at the finish life in the 'house' would be a bit uncomfortable for a while. I wasn't great at any sport but enjoyed them all, captaining the glorious third XV at rugby and opening the bowling for cricket's first XI, but the great thing about boarding schools is that you get to do everything. We had inter-house gymnastics competitions, swimming competitions, bridge tournaments and even singing contests, and all were entered with a very strong desire to win, which is probably why I find the state schools' move away from anything competitive desperately sad.

Our only means of escape was by bicycle or thumb. Bikes would be good for a Saturday trip to Woking for the cinema, but anything further required hitchhiking. Unfortunately, being spotted with my thumb out by a master blotted my chances of becoming house captain.

When the holidays came it was back to Oatlands and my mate Patrick who, fortunately for me, was at a local day school with a mixed sixth form so that, as our enthusiasm for Monopoly began to fade, he had connections with those mysterious members of the opposite sex. We still mucked about with fishing rods and box carts during the day, but the local youth club became the new centre of interest in the evenings.

I actually made my motorised sporting debut a couple of years earlier, not, as I had dreamed, on a racing circuit but on those waters of Iver Heath. Dad had designed a neat little two-seater water scooter with an outboard motor on the back and was trying to find commercial backing to put it into mass production. For once he'd come up with a concept that might even make him a rich man. Sadly a backer couldn't be found – and then someone invented the Jet Ski.

At the same time the powerboat world was introducing a Junior Runabout class for 12–16 year olds to go circuit racing – a sort of boating equivalent of karting – and Dad's little scooter was just the right length so we decided to convert one for me to race. Given one of the prototype fibreglass hulls, I cut out the motorcycle-styled saddle and handlebar steering, stuck a little seat on the floor and installed my own steering system. We were only allowed a maximum of 10 horsepower for the engines and Dad managed to secure the loan of a brand-new Mercury outboard which I ran in using a dustbin full of water that I'd roped to a tree. Only three boats turned up to the first race and although fastest in practice, I had an early lesson in the complexities of racing when the wash from other boats caused my propeller to 'cavitate' in air bubbles and lose its efficiency – leaving me to finish a disappointed last.

Back home Dad discovered that the bottom of the prototype hull had not been formed properly so I had to do all the work again, converting one of the early production models for the following season. The work was not in vain, however, and the new boat swept to victory. Unfortunately I was now about to turn 17 so the boat was sold to Andy Elliott who would go on to win the championship for the next four years and start a career that would lead to World Championship glory.

Not that I was too concerned, because turning 17 also meant that I was able to drive a car! I'd already driven up and down the drive to our flats a hundred times but, trapped at boarding school, I had to wait until the Christmas holidays, two long months after my birthday, before I could finally head out on public roads in Mum's Morris 1000 – taking her shopping as often as I could persuade her to go. After just a couple of weeks on the roads I took my test on 2 January 1969 and passed first time – the world was now at my mercy.

Fun though powerboat racing had been, the sport simply didn't have the same attraction for me. The only thing I carried forward into my car-racing career was the orange colour of my crash helmet – the regulation colour for all powerboat racers for maximum visibility when going for involuntary swimming exercises! No, motor racing was the only sport I was really interested in and throughout the fifties and sixties the most exciting days out were the trips to watch cars hurtling round corners, with my heroes sawing away at their steering wheels. We couldn't afford to go to many motor races but the Easter Monday meeting at Goodwood and the Boxing Day races at Brands Hatch were always musts.

We would splash out on grandstand seats and Mum would fill a huge picnic hamper with chicken legs and sandwiches to last all day – and thermos flasks filled to the brim with tomato soup. Kept warm with rugs over our legs, I could have sat in those stands all year long soaking up the atmosphere of 'my' world. Instead of the modern huff, puff and hype the commentary would be full of information, with detailed amendments to the programme and the line-up for the grid carefully copied into my programme. Lap charts would also be printed so you could record the race for yourself, and Michael became our family expert.

Of course all the drivers were superstars and I had many favourites, from Mike Hawthorn and Stirling Moss through to James Hunt, but one man stood out way above them all. A quiet gentleman who, in the manner of the day, would race saloons, sportscars and single-seaters all at the same event. A driver who I'd watched coming to prominence in his first single-seater race for Lotus at Goodwood in 1960 and who was tragically killed – still driving for Lotus – just eight years later. From the age of nine to 16, I idolised just one man... Jim Clark.

Just writing his name fills me with emotion. He should have been driving the new Ford prototype in the sportscar race at Brands Hatch on 7 April 1968, where Michael had taken me to watch, but Clark's loyalty to Lotus and their sponsors persuaded him to do the Formula Two race at the German Hockenheim track instead.

On our way home we dropped in at my aunt's house and the first words spoken when we entered were 'Isn't it awful news about Jim Clark?' Although some news had filtered through to those inside the circuit at Brands I'd had no idea, and it came as a total shock. Clark had had an aura of invincibility about him – surely no harm could ever come to such a supreme driver? If he had the best car he would destroy the opposition on the first lap and then cruise to victory; if not he would wring every last second out of any car and give it a result it simply didn't deserve.

Jim Clark raced in an era when Grand Prix drivers would drive in every type of event. He won the great Indianapolis 500, raced in NASCAR, stunned the rally world with his speed through the forests, and gained a generation of fans by chasing and often beating Ford Mustangs and Galaxies in his mostly three-wheeling Lotus Cortina. He would also put his reputation on the line by taking on the rising stars in Formula Two, and so it was that he lined up on the grid at Hockenheim in drizzling rain driving a Lotus that wouldn't run properly...

CHAPTER 4

LEARNING THE ROPES

The *Autosport* prize also included a one-week course at the Jim Russell Racing Drivers' School based at the Snetterton Circuit near Norwich and, fortunately for me, I just happened to be on sick leave from Wimpey so had the time to spare. A cartilage operation on my knee, which in those days meant carving open your leg, meant I was unable to walk on rough ground for a month – and that summer's work experience was building the M5 motorway.

Before I could go anywhere, though, I had to rent myself a lock-up garage, fix a tow bar to the Morris 1000 Traveller and find some seat belts and mirrors for the Lotus – apparently these were optional extras! Fortunately belt manufacturers Britax had their head office in Weybridge and – for the price of a sticker on the car – my first sponsorship deal was concluded.

With no M25 or M11, Norwich seemed a very long way away back then, especially in a ten-year-old car with less than 50 horsepower and drum brakes all round, towing a racing car on a trailer. Downhill with the proverbial wind behind I might occasionally stretch the speedometer round to 60mph, but it needed about half a mile to get it stopped from that sort of speed. Nearing my destination I began to hear all sorts of creaks and moans from under the car and, having finally made it to Snetterton, a quick look underneath revealed a front suspension about to tear itself from the chassis: next stop a garage with some welding equipment.

The one-week course was primarily designed as an introduction for overseas students and we all lived in bed and breakfast accommodation provided by the school – but while my class-mates would use the school cars to undertake their training, I would proudly use my gleaming new Lotus. Mind you, it would be an agonising wait to drive it properly as the lessons started with classroom theory, then driving up and down a straight to get used to the racing gearboxes, then walking through each corner one at a time, then driving through each corner one at a time, then finally lapping at 4,000 revs... come on, I'd been there already – just let me loose in my Lotus!

By the end of the week we were finally lapping at full speed – well, full speed to us, but way off the pace of a couple of former students who were now racing Jim Russell cars in public races and acting as our instructors. Emerson Fittipaldi had arrived on the school's doorstep a couple of years before and they'd helped guide the mercurial Brazilian's early career, first in Formula Ford, then quickly graduating to Formula Three. Now he was a Grand Prix driver for Lotus, while Belgian Patrick Neve and American Leigh Gaydos were two talented youngsters hoping to follow the same path. One would make it to the ranks of the Grand Prix grid, the other had just six weeks left to live...

With the course over, my public race debut was set for two weeks later at the Snetterton track on 2 May 1971, so I parked the Lotus in the school's garage and made the long trek home, floating in a world of make-believe and still unable to take it all in. The Jim Russell course had opened my eyes wide and the speed of the school's stars had woken me to the task ahead. I had begun to live the dream but knew I had a long road ahead of me.

The two weeks back at work on the M5 north of Bristol seemed like an age, but finally my first real race day dawned. The Lotus had come with just the one set of wheels fitted with Avon tyres that were the tyre to have – last year! The Formula Ford rules allowed you to use any production road tyres on five-inch steel rims and, for the first four years of the formula, two or three different makes had proved fairly equal, but then Firestone came out with a soft-compound 'special' – the Torino. They had to make several hundred thousand of the things to classify them as production tyres and there must have been some very unhappy customers who found them worn out after only a few thousand miles, but on the racetrack they were in another league. Unfortunately there was no way I could afford a set at that time, so I simply had to wait till I wore out the Avons. I couldn't afford any spare gear ratios either, which are essential if you are going to be competitive in single-seater racing. Before I did the school course I'd actually pulled the gearbox apart – with a friend writing down the bits in the order they fell out – as I began my self-taught path to being a racing mechanic. The Hewland manufacturers had, though, allowed me to swap the gears inside for a set that were at least about right for Snetterton. This was motor racing on half a shoestring!

My debut was in a non-championship club race, but the formula was so popular at the time that even for such a low-profile event there were still 45 entries split into two heats. I managed to qualify ninth in my heat, a couple of seconds slower than Neve and Gaydos who were in the other half of the draw, but a daunting seven seconds a lap off the Torino-clad front runners, albeit round the long 2.7-mile lap of the old circuit.

But I didn't really care how far I was off the pace: just being there on the inside of the fourth row for my first ever real race was good enough for me. For the four-car Brands Hatch school races we'd been restricted to using just 3,000 revs for the starts as the gearboxes were so fragile. Now I was in the middle of a pack and had no idea how to make a good start. I don't think I took a second breath for the first two laps as there seemed to be cars everywhere, but oh how the adrenaline flowed. As Steve McQueen so famously said, 'Racing is life. Anything before or after is just waiting.' Well, my world had truly come alive.

I somehow finished fifth – only 40 seconds behind after eight laps, so I must have been getting better. The grid for the final was set by your overall heat time which meant I lined up 11th of the massive field of 32 with Neve 7th and Gaydos 16th – we were definitely moving up in the world.

If I thought the heat was wild I now discovered the regulars had been taking it relatively easily to ensure making it into the final. All hell broke loose on the opening lap. As we exited the second corner a car off the road to my left cartwheeled along beside me, shedding bits and pieces as it self-destructed. This was the real thing, this was racing... I wasn't sure if I knew what I was doing but I was loving it. A solid 10th was my final position and the beautiful Lotus was still all in one piece – result!

The next race was back at Snetterton two weeks later, so once again I left the Lotus behind and set off to work for a couple of weeks during which I had the chance to do a deal with my first sponsor, Robert Trebble. Robert was, and still is, a racing nut who was unable to drive himself but wanted to get more involved in the sport. He'd advertised in *Autosport* to sponsor someone on a small scale, and a reply from me was just what he'd hoped for. He'd already backed another driver for a while and all he wanted in return was a lift to the tracks. He lived in London with his parents and either I would do a detour to pick him up or he'd get to a railway station en route. Extra mileage on my fragile tow car wasn't ideal, but the £10 per weekend made all the difference. Little did I know at the time that, apart from little bits here and there, dear old Robert would be my only real sponsor for what would turn out to be an often frustrating five years of learning my trade in Formula Ford – and it ended up costing him a lot more than our original deal. His wages working for British Rail and mine for Wimpey had to be stretched a very long way.

Nowadays this sort of racing apprenticeship is almost entirely done in the karting world, and by the time the Lewis Hamiltons and Jenson Buttons of this world are 17 they already have nine seasons of racing behind them. When they're first seen in cars they are on the pace from the word go, whereas we all had to work our way up the grid gradually as we gained experience. Back in the early seventies karting was still in its infancy and not really viewed as a serious training ground for racing drivers. Also, with racing cars being a lot less technical than they are now, especially Formula Fords, you didn't have to have a team manager, a race engineer and two mechanics in order to succeed. Indeed, my generation was mainly one of self-prepared 'transit van and trailer' racers doing everything themselves – being mechanic, van driver and racing driver all in one!

My second meeting was in a *Formule Libre* race – a hotchpotch of all sorts of single-seaters – but of the 26 starters, 11 were Formula Fords, so we had our own little race within a race. Despite a qualifying time a full three seconds faster than before I was only eighth fastest of the Fords and still a second off Gaydos and Neve – progress, but already I was getting impatient. We finished third, sixth and seventh after a race my diary describes as 'a fabulous dice', with the amiable young New Yorker bettering his Belgian team-mate on this occasion. After a bit of post-race banter, bravely boasting that I'd beat them both when we met again in a month's time, I loaded the Lotus on to the trailer, hitched it to the Morris 1000 and headed home

Sadly, the three of us never would meet again. While Neve and I would gradually battle our way on to the Grand Prix grids, Leigh was killed just two weeks later at Mallory Park when he hit a marshal's post side-on at high speed. After just three euphoric races I was brought right back down to earth, experiencing first hand the reality of the price a driver must be prepared to pay for the thrill that speed brings. The closeness made his death a very raw experience. I knew my sport was dangerous – after all, my hero Jim Clark, the greatest driver ever, had paid that ultimate price – but Leigh was just like me, a kid with a dream...

With a Formula Ford race taking place somewhere virtually every weekend, my plan for the year was to experience as many circuits as possible, and with trips to Thruxton, Silverstone and Castle Combe my confidence grew and the lap times dropped – especially as I now had my first set of Torinos. By the middle of July it was time to return to Snetterton and, with my new tyres almost worn out of tread, ideal for dry conditions, I shocked them all by qualifying third fastest for my heat which put me on the outside of the front row, a full *seven* seconds a lap faster than on my debut! Way back in 12th spot another American kid had joined the Jim Russell ranks – and Danny Sullivan was the one for whom the dream did come true.

Unfortunately there was a heavy downpour not long before the start and, while most swapped to spare tyres with more tread, I just had the one set of nearly bald rubber. Not that I really appreciated it would be a problem, I mean I didn't mind a wet track, and for three laps I hung on to the two hotshots ahead of me, wondering at my own brilliance. Then, suddenly, the car swapped ends without me ever knowing anything about it – I'd discovered aquaplaning! A swift 360 degrees and I had only dropped to seventh. I quickly fought my way back up to fourth before another competitor spun in front of me and round I went again, in sympathy. By now I was convinced there was something wrong with the car so I headed into the pits where the Jim Russell boys just looked at the state of my tyres and laughed.

The 15-lap final would be my ninth race in the Lotus 69 and, after my dramas in the heat, I would start it from way back in 25th on the grid. With the track now dry I somehow stormed up to ninth on that opening lap – the boy who had shown so much promise was going to show them! A lap later I was seventh and hard on the heels of the Palliser of Chris Pryer who had been on pole for the other heat.

Round the dauntingly fast Coram Curve, we headed for the notorious Russell Bend, back then a little right-left-right flick that could almost be taken flat out in top gear. It led on to the start/finish straight and a good exit gave a perfect overtaking opportunity. Perhaps distracted by my looming in his mirrors, Chris got it all wrong on the way in and slewed sideways in front of me, forcing me to jink right to avoid him.

Somehow I missed him, but the left 'flick' was now a *sharp* left at over 100mph if I was to avoid the earth bank looming large in front of me. I missed that but in so doing simply aimed myself head-on into the bank on the outside of the circuit. Eyes shut, massive impact, whump, thump, a powerful smell of fresh earth, then silence. Opening my eyes, blinking to clear the dust and dirt, all I could see was the sky above. The Lotus had rolled along the bank, embedding the rollover hoop and my head in the soft earth as it went, before ending up perched on top of it. Then my onboard fire extinguisher went off and the marshals joined in the fun with more of the same as soon as they arrived to help extricate me from the wreckage.

From the pits it must have looked very serious, but amazingly I was totally unharmed – which is more than could be said for my once-pristine Lotus. Having just begun to think motor racing was easy it was down to earth with a bang, in the most literal way possible.

Although we strapped the twisted remains of the Lotus on to the trailer and towed it back to its little Weybridge lock-up there was no way I was going to be able to fix this one myself, even if I could have afforded the bits it needed. My two-week summer 'holiday' was quickly booked and a week later I headed back to Snetterton and the helping arms of the Jim Russell Racing Drivers' School.

A month of hard graft later and thanks to both Robert's savings and all sorts of trade support we were back on the road. A battered £25 Ford Anglia van had replaced the Morris 1000 Traveller and I'd found someone to give a hand at weekends for the price of a pint. We now had a set of spare wheels and even a few spare parts which, along with the jack and toolbox, I'd neatly stow to one side of the rear of the van so that, for the long haul to the tracks in the early hours of the morning, mechanic Roy would lie down and sleep, and on the way back we'd swap the duties. Oh how lovely some of those deep sleeps were, bouncing home in the back of the van!

One of Dad's powerboat millionaires had agreed to a trial sponsorship period so the re-bodied Lotus now wore the blue and white stripes of Hilton Transport Services (HTS) and I began to mix some national championship events with the club races. With results just outside the top ten, or even just in the top three depending on the event, my experience was growing but there was still the odd rush of youthful over-enthusiasm.

After the Snetterton crash, Jim Russell had introduced me to Scholar Racing Engines where the father and son team of former stock-car racers Doug and Alan Wardropper ran their engine tuning business from the old control tower of the Second World War airfield at Martlesham Heath, just north of Ipswich. It was an introduction that would stand me in good stead for the next five years.

As is the case in all sports, there was a fair bit of bending of the rules in the early days of Formula Ford. The engines were supposed to be standard 1600cc Ford Cortina engines but you were allowed to rebuild them within the manufacturer's tolerances to optimise their performance – a process known as 'blueprinting'. Unfortunately there were always those who were tempted to 'optimise' by a little more than the regulations allowed. We all knew who had the 'bent' engines and it was hugely frustrating to see them power past on the straights and then hold you up in the corners. The sad thing is that if I had cheated I'd probably have prospered a lot more quickly, but the Wardroppers were great crusaders helping to clean up the sport and my own sense of wanting to play fairly meant that I just had to grin and bear it. Fortunately, during my time in the formula, the regulations began to be enforced a lot more thoroughly and the blatant cheats were gradually weeded out.

Of course the more often you rebuilt your engine the more competitive it would remain, but my budget restricted me to one rebuild every six or seven races. It was just after one such freshen-up that I took on the big boys at Castle Combe and, for the first time, found myself mixing it with the best. Sadly, a wildly over-optimistic move to slip into 3rd place behind the brilliant Tony Brise – who would surely have been a global superstar if he hadn't lost his life in Graham Hill's air crash – didn't come off. Spinning in the middle of the pack sent several serious championship contenders scattering in all directions, yet somehow I emerged unscathed to finish a chastened ninth – and spent the rest of the afternoon submitting my apologies.

That first unforgettable year came to an end at the Boxing Day meeting – not, sadly, at Brands Hatch but at Mallory Park. The schoolboy spectator was now well and truly on the other side of the fence: 25 starts had netted 23 finishes, without that first elusive victory, but a couple of third places hinted at some promise ahead.

The plan for 1972 was simply to be more of the same. With Formula Ford established as the only formula to be seen in for the ambitious young star, the budget-racing dream of Brands Hatch supremo John Webb had begun to spread across the whole world in a manner which even he could not have dreamed about. In Britain there were now three separate national championship as well as club meetings all over the country, so you could find a race somewhere virtually every weekend.

I was still beavering away in my nice warm university when we first loaded up and headed to Brands for a couple of January clubbies where I was now a regular top-three runner, picking up two thirds and a second and clocking my first fastest race lap and my first ever laps out in the lead – eventually losing a great battle to the wonderfully named Aussie, Buzz Buzaglo!

The first two national championship events were at Brands and Mallory Park and I was now quietly being tipped as one of the favourites to turn my early promise into serious results. Perhaps the pressure got to me and on a cold, wet day with snowflakes in the air I struggled to a disappointed tenth at Brands, but worse was to come at Mallory. Buried in the middle of the grid, the dash to the first corner turned into mayhem as that man Buzaglo got turned sideways and we all piled in. Well, I say piled in, but in fact, with my nose between two other cars, I was simply launched skywards as I rode over their rear tyres. Once again all I could see was blue, but this time I didn't get to eat the dirt as the Lotus landed heavily, still right side up, on the front left corner. Amazingly I was able to limp back to the pits with nothing more than a bit of bent suspension – or so it seemed at the time.

Despite winning the Lotus for apparently having a good idea of how to prepare a car for a race, in reality I didn't have the money, know-how or facilities to actually carry it through. Although nowhere near as critical as nowadays, it was still vital to keep the suspension alignment and weight distribution as near to right as possible.

My lock-up garage had neither lights nor electricity and the Lotus on the trailer could just about be squeezed in, so the only work I could do on it was outside in a yard in the daytime. I had to splash out on a couple of trips to a specialist race-preparation business to make sure everything was in order and then borrow wheel-alignment equipment at race meetings to keep a check on the toe-ins and cambers. Looking back, I'm amazed I ever got as far as I did, but as the 1972 season wore on, things definitely weren't getting any better. My lap times had stopped improving and I seemed to lurch from one frustrating weekend to the next. With so little money I was also constantly racing with the thought in my mind that even the smallest of accidents could mean the end of my season.

The HTS sponsorship hadn't gone further, so it was back to just Robert and me. I could see others hurling their cars at corners to find the limit, knowing that any damage could be quickly repaired, but it was a luxury I couldn't afford – and back then the 'run-off' used to consist of an average of ten yards or grass before being welcomed by a large earth bank.

The early-season results were littered with taps, spins and mechanical gremlins – some were my fault, others not. On one occasion, while changing the four ratios of the little Hewland gearbox that sat at the back of the car, I put the top gear in back to front so had to qualify with the engine screaming for its life in third – and this was at Thruxton, the fastest track in the country. As usual, with 60 or so cars turning up for the national championship rounds, there were two heats and a final. I'd still managed to qualify 18th for my heat, but the whole day was then spent climbing to 10th, starting 16th in the final and finishing 9th.

In between all the frustration we still went pot hunting at the clubbies and finally came away with that first, long-dreamt win, at Thruxton on 28 May 1972. Bizarrely, the one driver who for a while stood between me and that win was none other than my nemesis, Chris Pryer, who once again managed to spin in front of me. This time, however, I missed both him and the scenery to take an easy win and fastest lap. No longer the excuses when I returned for work the next day. The shortest answer is always the best.

'So how did you get on?'

'I won!'

Joy of joys!

Unfortunately it was only a temporary relief from the growingly frustrating season and, although I didn't feel so good about it at the time, it was actually another large accident that would finally turn my season round. A clubbie at the glorious Cadwell Park had netted another second place plus a fastest lap so I was hopeful of a good result in the national championship race there a few weeks later. Frustratingly, the best I could do in practice was only good enough for another grid position in the lower half of the top ten. When the flag

dropped – yes, it was still flags back then – 'Fiery' Frank Sytner made
a flyer from behind me and, in trying to pass a row of cars in front,
put two wheels on the dirt, lost control, speared across the circuit and
slammed me straight into the banking.

This time it was a lot more than a bit of bent suspension. The chassis
was obviously damaged as well, and there was no option other than a
full rebuild. Having already had a few bits welded and straightened by
Bert Ray at his south London workshop, the wreckage was duly landed
on his doorstep. Stripped right down, Len Wimhurst was the man
tasked with doing his best to straighten the chassis and he soon
discovered there was more than just the obvious problem – the whole
chassis had a twist in it and the heavy 'one-point' landing at Mallory
Park was the most likely cause. Half the year had been wasted trying
to drive a corkscrew round corners!

Another six weeks dragged by before I could get out again, but
suddenly I was back on the pace. The now 'almost' straight Lotus was
handling much better and a third at Castle Combe was followed by a
fifth at Brands and a second back at Cadwell Park – where my fastest
lap was 1.5 seconds quicker than last time there.

Unfortunately this surge of new-found speed was about to be
interrupted by the only injury I would suffer in my 30 plus years of
racing. Once again the occupational hazard of someone spinning in
front of me was the cause. This time I just clipped the culprit – and no,
it wasn't Chris Pryer – but the impact broke the steering arm so I
slithered to a halt at the edge of the road, ready to have the usual rant
at the cause of my downfall. As I went to push myself up out of the
car, however, my right arm collapsed under me: the combination of
the impact as I turned the steering had caused the radius bone in my
forearm to snap in two.

To make matters worse the race was at Oulton Park, just south of
Liverpool, and a long six-hour drive from home. Fortunately, with no
concerns about being sued for malpractice, the doctor at the track
(who could tell it was a clean break) suggested that rather than ending
up in casualty on a Saturday night, I should be driven home and report
to my local hospital the next day. Mind you, the biggest concern for

me was that the first ever Formula Ford Festival was just six weeks away and I *had* to be in it…

'We could put it in plaster and leave it for a couple of months, or we could put a plate on and then plaster for six weeks.'

'But I *have* to be racing then.'

'No way.'

'Plate it, but don't put plaster on, and I'll be very careful…'

I think they must have got the junior houseman to do the operation because the stitching that still scars my arm looks like 'knit one, pearl one' and one of the screws was so long that it stuck out the other side of the bone. For the year it was left in, if I wiped my brow with my forearm, I could feel it scratching me – from the inside! By being very careful, without the plaster, I was able to keep the muscles moving and maintain some of their strength. Unfortunately, in single-seater racing cars you change gear with your right hand so the situation wasn't ideal, but with my wrist well strapped I duly pitched up at Snetterton – along with the 88 other competitors who had arrived from all over the world.

With wet weather and limited daylight, the organisers decided to seed the entries for grid places in the four heats and my decidedly on-off year meant they placed me 28th. So I would line up seventh on the grid for my heat, from where I made it up to fourth – which put me seventh on the grid for the semi where I finished… fourth – which put me… seventh on the 30-car grid for the final.

It was another typical day that summed up the constant battle I seemed to have to establish myself. The funny thing is that the easiest place to be in a race is in the lead – the hard bit is getting to the lead in the first place. I'd shown the promise, but to fulfil that in motor racing you need to get everything together all at the same time: the car, the engine, the tyres, the gear ratios. It's still all about what that stupid competition was about but it always needs one very important ingredient – money!

The final was scheduled for 25 laps – a 70-mile race that would take us the best part of 45 minutes. It was so long that half of us didn't have fuel tanks big enough and had to jury-rig extras; I fitted one above my knees with a simple tap I turned after half an hour. Unfortunately I didn't make it to fourth this time and had to settle for seventh place, right behind Danny Sullivan and Patrick Neve, but it had been an amazing race with places constantly changing and it began an end-of-season tradition that continues to this day.

At the end of the year I did get to race at the traditional Brands Hatch Boxing Day race and finished the season on a high with another second place to take the season's tally to 39 starts and 35 finishes including *the* win and 17 other top-six finishes. Good but not good enough...

CHAPTER 5

The Breakthrough

For 1973 I really needed a new car. The Lotus was not only a bit tired but it was also getting a tad dated, as new manufacturers and new designers arrived on the scene. Formula Ford wasn't just a breeding ground for young drivers but also for young engineers, many of whom would go on to become big names in the Grand Prix world.

The production line of sponsor-chasing letters and approaches that would continue for many years to come was well under way, a soulless task that would bring the odd sparkle of interest among a sea of rejection but never hook the big fish. Doubtless my approach was very amateurish, but it was all I knew and all I had the time and resources to do. Another season began without having the budget really to do myself justice. I was working five days a week as a civil engineer, five nights a week as a mechanic, and then being van driver and racing driver at the weekend. It would be pretty much the same story for the next two-and-a-half years. Yes, more wins came and there were more finishes in the top six, but progress was frustratingly slow.

Another of my pleading adverts had brought me to the generous attention of Rick and Karen Burgoyne who offered me their garage in Feltham – complete with lights and power – while Rick became the new spanner man. Also Feltham based was fellow-racer Frank 'the fish' Bradley – purveyor of the finest jellied eels in the land – who just happened to be a dab hand at fibreglass repairs and paint spraying for which I was most grateful.

I was now a regular top-six runner in the national championships and the only one using a Lotus 69F. It was the last Formula Ford to be built by the famous marque and the production run had been fairly small, so it was quite a rare beast. While good in fast corners it didn't have the best traction out of the slow ones, so life was becoming a bit of a struggle.

Fortunately a helping hand came my way when the Hampsheir brothers, Peter and Brian, offered me one of their Elden Mk10 chassis plus gearbox at cost price. This was the manufacturer that had burst on the scene with the brilliant Tony Brise as their driver, but now they too were in the doldrums without a regular front runner to show off their wares. This was another great thing about Formula Ford being a 'free chassis' formula, because there were literally dozens of small manufacturers wishing to make their name and do deals with fast drivers.

My great supporters Scholar offered to lend me an engine for the new chassis so now all I had to do was sell my much beloved Lotus. The advert was short and to the point:

Lotus 69F. Tiff Needell offers the quickest 69F in the country. Complete with Scholar engine. Mk 8 gearbox. £1,500.

It obviously wasn't going to be easy to sell a car mid-season but, fortunately for me, the Austrian Formula Ford championship, which was mainly run on two dauntingly fast circuits, was being dominated by a driver in a Lotus 69F. When one of his rivals, Hans Meier, got to hear that mine was up for grabs he was swiftly en route to the Burgoyne's little lock-up.

A deal was done but, as is so often the case, Hans didn't have the funds instantly available. We made an agreement that I would load the car into a friend's transporter, which was heading to Austria for a European Championship event, and he would then pay for me to fly out to meet him and the car and pay me in cash… it was all highly dodgy and I felt a bit like a secret agent as I took off for Vienna and a dubious rendezvous. Fortunately the Lotus got there in time and, having checked all was in order, Hans pulled off into a lay-by en route back to the airport to produce the classic briefcase full of bundles of cash for me to count. I kept expecting a gun to be produced at any moment and was the happiest man by far on the plane back home.

My lovely Lotus was gone but it had served me well. My last race in it was round the glorious Cadwell Park Circuit and although it didn't produce a win, a second place was backed up with fastest lap. In two-and-a-half years it made 90 starts that produced 82 finishes with three wins and a total of 22 trips to the podium – except they didn't have top-three podiums back then! Indeed, it just used to be the winner doing a lap of honour driving his racing car, with helmet off, waving to the crowd: a nice tradition, sadly long gone.

Of course you don't tend to get deals on the best cars around. Although the Elden was brand new it was still a slightly dated design and not the chosen chassis of any of the championship front runners – which is why I got the deal in the first place. So although the reliability improved, the results sadly didn't: I was regularly the front-running Elden but still stuck in the wrong half of the top six.

The end-of-season gathering for the second Formula Ford Festival brought my first win in the Elden, but unfortunately it was only in a heat. This time I was graded tenth of the 110 entries and sat on the outside of the three-car front row with my old sparring partner Patrick Neve in the middle and championship front runner Derek Lawrence on pole. With no budget for any testing I'd had to put in new front brake pads before the race and, in soaking wet conditions, I hadn't been able to bed them in properly on the warm-up lap. If anything this might have helped me in the soaking conditions, where you need more braking on the rear wheels – and, having left Neve behind, I hauled in early leader Lawrence and sailed past for a morale-boosting heat victory.

All hopes of further glory were sadly dashed when I was lined up on the wet side of the front row of a fast-drying track for the semi-final and made a complete hash of the start. The problem was then compounded when I discovered just how bad my brakes were; by the time I'd got them working properly I finished a chastened 11th – all part of the great learning process, as they say – and 23rd on the grid for the final didn't offer much promise. Another demon opening lap quickly hauled me up to 14th, but then one ambitious overtaking manoeuvre too many saw me pitched off the road with broken suspension. Still, it was only my third retirement from 45 starts that year and I'd finished in the top three on 18 occasions. The results were getting better, but oh so slowly.

The following year, 1974, turned out to be simply more of the same. True, I now had the luxury of a battered green transit van to replace the Anglia, which meant we could sleep in the back and not have to pitch the tent, but that was about the only improvement. Even *I* was beginning to wonder if all the sacrifices being made were worth it.

The worst weeks were probably the 'engine rebuild' weeks – the luxury I could only afford every six or seven races. In the summer of '73 I'd been working at Wimpey's head office in Hammersmith so, having got back from a race late Sunday night, I had to be up early Monday for the commute to work in the van, from Weybridge, and then I'd head straight from work to the Feltham garage that evening. Overalls on, remove engine, load it in the back of the van and then head home to bed. On Tuesday I'd commute to work and then drive to Ipswich *and* back home in order to drop the engine at Scholars. Friday evening would see the same trip to Ipswich and back so I could install the fresh engine on Saturday, prepare the car and then load up for Sunday's race.

Before the motorways were built Ipswich was a very long way away, and I would always end up returning round London's North Circular road in the early hours of the morning, drawing up at traffic lights alongside lads of my age in their flash Ford Capris with eight-track car stereos booming away and an attractive girl in the passenger seat. And what was the glamorous racing driver in? A Ford Anglia van with one bungee cord round the gear lever to hold it in top gear and another stopping the passenger door flying open, with only my engine in the back to keep me company. It sounds completely ridiculous now, but I couldn't even afford to buy myself a simple car radio to break the monotony. On one occasion, doubtless half asleep at the wheel, I was a bit late spotting a red traffic light and had the hit the brakes as hard as I could only to find the passenger seat slammed into the dashboard by my poorly secured companion. Had the engine been sitting behind me I hate to think of the damage it could have done!

The fact that there were now three national championships and all sorts of regional ones meant that the races came thick and fast and only the very well-budgeted drivers did any testing. On the Easter weekend of 1974 I raced at Oulton Park on the Friday, Snetterton on the Sunday and then Thruxton on the Monday. Just to make life a little more hectic, the Saturday was spent getting a new wheel for the trailer after one of them overtook me going down the M1.

Through all of this I did manage to get my first national win and finished the year as runner-up in the 'Wella for Men' championship. Another 43 starts had been made with 41 finishes, three wins and 17 top-three placings. Good again, but not good enough to convince anyone to sponsor me in a Formula Three car or even the newly announced Formula Ford 2000 championship for cars with wings and slick racing tyres.

Frank the fish – who now ran an Elden like mine – did manage to get 'Durex' sponsorship on our cars for the Formula Ford Festival, where I was now graded eighth from 120. Unfortunately eighth is where I finished, so again it was good, but...

It was typical of Frank to pull off the first 'Durex' sponsorship – not being the shy retiring type – but, as is so common in our sport, as soon as the big teams see the opening they are in the door with all their high-profile marketing spiel and our hoped-for budget was snapped away from us.

And so we embarked on season number five. Although I still only had the same racing experience as a 12-year-old Lewis Hamilton, I was now 23 years old and becoming increasingly desperate to get my career moving. The hugely talented Tony Brise was about to make his Grand Prix debut at the same age, but he was one of the first to have had karting experience and most Grand Prix debutants at that time were over 25. Time was still on my side – just!

On the plus side, Elden had offered me the loan of their brand-new Mk17 model, so I was able to put my Mk10 up for sale. Better still, I'd picked up a slightly newer transit van and plucked up the courage to approach Wimpey's transport manager, Frank Keen, to see if he might be in a position to help me keep it on the road. Little did I know at the time that he had a son who had just started racing, but he still made me go through a long, pathetic drivel about 'any little help would be much appreciated' before simply saying 'What colour would you like it?' Sadly Frank is no longer with us – which at least means he can't get into trouble for abusing his powers – but that van was like a Rolls-Royce to me. No longer would I have to spend half my evenings working at just keeping the tow car functioning – not that Mum was too pleased at now having three transit vans parked in our road!

Tiff Needell offers his successful Elden Mk10C complete and ready to race with new Dunlops. Also two transit vans. 1966/68. Both taxed, MOT with tow bar fitted. Offers.

With others graduating to the new Formula Ford 2000 series I was considered as one of the favourites for the 1975 Formula Ford 1600 championships and, with the new car not yet ready, I started the season in the older Elden with a win and a second before delivering it to its new owner with a total of 65 starts and 62 finishes to its name.

Although the overdraft was greatly reduced, all I now owned was a very rusty trailer and a racing gearbox (everything else was on loan) but, just as things were looking up, what really mattered – the results – were dropping down. The Mk17 Elden was a disaster. I couldn't believe how bad a car could be. It was designed with a very narrow track to make it quick through the air, yet it was drastically slow in a straight line. Elden blamed Scholar; Scholar blamed Elden. We chopped the bodywork off the back, we stiffened the chassis, but whatever we did the thing was a pig down the straights and a pig round the corners.

I was now struggling even to make it into the top ten and I well remember how Rad Dougall, a young South African star who had just arrived in Britain to further his own career, commented that he thought I could be quite quick in a decent car…

All seemed lost, a career in civil engineering was looming large in my mind, but in that same mind I was still convinced that I wouldn't just be 'quite quick' in a decent car, I would be the quickest. The question was, how to get my hands on such a car?

In 1974 the Crosslé Car Company from Northern Ireland had loaned one of their new 25F chassis to promising British driver Richard Morgan who promptly blew the establishment away. He'd only got the car at the end of May but soon racked up enough wins to beat me to that 'Wella for Men' title, leap up every championship table going *and* take the end of season Festival at a canter.

The company wasn't new to the formula, having won the European title in the late sixties, but their cars weren't that popular on the English scene. However, with the 25F they'd certainly come up with something that worked, and lending a car to Morgan woke everyone up. Rival manufacturers protested against Morgan's engine, they protested against his gearbox, but nothing untoward could be found. It was simply a brilliantly engineered car that, among other things, put its power on the ground better than any other.

Over the winter the opposition had studied the 25F's advantages in detail and responded with similar designs, while Crosslé themselves brought out their own new model – the 30F. One of these was also to be loaned to the English scene, but my approach was in vain as Mike Blanchet was picked as the chosen one – while I got the Elden Mk17. Of course after Morgan's success there had been plenty of customers knocking on Crosslé's door, one of whom had been the eccentric Chris Hiatt-Baker, a wild child of the sixties who'd arrived on the scene and, in between odd flashes of promise, had systematically thrown his Formula Fords into the scenery at most of the tracks he visited. He'd also been known to smoke the odd weird-smelling cigarette but, hey, those were the days – we just all hoped he didn't smoke them *before* he raced!

Chris never appeared at the beginning of the season, however, and few knew what had happened to him until a little advert appeared in *Autosport* in the middle of June:

Unwanted gift, brand-new unused Crosslé 25F rolling chassis, £1,600 ono.

From the Bristol number and the style of the advert it had to be Chris. But where was I going to get my hands on £1,600 – around

£30,000 in modern money? But desperate times lead to desperate measures and I had nothing to lose.

'Hi Chris, it's Tiff. Look I simply have to buy your car but would it be all right if I didn't pay you for it until I sell it?'

'Yeah, far out! When do you want to come and pick it up?'

I'd hitched the rusty trailer to my gleaming new van before the phone line had even gone cold and was off down the M4 before Chris had any chance to change his mind. When I got to his Clifton address I found out why he hadn't appeared to race that year – he'd discovered hang gliding! Back then it was a relatively new sport and Chris had found the reality of actually flying 'as high as a kite' to be the thrill he'd been yearning for. He'd soon become a member of the famous 'Dangerous Sports Club' who, among other hair-brained stunts, would introduce bungee jumping to the world by leaping off the Clifton suspension bridge.

Chris had actually opened a school for hang gliding and it was in a dusty corner of his workshop that I found the passport to my future. I don't remember even stopping for a coffee. I kept him distracted with idle banter, wheeled the car out and strapped it on my trailer, convinced he'd change his mind at any moment, but he remained true to his word. His only stipulation was that I remove the 'Hiatt-Baker Racing' that he'd boldly emblazoned down the side and replace it with 'The High School for Hang Gliding'!

The date set for my Crosslé debut was 13 July, once I'd delivered the Elden back to its makers with 17 starts under its belt which had produced 14 finishes and just one third place. The venue was where my dream had started – back on the Brands Hatch Club Circuit for a round of their 'Townsend Thoresen' championship – and the race report began with the words:

'Tiff Needell set one of the fastest times ever seen in a Formula Ford to take pole position for Heat Two.'

The emotion was mainly one of huge relief. Even I had been doubting myself and yet now, after four-and-a-half years of learning it the hard way, years spent sacrificing everything for my dream and running my own car with precious little money and only half an inkling of what I was supposed to be doing, it was all so easy. Before this event I'd started 46 races at Brands and never won once. Now I would win the heat, with fastest lap, the final, with fastest lap, and go on to win 10 of the 12 races I contested there that year in the Crosslé... I was a shooting star again!

In the three main national championships Geoff Lees was storming to an incredible triple crown, and although I had beaten him in the opening heat of the year in my old Elden, I hadn't been able to touch him since. With the only series mathematically in my grasp at this stage of the season being the Brands Hatch one, that's where I concentrated my efforts and I finished the year with the 'Townsend Thoresen Formula Ford Champion' title to my name and was joint lap record holder into the bargain.

I did, of course, still contest as many national rounds as possible and I had some herculean dices with Lees – there was no love lost between the Atherstone garage mechanic and me! Having said that, while we raced hard we always gave each other racing room. I don't know if it is because most of us were racing on our own money or whether it was because the unforgiving banks were just a few feet off the road but we would never deliberately force each other off the track. In fact I well remember the day when Rad Dougall was driven off the Snetterton straight by his own South African team-mate Geoff Smailes and had a huge accident. Back in the paddock none of us could quite believe it had happened. 'What, pushed off on the straight?' Of course nowadays if you make a mistake exiting a corner and a rival begins to draw alongside that is exactly what every driver does. Now, if I was in charge of the rule book, things would be different.

At Oulton Park I put the Crosslé on pole and led my heat comfortably from Lees and Dougall only for the water cap to work loose, causing the engine to overheat and allowing Lees to get past on the last lap. Another bollocking from Scholar for my amateur car preparation and an engine too damaged to run in the final...

A couple of weeks later, though, I took pole position at Thruxton, set the fastest lap and led Lees home by over six seconds on a track where breaking away is never easy. A week later I beat him again at Mallory Park but lost the race to Dougall in one of the best dices I ever had – pulling 'round the outside' moves into the Esses being my trademark for the day.

Geoff got me back again in a wet, wheel-banging encounter at Thruxton but I saved my best for the final national championship round at Brands where I used the outside line once again at Paddock Hill Bend and was never headed thereafter. To be fair to Geoff, he was making sure he got the points to secure his amazing third crown so was driving with that in his mind – but I've never known a driver who likes conceding anything. Despite being off the pace for half the season, this race also brought me the small consolation of fourth spot in the premier national championship – but oh what might have been if I'd had that Crosslé at the start of the year?

My return to prominence also brought me the much yearned for promotion to the wings and slicks of Formula Ford 2000. Hawke Racing Car boss David Lazenby had somehow fallen out with his works driver Syd Fox in the car run by the charmingly cheerful Mac McKinstry and, just four weeks after my Crosslé debut, I found myself in the seat. With no testing I stuck it on pole position at Mallory Park, from where I made a lousy start and dropped back to fourth. Battling back I managed to salvage second by the end with fastest lap to boot. The man who beat me? Syd Fox! He'd managed to grab a drive in the works Palliser and certainly made his point.

I was able to fit in four more races in the Hawke DL14 and continued my Brands Hatch form with another pole position, fastest lap and first FF2000 win. At Oulton Park I spun myself back to 11th before recovering to fifth and then ended with two wins on the Silverstone and Brands Hatch Grand Prix circuits. My collection of winner's garlands was growing fast! Oh, and fourth in the championship, having only contested five of the 17 rounds.

My last Formula Ford Festival – and the last to be held at Snetterton before it moved to 'my' Brands Hatch – proved to be something of a disappointment. Rad Dougall and I worked together to try and pull

One of Great Uncle Sir Richard Fairey's Swordfish biplanes swoops in to cripple the Bismarck in May 1941.

Mum (far left) spent the war on the London stage dancing in productions like this one, with Arthur Askey, in 'Follow the Girls'.

War over, Goodwood is the place to be and Dad is there competing with his Ford V8 in the first Members' Meeting, in 1949.

The child of the fifties gets dressed up: the cool cowboy with big brother Michael clowning around in the background, but it's best clothes – and Dad's beret – for Goodwood with Mum.

At Torquay in 1961, Mum looks on anxiously from the steps as Michael and I stand on Tommy Sopwith's winning boat while Dad (third from right) chats with Jim Wynne's second-place crew after the Daily Express *Cowes Torquay race.*

A taste for four wheels – karting at Mallory Park in 1961.

Dad's News of the World powerboat in 1966.

Running-in my little Junior Runabout's engine (note dustbin)... and the euphoria of the first test, in 1968.

'The Summer of '69' – learning to slide in Mum's Morris 1000, and that first Formula Ford drive at the Brands Hatch school.

December 1970: Autosport launches a competition to win a Lotus 69F and four months later this 19-year-old wins it.

May 1971: my public racing debut with Jim Russell racing school mentor John Paine.

My third race and ahead of Patrick Neve for the first time – May 1971.

Hair-raising to say the least.

Crashing down to earth – July 1971.

DIY racing, with Roy and the Anglia van – and changing gear ratios again!

Victory at last. Thruxton, 28 May 1972.

No caption needed!

Durex debut with the Elden Mk 10C – Thruxton, October 1974.

The awful Elden Mk 17.

Classic Formula Ford action. Leading Rad Dougall and Geoff Lees at Mallory Park, August 1975.

First race – first win. The Crosslé 25F, Brands Hatch, July 1975.

While at Snetterton, the 'High School of Hang Gliding' prepares for take-off at the Formula Ford Festival.

Champion at last – Brands Hatch October 1975.

clear of the pack in our heat and our semi-final, but while it worked in one, it didn't in the other: a holed radiator cooked my engine again and put me out of the final. Cue more questions from Scholar as to why I hadn't put a stone guard in front of my radiator...

The year would end on a high, however, as I fended off the advances of a young Derek Warwick to take victory in what would turn out to be my British FF1600 swansong at the televised Brands Hatch Boxing Day bash. I was also then honoured with a Special Commendation at the annual Grovewood Awards where a panel of motoring journalists recognised the most promising young British and Commonwealth drivers of the year. The winner was 28-year-old Formula Two driver Brian Henton, with Lees claiming the runner-up spot. Nowadays, at the equivalent occasion – the Autosport Awards – you aren't even eligible if you're over 23.

The Crosslé added 27 starts, 24 finishes, 12 wins, seven seconds and three thirds to my mounting tally and the Hawke opened my Formula Ford 2000 account with those five starts, five finishes, three wins and a second. Finally, results that I could be proud of and results that secured me the works Hawke drive with McKinstry for the following year – a free drive with no bills to pay! Okay, I still had to help with the race preparation – and bring one of my Wimpey colleagues, John Quartermaine, along to help at the races but all the hard graft and sacrifice had finally paid off.

The year 1976 started, just as '75 had finished, with a win at Brands in a non-championship affair before the first round proper on the Brands Hatch Grand Prix Circuit a week later in a supporting race to the Formula One 'Race of Champions'. This was one of the last remaining traditional fixtures where the Grand Prix teams would turn out to show off their new cars or give new drivers a chance before the European Grand Prix season got under way. Most of the top teams were there.

Having put the Hawke on pole in wet conditions, here was the chance to show off my speed in front of the assembled Grand Prix team managers and I was determined to impress. The track was still damp when we lined up for the race but slick tyres were the only choice – and it was a combination that was well suited to my already slightly 'sideways' style. Sitting beside me on the grid was the menacing Ian Taylor. A Formula Ford superstar in my early days who then went on to be a Formula Three champion but never got the big break, Ian was now back in a lower formula and very determined not to be outdone by any young upstarts.

I didn't make the best of starts as we charged towards the newly reprofiled Paddock Hill Bend – the first such unfortunate 'chopping' of a classic corner to provide more run-off. Braking way too late I lunged up the inside and shot straight out on to the old circuit, taking Taylor with me. Fellow front-row man Richard Piper briefly assumed the lead before I carved back across the track and headed him off into Druids. The lead was mine and the stage was set.

On the opening lap I pulled out a *five*-second lead in the greasy conditions and went on to romp home 38 seconds in front of Taylor – who'd finished in the same place the week before. The Bottom Straight, behind the paddock where the Grand Prix managers were, is actually a long left-handed curve and in the damp conditions I was taking it full throttle in top gear in one long graceful slide: come on, watch me, sign me up, I'm here! Quite how many managers did bother to watch I'll never know, but Frank Williams was heard saying he saw 'some bloke disappear off into the lead and it all looked a bit boring'. So much for all my great ideas! But if the F1 paddock hadn't noticed, the motoring press certainly did.

'A Magical Mystery Tour is the only way to describe Tiff Needell's opening lap of the first 1976 APG FF2000 championship. This man deserves to be in a much higher class of racing now.'

Even the national newspapers were now beginning to take notice. 'Needell on a Racetrack' was the *Daily Express* headline:

'Tiff Needell, like James Hunt, is a handsome six-footer, full of the courage and skill that could make him a Formula One world championship contender within two years.'

I'd also appeared on the kids TV programme 'Magpie', courtesy of cousin Penny who worked there, teaching Jenny Hanley to drive my Crosslé. I say 'my' Crosslé but of course it was still really Chris's, although it was about to be bought by my brother Michael who'd recently driven off to South Africa in a Land Rover with three of his mates and now wanted to start racing himself, down at his local Cape Town track.

But while it was all very well getting this nice publicity, there still wasn't a queue of teams rushing to sign me up. Driver managers were few and far between and you simply used to wait for the call to come. If anything it was the motoring journalists who pushed your name forwards, and I was very fortunate to have *Autosport*'s Chris Witty championing my cause.

Of course after such a great start to the season things could only get worse... at Mallory Park for round two 'that man' Syd Fox sat on the outside of the three-car front row with me in the middle. Unfortunately three into one didn't go as we headed for the first corner. Syd made the best start and edged my way, so I squeezed pole man David MacPherson towards the pit wall and, after a tangling of wheels, we all nearly ended up in the famous Mallory lake. Naturally, with me in Syd's car etc., etc., it all blew up into a major issue but this, so often, is what motor racing is all about.

There was more woe in the next round when the steering broke at the start of practice, possibly as a result of the Mallory shunt, leaving me 14th on the grid and then, having battled up to third, the wing broke. Next time out I was on the front row at Thruxton and, for once, decided to be cautious and back out of a challenge for the lead at the first corner, only to get whacked up the back...

I should have waltzed to the title but pole positions, wins, second places and lap records were too frequently interspersed with dramas out of my control. Even the weather contrived to work against me as that roaring hot summer of '76 exposed a cooling weakness on the Hawke which sapped the engine's power. In the end it boiled down to a last-round decider between Taylor and me at Mallory Park with the points so close that whoever finished ahead would take the crown.

At the penultimate round at Cadwell Park we'd debuted the new Hawke DL16 with another pole, win and lap record and, having seen Taylor spin off in my mirrors, thought I'd won the title as well but, with so many others also in trouble, he was still able to salvage second place.

With everything to play for we somehow both managed to enter two cars for the final round, where 38 entries were split into two practice sessions and the fastest 25 overall making up the championship grid. On what must have been the most stressful day of my life I found the DL14 handling badly and the DL16 down on power. One would put me fifth on the grid, the other back in eighth – and Taylor was on pole. With none of the modern-day telemetry at my disposal, trying to explain all this to both Hawke and the engine tuners from Holbay wasn't easy. It was all a matter of how I 'felt' and, in the end, I went for swapping the engine from the 14 into the 16 and opting to start back on the outside of row three.

To this day I'll swear I didn't jump the start – but I led into Gerard's! It was simply the perfect start and, as the field in front bunched to the inside, I simply swept round them all. To make matters better Taylor had slipped to third, but all too soon his orange Dulon was looming large in my mirrors. Despite setting a new lap record I didn't have the consistency to pull away and he slipstreamed along the outside of me into Gerard's on the fourth lap. With wheels almost touching we completed the whole high-speed, top-gear corner absolutely side by side. I knew I would now be on the inside for the Esses and could retain the lead but then, over the bump exiting the corner, my engine revs suddenly soared and I momentarily lost momentum. We had yet to fit the new car with a left footrest and I'd accidentally 'leant' on the clutch pedal. In that instant the championship was gone. In motor racing attention to detail is everything.

I lost the championship by one solitary measly point. Out of all those frustrating retirements, I just needed one more point. The only consolation was that I won the 'Dunlop Pole Position' championship based on qualifying results by a massive 40 points, but that did little to wipe the smile off Taylor's beaming face.

Three weeks later Rupert Keegan was in a similar points position in the last round of the British Formula Three championship. The 21-year-old son of the British Air Ferries founder was my complete opposite, a super-confident playboy with a budget that allowed him to develop his abundance of natural talent quickly by simply going faster and faster till he fell off. His Formula Ford career had been littered with accidents, but he'd matured well and now led the most prestigious national championship of the year. He'd qualified on the outside of the front row with his rival, Italian Bruno Giacomelli, sitting on pole position. The odds were against Keegan but, when he lined up on the grid, he aimed his car at an angle towards the inside of the first corner. When the flag dropped he headed diagonally across the track aiming for that first apex – the fact that Bruno's car was in his path didn't seem to matter. He simply took himself and Bruno out of the race and claimed the title!

He won his championship in a similar way to how Michael Schumacher would when he ram-raided Damon Hill in Adelaide. It was something I could so easily have done, with Taylor on my outside round that long Gerard's Corner, yet I'm so glad I didn't. Maybe that would now be regarded as a weakness in the modern 'winning is everything' world of sport. I certainly never thought of myself as the 'first loser' when finishing second. I mean, there I was doing something most people only dream about and one man was ahead of me – but there were over 20 behind us.

Mind you, I was quite grateful about Rupert's move because I just happened to be a couple of rows behind him in that Formula Three decider. No longer having to pay for my racing, I'd suddenly found myself in a very unusual position: I had a bank balance that was in credit! Fortunately there was a little one-car Formula Three team just up the road and they just happened to have a car for hire.

Team Safir was formed when Peter Thorpe took over the Token Formula One project with its designer, Ray Jessop. They only entered a couple of non-championship events before the money ran out, so they decided to have a go at the F3 market and built a couple of RJ05 models. The first was used with some success in the 1975 season by

Patrick Neve; the Belgian's career continued somehow to be linked to mine. Sadly Ray died unexpectedly and, while Peter persevered with the project, with no budget for '76 the car had been sitting in their Walton-on-Thames workshop until I arrived with all my worldly savings. My debut was at Oulton Park in July and, having qualified a steady seventh, I finished an encouraging fourth – one spot ahead of that other nemesis of mine, Geoff Lees, who had similarly scraped together a budget to race a Chevron.

A fifth and a couple of sixths followed before we arrived at that Thruxton finale where I very nearly repeated my demon start from the outside of row three. With Keegan removing half of the field in front of me I did actually arrive at the first corner in the lead, but with the surviving front-row man Conny Andersson on my inside and in a determined mood. Trying to hold on round the outside merely pushed me wide and allowed both Conny and Lees to get past. When the Swede retired it was back to being just like the old Formula Ford days, but this time Geoff had the upper hand and I would have to settle for another second. Nevertheless, I had made my mark and people had taken notice.

But that still wasn't the whole story of 1976 because I hadn't quite finished with Formula Ford 1600. The Hawke factory had got me back to my roots to help both promote their models overseas and try to help their lead driver, Derek Warwick, win the European Championship.

On my overseas racing debut in the dart-shaped DL15 I claimed pole position by a clear 0.7 seconds at the old, ultra-fast Zandvoort Circuit in Holland, upsetting the locals no end in one of their Benelux Championship events. They managed to make amends in the race, though, by giving me a lesson in the art of slipstreaming that would come in handy a couple of months later – but third place was still a great result.

The next event was a far more serious affair – a round of the European Championship where Warwick and Hawke were fighting an intense battle with a whole bunch of Crosslé drivers. The venue was the Jyllands Ringen and the race was billed as the 'Danish Grand Prix'. With the cream of that year's Formula Ford crop assembling for the event, the British drivers all ended up in one hotel and, enjoying my 'vacation' from the pressures of the FF2000 season back home, I thought I'd have a couple of those small draft beers on the night before qualifying. Well, as the conversation wandered on, with the assembled ranks telling me how tough the competition was that year, whereas last year there had only been me and Lees that were any good, I might have had a couple more...

By the time we went to bed the world had turned to full 'room spinning' mode whenever I tried to shut my eyes. I'd only ever been able to drink a couple of pints before getting tiddly and obviously this foreign stuff was a bit stronger than I'd thought. It seemed to take a long time to get to sleep, and when I awoke with a head-splitting hangover I felt decidedly guilty – right up until the moment I stuck it on pole position, fastest of the 50-car field!

Warwick was in the other heat and, after we'd both gained victories, we lined up side by side on the front row for the final with me on pole as mine had been the faster heat. Now obviously Derek had to win, but we didn't want to fall over each other and let the opposition take advantage, so it was agreed that if I got into the first corner in the lead I'd get my head down and hopefully we'd pull away. Then, on the last lap, if we were clear I'd let him by for the win.

All went as planned and the pit signallers – unusually situated at the beginning of the start/finish straight – counted down the 15 laps. So, the lap after the board had read 'P1 – L2' I naturally expected to be greeted by 'P1 – L1' and the signal to let Derek by. Instead all I saw were a lot of people jumping up and down and only after I'd taken my eyes off them and then my mirrors did I look up to see a man waving the chequered flag at me. I'd won the Danish Grand Prix with all four wheels locked up in a futile attempt to let Derek by. At first we thought the pit crew had miscounted the laps but, on checking the race time in the results, it became obvious that they'd brought out the flag a lap early – and the flag is the flag. The magnificent trophy I thus received hangs on our kitchen wall to this day – an engraved copper frying pan!

All this meant that, when we arrived at Zandvoort for the championship decider, Warwick winning the title was going to be that little bit more difficult. Hawke *v*. Crosslé had virtually boiled down to Warwick *v*. Ireland's David Kennedy. But Kennedy had to win with Warwick third or lower to take the title, so the odds were on our side – and it still remains the most exhilarating, heated, tactical, dirty race I was ever involved in. It turned out to be more like an unbelievable Hollywood script than reality. The top ten qualifiers were all either Hawke or Crosslé drivers, three of 'us' against seven of 'them', with me on the outside of the three-car front row the best Hawke, Kennedy fifth and Warwick back in ninth.

Slipstreaming down the monstrously long straight, we ran like a pack of wild animals, sling-shotting past and then daring each other to brake later and later into the famous Tarzan Hairpin. The hairpin is followed by a much tighter section that led out to the fast back curves so, as soon as I got to the front of the pack, I deliberately slowed the pace through the twisting section. This bunched up the cars behind, giving Warwick every chance to work his way forwards. Meanwhile a spate of Crosslé whccl-hub failures was beginning to balance the odds.

With just a few laps left it was down to Warwick and me versus Kennedy and Dutch star Maarten Henneman – and I was now driving minus a nose cone that had been a casualty of the war. We all knew who had to finish where so when, with two laps to go, Henneman headed out the back in the lead, Warwick and I jumped Kennedy. Weaving from side to side with the frustrated Irishman trapped behind us we slowed the pace to such an extent that the Dutchman disappeared out of view. With no TV cameras to tell the tale we'd mugged poor old David good and proper.

Starting the last lap Henneman's pit crew waved wildly to slow him down and, in his confusion, he even spun at Tarzan all on his own. Still seeing no-one behind him he assumed we'd all crashed and continued round to a victory that ensured Derek Warwick and Hawke were crowned European Champions.

One more Hawke PR trip to the short circuit at Hockenheim in Germany brought the season to a close with another second place and my tally of Formula Ford 1600 starts up to 204 with 187 finishes, 22 wins and a total of 77 top threes. Formula Ford 2000 had added 21 starts, 5 wins and 12 podiums to that total. Surely now the apprenticeship was over and a permanent graduation to Formula Three would be in the offing?

To put the proverbial icing on the cake, I received the ultimate accolade of the Premier Grovewood Award from the newly crowned World Champion James Hunt at the end of the year. I was now officially Britain's most promising young star and ready for take-off!

CHAPTER 6

The Civil Engineer

While the dream had always been the racing driver, the career in civil engineering hadn't been something picked out of a hat. A dream was a dream but I was going to make sure the education my parents had gained for me wasn't wasted – if, as all bar me believed, the dream didn't work out. In any case, I'd always thought I was going to have to pay for my racing myself, so the better the job the better the earnings.

Thinking of a career when you are just 15 or 16 always seems to be an impossible task. The last thing you actually want to think of at that age is settling down and doing one job for the rest of your life. So what's it to be? Doctor? Bank manager? Train driver? No-one really seems to have a fixed idea but, as maths was my best subject and two of my uncles were accountants that was my first 'obvious' choice. Fortunately for me the school ran a series of career lectures presented by a wide variety of companies – one of which was George Wimpey & Co. Ltd.

With a presentation that included the building of the new Ascot grandstands I suddenly saw a job that needed my mathematical skills but at the same time got me out and about on building sites, creating dramatic structures that would last for ever. When I then learned that they offered sponsored scholarships for five-year sandwich degree courses at the City University in London – with paid work for half the year – it seemed like the perfect job for me. Now all I had to do was get one of those dozen or so precious scholarships that were on offer.

I'd passed mathematics A-level in the lower sixth form when I was 16 so that, added to my seven O-levels, at least gave me some academic credibility, but the destination of the scholarships was mainly decided by an interview – and job interviews just have to be the worst days of your life. Do you really 'relax' and just 'be yourself'? Of course not, you desperately try to be the person you think the interviewer wants you to be.

At the same time I was working on my pure maths, applied maths, physics and chemistry A-levels, and wading through the university application forms trying to decide where to go if Wimpey didn't want me. On top of all that I was trying to grapple with the extra complication of having to learn how to handle girlfriends – growing up was just getting harder and harder! Fortunately Wimpey decided I was the man for the job – or at least the boy they'd interviewed was – and the City University came up with a generous offer that allowed me to drop chemistry and concentrate on the other three subjects, which I duly passed.

After the close control of boarding school it took me quite a while to settle into life at university. Wandering around the many different buildings trying to find lecture rooms, not knowing anyone to ask advice while trying to understand which books I needed to buy for which courses… for a while it was a very lonely and slightly scary transition. There must have been about 50 of us on the course and we were immediately immersed in a constant stream of lectures – all day, five days a week. After the relaxation of my 'summer of '69' this was back to work with a bang! I think we had something like seven subjects for that first six-month semester with exams on all of them in February. It was like doing seven more A-levels all at once. It certainly wasn't the casual, relaxed stroll that is so often the image of university life.

After my gentle introduction to working on the Witham housing estate in 1970, my second summer, building the M5, was a much tougher assignment but also a much more rewarding one. Seven of us trainee engineers were spread out over several sections of the route to the north of Bristol and we all joined together to live in one house in the Filton area of the city.

Our 11-hour day would begin by boarding the Wimpey bus that

picked up the workforce in the early hours of the morning, joining the many Irish labourers that the company was so famous for employing in those days – hard-working men whose families remained back home while they earned their living. Lovable though they were, I can still well remember the 'characterful' aroma that would greet us as we boarded that bus, a less than subtle whiff of 'hard work' blended with a drop or two of fresh 'golden nectar'!

On the section I worked, all the big earth moving had been done and my main task as a setting-out engineer was to lay out the precise lines and levels for the motorway itself, as well as for the Michaelwood services that were to be built in my stretch. 'Profile' boards had to be erected, to give the correct levels for the surface, and posts with nails in the top would mark the centreline. Occasionally half a day's work could be wiped out by an errant digger, but it was hard to get angry when the gentle Irish lilt explained the situation. 'Sorry, Mr Engineer. There's been a wee accident. Would it be possible to replace them little boards you just put up?' The worst problem was mainly the heat and the dust of a hot and dry summer. Either side of my section they were still cutting through some hills and filling some dips using giant earth movers that drop their bellies, scrape away the surface and then transport their load to the dropping zone – via my section.

So there I was, with my theodolite mounted on its tripod, trying to communicate with my 'chain boy' assistant setting out the centreline, with these monstrous machines continually blasting past, just feet away, billowing dust in all directions. On many occasions, especially if the boys had had a couple of beers the night before, I would retreat to the shelter of the cool, dark storm-drains that lay underneath to enjoy a brief respite.

At this point it's probably a good time to make a small confession. Unbeknown to all, there is a small kink in the M5 just south of those Michaelwood services! The problem stems from the fact that there was an existing road across this area of cutting, which also happened to be in the middle of a long curve of the motorway. Now, what you do in these circumstances is cut up to the road on each side, build a new bridge to take the road's traffic and, when that is finished, cut away the old road and join the motorway together. The only trouble was, my two curves on either side missed each other. After a bit of fudging I did manage to make a line that looked smooth enough to the naked eye, and I just had to hope the resident engineer didn't get to check that piece of the curve. At 70mph no-one was going to notice, but if anyone is thinking of taking their Bugatti Veyron for a late-night top-speed test I would suggest an element of caution...

Despite the long hours, occasional demands for Saturday work and the fact that I was now also a racing driver most Sundays, it was a very involving project to work on. 'My' piece of the M5 might not be quite as glamorous as those Ascot stands – which have in any case now been replaced – but it will always be there for all to enjoy.

A year later and I was back on the housing estates, this time one near Maldon in Essex, and I rented a room in the delightful little village of Tollesbury. While it was a relatively easy year workwise it did bring about the rather unwanted experience of the inside of one of Britain's police cells and a visit to the dock at Chelmsford Crown Court to defend a charge of nicking bricks!

It all began when Mum wanted a small wall built in front of our Weybridge home. Just a couple of feet high and 15 feet long, it would need about two hundred bricks. Now I already knew from my previous experience that Wimpey engineers were allowed to take small amounts of building materials for their own personal use. You couldn't slowly build a complete house, but you could have the odd bit or two, so I brought home a few samples, asked which she liked the best and planned to bring them home in the Anglia van in two goes on Friday nights. But bricks are dusty things, and on my second run, as usual, I loaded up the bricks after work, covered them in a blanket and headed for home; I hadn't gone a hundred yards before blue lights were flashing in my mirrors.

My only concern was for my driving licence. Had I been speeding? No. Was the van roadworthy? Maybe... Now, to be fair to the officers of the law, I was a scruffy 22 year old with hair down to my shoulders, wearing shorts and driving a clapped-out Anglia van – not exactly a management image. However, after a short discussion about who I was, they quickly got round to asking what was in the back of the van.

'Bricks, officer.'

'And why is they concealed under this 'ere blanket?'

'Because they are dusty, officer.'

'So where's the copper piping?'

'Copper piping, officer? What copper piping?'

It turned out that, before I arrived at the job, there had been a break-in and a large amount of copper piping had been stolen. The police had been keeping an eye on the site just in case the villains returned and they'd spied me loading my bricks and obviously decided I was their man.

'If you would kindly step out of the vehicle we would like you to accompany us to the police station.'

That got me worried! I had no knowledge of the copper piping, but I soon found myself stuffed into the back of a police car, with a police officer about to drive my van – with its bungee strap keeping the door closed – to the Maldon police station.

Having explained my side of the story nobody seemed convinced. My Mum was phoned to see if she did indeed have a pile of bricks outside her house – which naturally put her in a right old state – but I didn't know any of my employers' private numbers and they were now all gone for the night. Finger-printed, shoes and belt removed and I was stuck in a cell! I know they were all trying to do a tough job, but unfortunately I now had first-hand experience of the way you can be very much presumed guilty before being proven innocent. As time seemed to crawl by the little sliding hatch in the cell door would occasionally be flung back and pressure would be applied.

'Tell us about the copper piping and we'll forget the bricks.'

'You can forget about your career now, you won't even have a job come Monday morning.'

'If you're not in enough trouble with the bricks there's a long list full of charges concerning your van. The brakes are so bad my fellow-officer nearly had an accident.'

The van, the van! I'd almost forgotten about that side of the problem.

It must have been parked right outside my window because I could hear them unloading the bricks, counting them out one at a time. After more interviews – and more time soaking up the delights of a Maldon police cell, despite my best protestations of innocence – I was eventually charged with brick nicking and released on bail. I still have no recollection of being offered a solicitor but I assume there must have been one provided for me, and that was that. I nervously collected the Anglia's keys and drove very slowly back to Tollesbury.

Fortunately the office was open the next morning and I soon had a senior Wimpey man informing the police that, yes, engineers were allowed to take a small amount of building materials so would they please drop the charges. To everyone's amazement they decided to say no. The charge was in the books and they would see us in court.

So there we were in Chelmsford Crown Court, a full-on jury of '12 good men and true' and me standing in the dock as the accused. My barrister opened with one of those approaches to the judge, pointing out the futility of the case and what a waste of time the trial was going to be. He'd hoped for a quick dismissal but no, the prosecution intended to prove that I didn't actually know that I was allowed to take anything so therefore I would be guilty as charged.

The only good thing about it all was that I had some very flattering testaments, on oath from both Wimpey and the City University, to point out what a thoroughly nice young man I was. After the case had been heard and I was 'led below' to await the jury's findings, the court officer with me said he'd never heard anything so stupid. I'd even thought I'd seen one of the jurors wink at me so I was fairly confident of the 'not guilty' verdict that was duly announced.

Of course there was still the matter of the van, and I can only assume they were so embarrassed by the courtroom result they decided not to take it any further. The bricks were returned and the wall still stands to this day but, for the rest of my time in Maldon, I drove around very slowly...

My fourth and final summer of work experience was in the estimating department at the Hammersmith head office, where I spent most of my time working on the bid to build the Newmarket by-pass. I actually quite enjoyed the task of working out that 'if it took one man and one shovel one hour to dig one yard of a ditch it would take 387,629 men two months to build the by-pass'. The silly thing was, though, that once you'd worked out the cost to the final penny you simply doubled it for the estimate! Anyway, Wimpey won the contract and *only* lost about a million pounds building it. Maybe estimating wasn't for me after all.

By the summer of 1974 I'd donned the mortar board and gown, received the scroll and become Tiff Needell B.Sc. (Hons), a graduate of the City University with a scraped-through third class honours degree in civil engineering. I was now a full-time engineer in the structural design department in Hammersmith. Initially this just meant checking drawings and calculations made by others, but it wasn't long before I was given projects of my own.

Reinforced concrete was my speciality and, among other things, there's a five-storey office block in Basingstoke and Wimpey's own new office extension that still stand today thanks to my calculations – indeed I'm particularly proud of the grand columns and curving ramp that lead up to its mezzanine car park!

In a large open-plan office, work was always relaxed and fun. Elastic bands would regularly fizz past your ear or land with a stinging smack, while lunchtimes would be spent either down the pub by the river or playing three-card brag for money in the boardroom. Fortunately the stakes were small as I soon learned that my optimistic approach to gambling was a losing one.

While most of my fellow City graduates filtered off to solid careers in consultancy work and grandiose oil-drilling projects, I happily settled in to the nine-to-five slot at Hammersmith, with my bosses being very understanding about the bit of extra time I needed off for my racing – and then, of course, I got the van so my loyalty was confirmed. Mind you, there was many a day when I would manage to prop myself up on my drawing board, chin on elbow, and quietly have a little snooze as the effort needed to race every weekend and work every week took its toll. I was more than happy with the career I'd chosen, but by the end of '76 the dream one wasn't doing that badly either.

CHAPTER 7

Turning Professional

While the 1976 season had undoubtedly ended on a big high there was still no guarantee that my racing career was about to take off. James Hunt had just won the F1 World Championship in dramatic style and motor racing was getting plenty of good news coverage. The Grovewood Award had headlined me as the 'next Hunt' and I couldn't have been more flattered, but while the £1,000 that came with it was big money to me, I needed £35,000 to secure a Formula Three drive – and that was £34,000 more than I had.

Sponsorship letters were being posted out by the sackload and there were many supporters networking my name wherever possible, but the most frustrating thing about the sport that I had fallen in love with was that someone had to pay for it – and pay a lot. Another season in Formula Ford 2000 was on offer thanks to Mac McKinstry and Hawke, but I felt I just had to move on.

One friend who was trying to further my cause was racing driver-cum-journalist Tony Dron, who'd battled with Hunt in his early Formula Ford days in the late sixties and had just managed to get himself back into the single-seater world by persuading the British Leyland parts subsidiary Unipart to sponsor him in Formula Three. Then, as now, the engines for the formula had to be based on two-litre production car engines with an air intake restrictor to limit the power and improve reliability. For Unipart this obviously had to be a British Leyland engine and the one chosen was from the Triumph Dolomite Sprint.

At the time, apart from a smattering of Ford powerplants, virtually everyone was using the Toyota twin-cam engine tuned by the Italian

Novamotor company – as I had in the Safir – which was part of the reason that Dron had managed to persuade the flag-waving patriotic company to take on the challenge. It had been their first full season in 1976 and it had been fraught with all the usual teething problems, but Tony had got the car into the top six on several occasions and ambitious plans were being drawn up for a two-car team for the 1977 season.

It now seems strange that none of us had personal managers to help us negotiate our deals so, when Tony gave me a quiet call to let me know he'd put my name in the frame for the second drive, I did as asked and waited for the call. Ian Taylor and I were the obvious candidates but, although he'd beaten me to the FF2000 title, he was about to turn 30 and had already been an F3 champion back in 1973. Surely I was the more promotable choice? What I didn't know was that team manager Alan Howell had been Taylor's team manager at that time!

When the rumour began to spread that Taylor was to get the Unipart drive it felt like my only realistic hope had gone. Sitting by telephones waiting for them to ring is the most depressing part of a racing driver's life; there are so few opportunities that are chased by so many hopefuls and news of another lost chance makes you sink with despair. So when I answered the phone to find Alan offering me a drive I thought he was trying to wind me up.

'But I'd heard Ian had got it!'

'He has – and we want you in the other car.'

I was now alternately climbing the ceiling with euphoria and sinking to the floor with guilt, because poor Tony had obviously been the one squeezed out. Fortunately he was offered a drive in a Dolomite in the British Touring Car Championship where he excelled – winning his class for the next two seasons – but as awkward goes, that was awkward.

Just getting the drive was all I really wanted, but the next thing I knew was that they were offering to pay me *and* provide me with a company car – a white Triumph TR7 with red and blue stripes. I had arrived! Okay, with £40 a week I wasn't moving to Monte Carlo and it was actually a little less than my current salary, but Tiff Needell was turning *professional* racing driver. Wimpey gracefully accepted my resignation and offered to keep my job 'on hold' for the next two years but, as far as I was concerned, on 31 January 1977 I became a retired civil engineer.

The team planned to do the full British Championship, take in a few European Championship rounds and enter the blue riband Monaco Grand Prix support race – this was where I needed to be. Although it was obvious that Alan saw Ian as his number one – as it was he who got the new March 773 car while I made do with Dron's updated 763 chassis – we all soon gelled as one more or less happy family.

Alan was a typical old-school mechanic who lived as much for the fun of it as the results we all strove to achieve. He'd worked for James Hunt in his F3 days and been part of Graham Hill's Embassy Grand Prix team – and only at the last minute failed to take a place on the ill-fated flight home that took the lives of Hill, his young driver Tony Brise and three other team members when their light aircraft plunged into the ground approaching the Elstree aerodrome. Fortunately for me, the sterile world of sports drinks, diets and endless fitness training had yet to arrive. Instead, Alan would take us to the pub down the road from the Brentford workshop for beer, lunch and endless games of bar billiards.

Of course my new team-mate had only just finished being my greatest enemy and, while I had always been friendly with the rest of the grid, Ian's approach seemed to involve having to hate all the opposition. Naturally I wasn't quite sure how we'd get on, but we soon developed a strong friendship and had many a good laugh with each other – still clashing on the track but good mates off it. The aggro was just his way of handling the competition.

The first race of the year was supporting the big International Trophy race on the fast Silverstone Grand Prix Circuit – and we lined up first and third on the grid. Engine tuners Holbay had had a busy winter of development and had obviously come up trumps. What a year we were going to have! Obviously I was a bit niggled that Ian had the newer car, and I always knew that if one engine were slightly better than the other then he would get it – but hey, I was being paid to race and I'd get on top in the end.

The race didn't go quite as well as we'd hoped, though, as my former Formula Ford sparring partners Stephen South and Geoff Lees spoiled the party, South pushing Ian to second and Lees demoting me to fourth – quick in qualifying, we obviously needed to work on our race set-ups, but that would surely come with time.

Round two was at one of my favourite circuits, Thruxton: another super-fast track that seemed to suit our Dolomite powerplants. Once again the grid lined up in the order Taylor, South, Needell. This time, though, in wet conditions, it was my turn to push South all the way to the line, as Taylor faded first with a bad start and then with an over-revved engine. Even now it's hard to believe that those first two races would be my best of the season...

The problems began as soon as we hit the tighter tracks. While our top-end power advantage had been our ally, now our lack of low-rev torque was our enemy. Suddenly we were battling just to stay in the bottom half of the top ten. A trip back to Thruxton was blighted by some bad fuel, and then we headed to Monaco...

The 65-car entry was to be split into two 20-car heats, so the slowest 25 drivers wouldn't even get a race. Then the Formula One teams suddenly wanted another practice session for some reason or other and they scrapped the heats – so now the slowest 45 wouldn't get a race. Down on torque, there couldn't be a worse circuit than the tight confines of Monaco, and with over 30 cars in each session it was chaos. Without ever actually crashing I think I hit just about every barrier there was to hit in my efforts to make it, but I came up 0.8s short, 32nd overall with Taylor 35th – and all this with Unipart's enthusiastic PR machine making a documentary about its young stars! Little did I know that this would be a rehearsal for my return on the big stage three years later.

We now got into the vicious spiral that so easily overwhelms a team in trouble mid-season. Drivers moaning about engines, engine tuners trying modifications without time to test them fully, sponsors threatening to pull the plug, engine tuners blaming the chassis installation – we had it all. The team even bought a rival Chevron chassis and put an engine in that, but the result was inconclusive.

Both Ian and I were driving on the ragged edge, regularly upsetting our midfield opponents as we wove around on the straights to stop them passing or dived inside them with desperate overtaking manoeuvres. At the European Championship round at Donington in August I even found myself slammed into the barriers by my team-mate – and having returned to the pits on foot I would have to be asked to apologise to the Unipart guests in the garage at the time for my colourful description of what I thought of Ian at that precise moment.

October would see the last three races of the season but, after I'd blown three engines during the course of retiring from the first two, the team pulled the plug with one race left to go and rumours began that they wouldn't be back for the following season. The job held for me back at Wimpey was suddenly looking like an option.

There was, however, one last roll of the dice to come in 1977. My South African mate Rad Dougall had taken on my mantle as the Formula Ford 2000 star, racing a works Royale sponsored by the Toleman Group. Working at the race team's factory, he had been helping run Toleman Group directors Bob Toleman and Alex Hawkridge in a pair of FF1600 cars the year before. Tragically, Bob was killed in an accident at Snetterton towards the end of the year, so Alex switched from driving to managing and, supported by Bob's brother Ted, backed Rad's FF2000 season.

I'd met both Bob and Alex when my brother raced against them in the Crosslé he'd bought from me on a visit to England, before he shipped the car to South Africa. During the '77 season we'd kept in touch, and Alex had occasionally asked my advice on where I thought Rad should be going next. While that was all good for Rad I was now the one who needed help and, with my F3 career going pear shaped, I was desperate to salvage something from the season. Coincidentally, Unipart's withdrawal from the last race of the year left me free for the weekend of the European Formula Two finale at

Donington, where a seat just happened to be going in Fred Opert's race-winning Chevron team.

Alex is one of those men who makes things happen, and before I knew it my subtle hint had become a reality. A deal was done and I was to make my F2 debut on the weekend of my 26th birthday – old by today's standards, but definitely not too old back then.

There was only time for one hour's testing on the day before official qualifying, but the power of the car had been a revelation, its Hart engine firing me forwards at an awesome speed. This dream was just getting more and more exciting. Unfortunately, just 20 minutes into the final 90-minute session that really mattered, the belt that drove both fuel and oil pumps broke and I was stranded out on the circuit. As soon as the warning light had come on I'd switched off, but now there was the extra worry that the engine had been damaged – life is never easy as a racing driver.

My early demise left me stranded back in 20th place on the grid but my confidence had been growing and, having got used to the extra power, I was just beginning to use it to its full advantage. In the race I fought up to 13th place on the 13th lap of the 13th round of the European Championship and was having a great dice with rising Italian star Elio de Angelis when the engine broke. Happily the dreaded curse of superstition has never come my way but, just for once, I was tempted to believe that fate had it in for me. There are plenty of drivers who always have to put their left glove on first or get into the car from the right side or wear their lucky underpants... it must be a real pain and is something I'm delighted to have avoided.

So that was it, a season that had started with so much promise had ended in terminal disappointment, and all I could do now was get through a miserable Christmas waiting to hear if Unipart intended to continue. Even if they did, would the car be any good? There was certainly nothing else in the offing, the sponsorship letters were still bouncing back with polite refusals and the only other option was civil engineering.

Fortunately for me, Unipart determined to continue. Alan Howell and Swindon Engines had to fall on their swords and Dave Price was put in charge of an all-new team with two March 783 chassis and Dolomite powerplants now tuned by Swindon Racing Engines. Unfortunately none of this changed the results! The cars looked great in a new patriotic Union flag colour scheme and optimism sprang eternal within the team, but the new engines weren't working well and, having missed the start of the season, Ian and I began our year by doing alternate races with the one usable engine we had. There was the odd flash of promise, but when the decision was made to drop the big trip to Monaco things reached an all-time low.

We did, however, get to do two overseas races, the second of which was perhaps the highlight of the year. The first, at Dijon in June, only served to introduce me to a young French star of the future by the name of Alain Prost. Alain was suffering the same 'character-building' career as me as he battled to develop Renault's new F3 engine. We lined up way back in 19th and 20th places, sharing the 10th row of the grid for this round of the European Championship, and we drove ourselves to the ragged edge simply to end up 10th and 11th.

A far better result – or I should say performance – came a couple of months later when we set off to the ultra-fast Osterreichring for a race that supported the Austrian Grand Prix. With its high-speed swoops devoid of any demands for low-speed acceleration, the Dolomite once more came into its own. The circuit also suited my driving style, which I'd adapted to cater for our lack of horsepower by running less rear wing to reduce drag, and then living with a consequently very twitchy car.

After the embarrassment of Monaco the year before Unipart had chosen this race to make another PR film and, to make sure of at least one good story, placed Niki Lauda's cousin Thomas into one of our last year's cars. Not that we ended up needing a publicity stunt, as I planted my car on the front row of the grid for the race with Taylor back in 14th and Lauda 23rd. It was an uncomfortable weekend for Ian as, after all the disappointments, I think he was beginning to lose motivation quicker than I was and he just didn't seem to be on the pace all weekend. If he had been the unofficial number one the previous year, I was now definitely the team's favourite.

With Dave Price's eternal enthusiasm and optimism urging me on we all thought this could be our day. Both pole-man Guido Pardini and I had lapped faster than when the European Championship had visited the circuit, and the Italian obviously had one of the best Novamotor Toyotas in his Ralt chassis.

The novelty of a rolling start saw me taking an over-cautious approach and initially drop to third, with rising American star Bobby Rahal snapping at my heels. By the time I'd moved up a place Pardini was three seconds up the road, but gradually I hauled him in and we began a tremendous high-speed duel. The little Italian's Ralt was still quicker than me in a straight line, but I eased back just a fraction entering the glorious high-speed swoops and then built a slightly higher corner exit speed to edge back closer and closer, little deft touches of opposite lock constantly catching the wandering rear end. This was what I lived for!

As the race neared its end Guido started becoming more and more defensive, taking the inside line into some corners. On a couple of occasions I dived down the outside and hung on all the way round the final Rindt Curve leading on to the finish straight, but each time the Ralt would edge back in front before we reached the finish line. I could see little Dave leaping up and down in the pits and the whole team was hanging over the wall willing me on.

I was trying to work out a plan of what I would do and where I would do it. The last-corner idea wasn't going to work, but I'd noticed Guido was getting slower and slower in the second Texaco Curve. So that was it, there could be no rehearsal to give the game away and it would have to wait for the last lap or he would simply waft back past on the straight. I was going to dive inside him on the tight left-hander before the final corner and win the race... but then the engine stopped. This time it wasn't even an engine fault, simply a dud battery that ran out of spark – I had to shield my eyes to hide the tears that flowed. When you work so hard to achieve something and come so close to making it happen it's hard to stop the emotion pouring out.

Apart from being involved in the massive 16-car pile-up at the start of the British Grand Prix support race – which seems to feature on all the 'best crash' videos – the only other real highlight of another dismal year in Formula Three came courtesy of a timely shower of rain as we sat on the Cadwell Park grid. Loving the circuit, I'd dragged the March to fourth in qualifying, but that was still over a second slower than pole-man Nelson Piquet who was in the middle of a record-breaking run of victories.

Fortunately the arrival of rain saw most of the opposition panicking and switching to wet tyres. By the time the flag dropped only Nelson and I, of the front runners, still had slick tyres on our cars. It felt like a re-run of my Brands Hatch FF2000 race; I just love these conditions, where the car is continually 'alive' in your hands. After slithering back a few places early on, by half-distance I was glued to Piquet's gearbox and we were dicing for the lead.

While Cadwell is probably the most exciting track in Britain to drive round on your own, it is narrow and overtaking opportunities are rare, so all I could do was hope to pressure Piquet into making a mistake – but it wasn't something he was about to do. Resisting the temptation to give him a subtle nudge, I duly followed him home for a morale-boosting second with the consolation of fastest lap – for which I would be honoured with the prestigious 'Big Balls' trophy at the end-of-season awards!

While these brief demonstrations of my talent helped keep my name in the frame as one of the drivers with a future, it is results that really count and, while journalists continued to appreciate my plight and were sympathetic to my cause, my career was going nowhere. It was something of which I was all too aware. The Unipart backing had been brilliant but for all the effort they put in they received poor reward – and I needed to move on.

While my career was stalling, Rad Dougall's seemed to be soaring. Alex and Ted Toleman had decided to skip F3 completely and run him in Formula Two in a March 782 BMW. In an extremely competitive season it was a tough learning curve, and after a brilliant third in the opening round at Silverstone Rad had only managed one other top-six finish.

Now one of the downsides of being a racing driver is that you have to sometimes take on the personality of a vulture – even if it's one of your friends who is suffering. So, with Rad struggling slightly, I obviously kept in close touch with Alex and the Toleman Group. My perseverance paid off with an offer once again to drive in the final round of the European Formula Two Championship, this time at the German Hockenheim Circuit that had so cruelly claimed the life of my hero, Jim Clark.

The team had kept a spare chassis on standby for the season but, as this was the last round, it would be free. With the help of a deal to run one of Heini Mader's BMW engines they were able to enter two cars – and in my mind they might want to enter two cars for the whole of the following season. The only problem was that the race clashed with an F3 fixture, so I had to try and get myself released from that. Fortunately Unipart were very supportive of my career and they realised it was an opportunity not to be missed so once again they gave me the weekend off.

Best news of all was that Hockenheim was *my* kind of circuit. Huge long straights were cut in half by a couple of fast chicanes and joined at the top by the magnificent Ostkurve, a corner where you arrived flat out in top gear, dabbed the brakes, dropped from fifth to fourth gear and then committed yourself. Brilliant! At the other end of the straights lay the tight twists and turns of the stadium section, enveloped all round by vast tiered grandstands. To be quick down the straights you needed to run as little downforce as possible, so the tighter turns demanded delicate throttle control. While the regulars had already visited the track earlier in the year, I had only ever done the one race round the short circuit in the Hawke Formula Ford so I had some catching up to do – and with 42 cars vying for 26 places on the grid the first target was simply to qualify.

With the team managed by former driver Tom Walkinshaw – who was heading towards creating Le Mans-winning Jaguars – and engineered by Rory Byrne – who would go on to design Grand Prix-winning Ferraris – it certainly didn't lack for anything and I was instantly at ease in a car that just seemed to be made for me. For once, I had the best of everything.

There were quite a few of my old British F3 sparring partners there – Lees, South, Derek Daly and Ronnie Peterson's Swedish protégé, Eje Elgh. Eje had become a close friend and had been the person to introduce me to the wonders of their favourite Scandinavian schnapps, Aquavit – I don't think I sobered up for three days! Anyway, Eje reckoned I would do well just to make the grid.

But I would actually do more than just make the grid, for after the two timed sessions I would start seventh for my second F2 race – one place in front of Rad, who I seemed to have spurred on to one of his best results for a while. In fact, had the session not been suddenly cut short by five minutes, just as I was putting on some fresh tyres, it could have been even better. Over the long two-minute lap, just a couple of tenths would have elevated me to fifth!

I wasn't just 'walking tall' – I was floating round with a big grin on my face. My name seemed to be buzzing round the paddock and there actually seemed to be a lot of sympathy from those who understood my trials and tribulations of the previous two years. Even soon-to-be McLaren supremo Ron Dennis, whose Project Four team was running a couple of cars, was impressed! Obviously things were a little awkward with Rad, but we knew each other well and he knew that the Toleman team was still very much *his* team.

The race was a two-part aggregate affair with the overall results decided by the combined time of the two 20-lap races. Rad got the jump on me at the start so I felt obliged to settle down behind him and keep out of trouble but, when he was pitched off into the barriers at high speed, I was left to battle on my own, getting involved in some frantic slipstreaming action. For most of the race I was contesting fifth place with the Project Four pairing of Eddie Cheever and Ingo Hoffmann, with South in the mix as well. Eddie was struggling with blistering tyres, but when I went to pass, flat in top on the way down to the first chicane, he gently eased me on to the grass. Welcome to F2, I thought. The big boys didn't appreciate the upstart. Assuming this was the norm, I returned the compliment to Hoffmann a couple of laps later – and after the race he went ballistic! So, it was just a Cheever thing, then...

When Cheever eventually pitted for tyres, and Daly had a puncture, I was elevated to fourth and determinedly held on to that position to the finish – beaten by Lotus Formula One reject Brian Henton, who was trying to re-establish his career, and the two works March cars of champions-elect Bruno Giacomelli and Marc Surer. I would start my third F2 race from the inside of the second row.

When Henton suffered a gearbox glitch at the start of the second part he was swamped by the pack, while the third works March of Manfred Winkelhock pushed me back to where I'd started, in fourth. It took me six laps to dispose of the German and I soon pulled clear, at one stage holding the race's fastest lap as the two March drivers in front held station. I was going to be third, going to be on the podium in front of one of the biggest crowds of the year...

Then, hurtling towards the entrance to the stadium section, a connecting rod bolt broke and the engine exploded. The flailing rod punched two big holes in the cylinder block and the hot oil that escaped erupted in a fireball. With the flames being sucked into the cockpit by the slipstream it was getting mighty hot where I was sitting. Having braked to what I thought was a safe speed, I undid my belts and stood on the seat as the car rolled into the view of the crowd. Unfortunately what I thought was about 20mph was more like 60mph, so my plan to jump clear didn't look so good! Luckily the oil fire subsided as quickly as it had started so I meekly slid back down into the seat and brought the car to a halt.

From where I parked I could walk back across the infield to the paddock, and the raucous approval from the knowledgeable German crowd simply caused the tears to well up yet again. Once more I had been so near yet so far on the big stage. Surely this time someone would sit up and take note? Surely Toleman would run two cars for the following season...

Meanwhile, back in England, the Unipart saga was beginning to come to an end. As a stand-in, Dave Price had engaged the talented Kiwi Brett Riley, who he'd run the year before on a very tight budget, and they'd been testing ahead of the race. The story goes that Brett in 'my' car had been consistently quicker than Ian, and when Ian got him to try his car he too couldn't make it go any quicker – so Ian elected not to race. At the end of two hard years with a project he'd put so much effort into he wasn't going to turn up and be embarrassed by a new team-mate – and you have to see his point.

We were, in any case, into the full circle of engine tuners saying the engines were all the same and drivers, as drivers always do, insisting that 'theirs' was definitely down on power on the others. There was also the question of our own efforts. Dispirited drivers often don't perform to their best ability, new blood can bring an injection of enthusiasm – and so, on my return, I found Ian had 'stood down' permanently.

When I was then left trailing by Brett at the next two races my whole world started to go pear shaped – especially when he led at my home circuit, Brands Hatch. No, they hadn't switched the engines. No, there wasn't only one good engine. No, there was no favouritism towards Brett, I just needed to sort my chassis – the mood wasn't good. Having just raised my stock in Germany I was being made to look decidedly second rate in my own team.

With a big gulp of self-confidence I insisted that, before the final two races, we go to Goodwood to test and, having set a time in my car with my engine, we'd swap the engines. This was no two-minute job and something I'm sure none of the mechanics were too keen on just to soothe my ego, but I reiterated that it had to be done – and after the test, Brett's engine stayed in my chassis and he was never in front of me again... To be fair to everyone, we were all trying in our own way to get the best result for the team. Engines that perform well on the test bed sometimes don't reproduce that form when installed in a car. Perhaps Unipart already saw Brett as a driver for the future while they knew I wanted to move on. It's all part of the very complex world that makes motor racing such an intriguing sport. The mind is a very complex thing.

Anyway, I actually came within a squint of winning the last round of the championship back around the high-speed curves of Thruxton, losing out by a scant three-tenths of a second – even if I did have to stick poor old Thorkild Thyrring on his head to get him out of the way! Somehow this second place added to my other at Cadwell plus all sorts of lowly top-six results saw me climb to fourth overall in the championship, but well behind the dominant trio of Nelson Piquet, Derek Warwick and Chico Serra. We'd all make it to Formula One, but some would be more successful than others.

There was no doubt the Unipart act was finally coming together. Swindon Racing Engines could obviously make one good engine – even if it still wasn't quite good enough – so surely they could make more. But would they ever be regular winners? While in its own element, able to breathe as much air as it wanted, the Triumph engine was one of the best, but the fact that all its 16 valves worked on one camshaft always seemed to me to be a potential Achilles heel – surely less efficient than two when 'getting going' was critical and when its air intake was restricted. Not that my layman's theory seemed to carry much weight with the engine tuners!

So it was that another winter of discontent loomed, another Christmas not knowing where I was going. Unipart were being very positive about the future, but could I really do a third season in F3 – and that age thing was beginning to become more of a concern. It was going to be hard to walk away from a paid drive, but then there was also the growing rumour of that second car at Toleman...

CHAPTER 8

FORMULA ONE BUT NO
GRAND PRIX

For a racing driver, the problem with Christmas and the New Year is that everything comes to a halt. Just when you want to be knocking on the marketing director's door to convince him that an association with 'the next James Hunt' is a brilliant idea, he's either off down the boozer for the Christmas party or sunning himself on a Caribbean beach.

If I stayed at Unipart I would have to start winning races again. It doesn't matter if everyone understands you don't have the best equipment; as soon as you stop winning your star begins to fade – and I hadn't won a race for two years. Reaching the top in motorsport is all about momentum and mine had ground to a halt. The only alternative to not winning was to do something different. So could the Triumph Dolomite finally be made into a winner? If I walked away, would Brett Riley win every round of the championship and be snapped up by Ferrari? All of this was twirling round in my mind, but I kept on thinking that if two of the top engine tuners had spent three years trying to make it work, surely it never would – but then I remembered way back to those first two races of 1977 when we *were* the cars to beat! How could it all have gone so wrong? The potential must still be there…

Obviously I'd been keeping in touch with the Toleman situation and there were indeed plans brewing to run two new Ralt chassis in the European Championship – but there were also rumours that they were considering bringing Brian Henton into the team to use his experience to develop the new car and help Rad progress. Maybe it hadn't been such a good idea out-qualifying him at Hockenheim! Henton's race there had ended in a massive accident when he had a territorial dispute with my mate Cheever. His car was destroyed and, running on his own money, it looked like the end of a once promising career. The sympathy vote was also in his favour.

With the Toleman drive such an obvious place for me to go I made another basic mistake by putting all my eggs in one basket. Only years later did I discover that, after my Hockenheim performance, March supremo Robin Herd would have somehow made things happen if I'd come knocking on his door. He had assumed I was going Toleman's way, and with them switching to the rival Ralt chassis he wasn't to know any better.

There was, however, one other option that was looming large on the horizon. A British Formula One Championship had grown out of the ashes of the old Formula 5000 series and it was about to receive a boost by the arrival of sponsorship from model racing makers Aurora. With three races on the continent and a dozen at home it looked an attractive alternative.

John Surtees had given the series extra credibility by announcing that, after 19 years of struggling to run his own Grand Prix team, he was quitting the World Championship to concentrate on other fields – like the Aurora series. The *Sun* newspaper report even went on to say that he would 'probably use Tiff Needell, one of Britain's most promising young drivers'! I had had a meeting with John, but of course while he was keen to put something together and underwrite some of the cost, sponsorship had to be found.

Mind you, that wasn't the only opportunity going because former driver and preparation specialist Graham Eden had put together a package to run three promising young drivers for a third of the season each in the unique and never raced Chevron B41 Formula One car sponsored by my old friends Durex – who, coincidentally, had just ended their Grand Prix deal with Surtees.

Now, one of my main faults is that I always feel happier when I'm in a comfort zone. I don't like boldly leaping forwards into the unknown when there is an easier path to take. I didn't want to leave the security of Unipart, but finally I knew I had to. There were opportunities out there and, like the March deal, they might not come my way if everyone assumed I was sorted. After much deliberation I finally made the great step into the unknown: unemployed – apart from labouring for a friend on a building site – I launched myself into a freelance world where I would pretty much stay right through to the present day. I was now 27 years old, still living at home with Mum and Dad, but still living the dream. I could never be grateful enough for all the support that Unipart had given me, but I just had to move on – and of course, as it turned out, it wouldn't be the end of our relationship. As soon as word spread that I was leaving Unipart the phone began to ring with a string of hopefuls wanting to take my place – and one of them had a very distinctive accent.

'Hello, my name is Nigel Mansell and I want your drive.'

Now I gave Nigel exactly the same advice as I'd given the others, but it was he who got my drive – and then of course it would be Mansell who would eventually be the next James Hunt! At the time, the talk was all of Henton, Keegan, Lees, Warwick, South or me being the next British World Champion but, after British drivers had claimed ten of the first 27 championships, we would have to endure a 16-year break before 'Our Nige' did the business.

The first option to fall by the wayside was the one I really wanted – the Toleman drive. Alex made the call and pretty much told me what I'd expected was going to happen: the man with experience had got the nod. Inevitably there was talk of 'maybe next year', but that's never what you want to hear, and with Brian being such a good driver it was pretty hard to argue against their choice.

By now most of the sponsorship approaches that had even yielded the slightest interest were beginning to come back with the standard 'our budgets for this year have been allocated' answer – so the Durex scholarship was fast looking like my only hope. Like every young ambitious driver I had, so far, been completely focused on that one ambition – to be a Grand Prix driver. But there comes a time when you realise you must begin to glance sideways. Only about 30 drivers across the world are engaged at the pinnacle of our sport at any one time, fewer than a single football club's squad, so in reality your chances of gaining one of those spots are desperately small.

By now I had actually signed on the dole. At the interview I had been asked what my 'profession' was and got rather a strange look when I simply stated 'racing driver'! Of course you can't just name a job when filling in such a form, they need codes to put you in a category – and to both my own and my interviewer's amazement she found it in her big book, bracketed with driving instructors, bus drivers and lorry drivers. Having informed her that 'No, I wasn't looking for an opening in any of the alternative occupations', I joined the weekly queue for my cheque.

The decision had thus to be made to start looking at alternative forms of the sport where there was the possibility of making a living, whether it was in single-seaters, sportscars or saloons. March were looking at taking a BMW M1 to Le Mans for a trio of British drivers, which was certainly a race I'd always wanted to do, while Tom Walkinshaw was busy setting up the 'BMW County Championship' for a grid full of identical 323i cars. He kindly put my name forward for one of the drives, so there were possibilities in the pipeline.

However, to my great relief, my campaign for the Durex nomination came up trumps when I was selected to do the first four races of the season, starting with the opening round over at the Belgian circuit of Zolder – more omens for the future! Graham Eden's Chevron was a one-off that had been designed some three years earlier but never raced so it wasn't exactly a known quantity. I had a brief test at Silverstone before we went and nearly destroyed the car on my out lap. In cold wet conditions, crossing the famous 'river' that bisected the track diagonally in the braking area for Club, the car simply swapped ends in the blink of an eye. I didn't really do any correction and the car completed a swift 360-degree spin and just continued running. I didn't think it necessary to tell Graham...

The Chevron was powered by the ubiquitous Ford Cosworth DFV and, once my heartbeat had returned to normal, I soon became yet another dedicated admirer of this engine which had won its first Grand Prix in the back of Jim Clark's Lotus some 13 years earlier. Without the complex electronic management systems of modern engines it was embarrassingly difficult to trickle out of the pit lane without stalling, and it would feel rough and uninterested until the revs moved over the 7,000rpm mark – then it would chime in with a sudden wall of power and simply the sweetest of sounds as the rev counter rapidly headed for its 10,500 red line.

Arriving at Zolder for my Formula One debut there were just Graham with the Chevron in a truck, his part-time fireman mechanic, me and my mate Phil to help out. This was Formula One on a budget! With the Chevron being so new we suffered all sorts of teething problems that limited us to just 16 laps of running in the dry and left me back in ninth on the grid. Fortunately, just before the race there was a shower of the rain and, although the track remained mainly dry, the organisers declared it a 'wet race'. This meant they wouldn't red-flag it if it rained, so with the track not really fully wet the only option was to start on slicks – my kind of conditions.

It was almost the dream debut – but not quite. After over an hour of 'on the ragged edge' racing with the occasional light shower keeping the surface nice and slippery, I was challenging for the lead with one lap to go. But, just as at Cadwell Park with Piquet, I couldn't quite pull off the pass as David Kennedy got his revenge for the Zandvoort stitch-up and held me off by a fifth of a second at the line. It was an euphoric result – and the day ended with all the glamour of helping Graham to load the truck before sitting down for a simple beer with grins all over our faces.

Unfortunately there was no way the rest of my drives in the Chevron were going to reproduce such a result unless the weather came to my aid again – and it didn't. The car simply wasn't competitive enough, despite Graham's every effort to improve it, but the Durex Award had given me what I needed – the experience of a drive in a Formula One car and a headline result to go with it – even if I was now once again effectively unemployed.

Then came the sort of opportunity that arrives increasingly rarely as the safety of our sport thankfully gets better and better: a mid-season chance of a Grand Prix drive. The opportunity didn't even come from a motor racing crash but from an injury to Patrick Depailler in a hang gliding accident – not that I was in the frame for a drive in his race-winning Ligier, but instead in the Ensign N179 DFV that Derek Daly had quit in the hope of getting that drive.

Being free from any other commitments and now armed with Formula One experience my name was soon on the list of possible replacements. This time the phone brought the almost unbelievable news that eight years after winning a magazine competition Tiff Needell was set to head to Dijon in France to make his Grand Prix debut! Admittedly, it was probably in the most ugly and ungainly car on the grid – not that it had been on the grid very often, as Daly had only managed to qualify it once – but little did I care.

All I had to do was apply for the newly introduced Grand Prix Super Licence and my ten-year-old Ford Capri and I were going to be on the road to France. But then circumstances intervened. The war between Bernie Ecclestone and Max Mosley representing FOCA – the constructors' association – and the Paris-based world governing body, FISA – ruled by its autocratic president Jean-Marie Balestre – was just beginning to break out and the French said... 'Non'!

The Super Licence had just been introduced to prevent the increasing number of average drivers who were trying to buy their way into Formula One with insufficient talent but a huge stash of cash – mobile chicanes were not what the pinnacle of our sport needed. The French therefore came up with all sorts of qualifications that would need to be satisfied, but the basic ones were that you either had to finish in the top five of either five F2 races or ten F3 races over a two-year period. No problem – except when you looked a little more closely the wording said 'international' races.

Now, since Formula Three had begun the British Championship was without doubt the most prestigious and competitive series going. Drivers came from all over the world to prove their worth. From Brazil to the USA, Australia to Sweden they all came to Britain, but little did anyone really notice that the races were run on 'British' permits. This simply saved the entrants from having the extra cost of FISA officials at every race, but in no way did this dilute the challenge of the series.

Of course the French couldn't be blamed on their own. Britain had an RAC representative on the FISA Council and someone should have spotted this potential contradiction – but they didn't and so none of my F3 results counted, and nor did my Aurora efforts, nor my F2 finish as that was just 'half' the final result. No, on paper I was stuffed. Surely they would see the nonsense of the ruling and hand me a waiver... 'Non'!

Ensign boss Mo Nunn appealed to them, the RAC appealed, Bernie Ecclestone and Max Mosley supported my cause while I simply wore the carpet out, pacing up and down by the phone. I simply couldn't believe this was happening. I'd got something I'd sacrificed everything for and it was about to be taken from me by some bureaucrats in Paris.

But taken away it was, the best week of my life had just turned into my worst nightmare and, with just a day to go before the race, Nunn's only realistic option for a driver was... a Frenchman. And a Frenchman who'd started his Formula Three career by racing against me in the British F3 Championship! Indeed, in 1977 Patrick Gaillard had more often than not been behind me in my recalcitrant Unipart March but had gone on to be one of the stars of the '78 European Championship and so had qualified for his Super Licence.

By now the effort of picking myself up and pushing onwards was beginning to wear a bit thin, but at least my season was far from being over. I still had a couple of Durex races to do, Bernie and Max fixed me a drive in the BMW M1 Procar race supporting the British Grand Prix (a Grand Prix which had no English drivers in it, as I had to endure the sight of Gaillard racing in 'my' Ensign) and, while the March Le Mans entry hadn't materialised, I was enjoying some brilliant door handle racing in the BMW County Championship. There was also an outing sharing Stuart Graham's 'Brut 33' Capri at Silverstone's Tourist Trophy event where we finished fourth overall and won our class. I was a winner again at last!

But perhaps what would the most significant move in my career came with a few opportunities to race out in the Far East – and they were going to pay me. The first trip was for a round of the Japanese Formula Two Championship courtesy of March's Robin Herd. He wanted me to help improve the fortunes of their new 792 'ground-effect' model which was proving tricky to sort out – the fact that he wanted me to tell the Japanese teams to swap the front springs for the back to make it work would lead to much disbelief and oriental head scratching.

Flying the cheapest way possible meant that my first ever long-haul flight would be in an Aeroflot Ilyushin 62 that looked like a VC10 copy. March's James Gresham joined me on the trip from London to Moscow and then on to Tokyo, and we took something like 20 hours to get there. Still in the thick of the Cold War, it was a bizarre experience – and if you think modern budget airlines are 'no frills' this beat the lot. For starters, the cabin was pumped with air that appeared to have been sanitised by toilet disinfectant, while the glum welcome from the stewardesses promised a long and boring trip. There was no in-flight entertainment at all – not even one single film – so we just sat there, read books or tried vainly to elicit even the slightest of smiles from one of the crew. Yet this was very much a part of why I'd wanted to be a racing driver in the first place. To travel the world in whatever direction the sport took me, to experience different cultures, different tracks and different competition – the fact that the Aeroflot experience was so bad was actually all part of the enjoyment, especially as I wasn't paying for it!

There were no such problems when we landed in Japan, though; this was a properly foreign country and I was instantly taken by the service, the enthusiasm and the politeness from everyone around us. Two days in Tokyo saw us bartering over the price of watches, calculators and cameras in the bustling back-street stores and getting completely lost in a city that has no street names to guide you and, at that time, not even any signposts in English.

The Bullet train whisked us the 250 miles westwards to the Suzuka Circuit and proved a stark contrast to my British Rail experiences. The food trolley would enter your carriage and the servers would gently bow to the occupants before offering all sorts of weird and wonderful treats, then gently bow again as they left. Courtesy, respect, charm – however you like to look at it, it was a refreshing touch.

Suzuka Circuit is, of course, still one of the greatest, but back then it was even better. Now the Degner and Spoon Curves have had their flowing contours abruptly altered, with entry points now earlier, as with Paddock at Brands and Copse at Silverstone. While this provides greater run-off it loses the deep, more challenging entry. These great old corners were designed to have slower entries and faster exits but sadly their 'modernisation' has made them the opposite, thus reducing the overtaking opportunity. On top of that, the final stop-go chicane had yet to be installed so the last corner was an unbelievably fast right over a blind crest... magic!

Once again I was thrown into a new car on a new circuit and with very little time to get used to either – especially as the Hong Kong customs had decided to delay the car for a couple of days. The 792 was March's first 'ground-effect' car using the dark art of accelerating the airflow under the car in order to create a negative pressure that would literally suck the car into the ground. After Lotus had dominated the '78 World Championship with such effect this would now be the future of all car designs – and it might be argued our sport would never be quite the same.

Ground effect demands that the chassis of the car is kept close to the ground and at as constant an attitude as possible, so suspension travel is its enemy. Until now we'd balanced our racing cars with controlled pitch and roll, transferring load from one corner to the other in a manner that gave us the grip and feel that we wanted. With ground effect the cars demanded to be jarringly stiff and driven as if on rails. Before designers learned to control the effect, some cars would start bouncing up and down on the straights – porpoising, as it was called – as the car would suck itself so low it would block the airflow, then suddenly lose that suck and leap back upwards only to be instantly sucked back down as the airflow resumed. Blurring your vision, it was like driving a Pogo stick at 180mph.

Despite all this I was quite chuffed to qualify sixth on the grid and go on to finish fourth in a field full of Japanese superstars that included Satoru Nakajima, who would soon be gracing the Grand Prix grids for Lotus. Blindingly quick in his homeland, for some reason Satoru never seemed to be able to replicate that form when he travelled overseas, perhaps missing the physiological warmth his very different world provided for him.

After the race I was handed my prize money in one of those classically decorated envelopes that you see Sumo wrestlers receive after their bouts and, after downing a huge frosted glass of Asahi draft, I headed to my room in the Suzuka Circuit Hotel to discover its contents – a wad of brand-new 10,000 yen notes! I threw them up in the air and watched them flutter down on to my bed. I'd only earned about £2,500 the previous year and there must have been £1,000 right there, in cash. It was time to sign off the dole...

My next adventure would send me further south, into the steamy tropical world of Malaysia, where the local Unipart franchise had asked if one of their UK drivers could make an appearance for a Formula Pacific race. With Riley and Mansell too busy, the now freelance, have-helmet-will-travel journeyman driver was assigned the task.

This time I flew in a British Airways Boeing 747 – the original jumbo jet – and oh what a difference. It was party time all the way! Being a happy smoker back then, I used the trick of taking a non-smoking seat – you don't want other people blowing smoke over you – and then wandering down the back for a puff. With just two films for the whole trip and no 'entertainment' consoles I wasn't the only one on the move and parties of smokers and drinkers used to gather down the end and while the time away.

Landing at Kuala Lumpur there were no jet bridges to connect the jumbo to the terminal so we got off down some good old-fashioned stairs and walked to the terminal. But exiting the plane was an experience of its own as, for the first time, I felt the effect of dense humidity. It was if someone had just covered my mouth with a hot, wet towel scented with tropical spices. Walking across the tarmac on a dark evening I felt as if I could be Humphrey Bogart in *Casablanca*. This was what the excitement and romance of travel was surely all about.

Once again customs officials had decided to delay the arrival of my racing car – this time in Singapore – not that it was a brand-new machine but a three-year-old March 76B imported from Australia. When it did arrive it was in a fair old state, and it was all the team could do just to get it on track for some running the night before the grandly titled 'Selangor Grand Prix' at the Shah Alam track just outside Kuala Lumpur. With paint that was barely dry, porous wheels leaking air, a gear linkage that didn't want to engage gears and myriad minor niggles it was all a bit of a disaster – not to mention the fact that I was still trying to get to grips with the idea of driving a racing car while sitting in a sauna. I somehow got to the finish, despite a wheel trying to detach itself, and it wasn't long before I was drinking another refreshingly cool beer in the bar and getting to know the Aussie and Kiwi stars who were regular visitors to these events.

Unipart wanted me to return in about a month's time to race for them in the Far East's big event, the Macau Grand Prix. This is held round the streets of what was then the Portuguese colony that lies to the west of Hong Kong – now, of course, both have returned to the control of the Chinese. It was an event I wanted to do but not in that tatty March so, with time on my hands, I agreed to return to Kuala Lumpur in a couple of weeks with an English mechanic, do a thorough rebuild of the March and then go with it to Macau for the race.

Toleman mechanic Barry Foulds was my man for the occasion, and with a job list that would normally take a month we were busy boys – well, Barry certainly was. I did a lot of heckling and handing of spanners but mainly suggested it was surely time for a beer. Exhausted by the oppressive heat we didn't even go out on the town much, but at least the March was progressing nicely. Barry was welding in all sorts of extra braces to stiffen the chassis up a bit and he managed to overwork himself to the extent that his ankles suddenly swelled up in the heat and he was ordered to sit down for a day.

The fact that he managed to do this on the day we had to replace the rubber bag tanks seemed to me to be more than just a coincidence. Racing car fuel tanks are like bladders that are filled with plastic foam to stop the fuel sloshing about and to slow down any leaks. Someone had been using aviation-grade 'Avgas' in the car, which rots the foam, so they had to be replaced. The tanks on the March were long sausage-shaped things down each side of the car and they were perfectly shaped to fit the contours of the monocoque chassis – the problem was you had to push them in via a small hatch at one end. With the rubber gripping the inside of the tank the only way to do this was with liberal use of talcum powder. So there I was, in the stifling heat of a Kuala Lumpur workshop, covered in white powder, streaked with rivers of sweat, trying to shove this great rubber sausage inside the car, with Barry alternating between shouting instructions and falling about laughing!

Quite how we got it all done I'll never know, but we made it to Macau and readied our little team for the race. The Macau track is like a wild, stretched-out version of Monaco with a huge long straight broken by a couple of flat-out kinks and then a switchback 'mountain' section with no room at all for error. In 1979 the booming expansion of the area had yet to really get under way, and where there are now huge hotels built on reclaimed land to the left of the straight there was simply water – and coming out of the last corner there was little to stop you going into it if you got it all wrong.

There was still plenty of poverty in the region, with the centre of the circuit an area of semi-jungle inhabited by families living in shanty accommodation complete with their livestock. We were given garage space alongside four other cars in an old army Nissen hut, and I was shocked to discover an identical building alongside was housing what must have been a couple of hundred Vietnamese boat people. The end of the Vietnam War had seen vast numbers fleeing the new communist regime in their small boats and I found this a very humbling experience, embarrassed by my decadent western lifestyle.

Traditionally the event was a big battle between the two rival teams assembled by Hong Kong businessmen Teddy Yip and Bob Harper, who had imported Grand Prix stars Riccardo Patrese, Rupert Keegan and Derek Daly for the annual clash. However, I was to find that the little three-year-old March that Barry and I had built was up to the challenge of the stars in their new cars.

Revelling in a car that just seemed to do what I wanted – and a circuit that once again demanded the kind of low-downforce set-up that suits me – I shaved every barrier to plant 'Team Unipart' fourth on the grid. When pole-man Patrese fluffed his start I tagged on to the back of the Ralts of American aces Kevin Cogan and his 'Flying Tiger' team-mate Bob Earl for the early part of the race. I held off the Italian Grand Prix star for as long as I could and then, just after the half-way mark, a rod in the gear linkage simply sheared off, due to old age! By then I was running a solid fourth, well clear of the eventual third-place man. There was huge disappointment but great pride in what we had achieved – and simply driving round that circuit right on the edge of control had been one of the greatest buzzes of my career. I'm still able to re-live every corner in my mind.

Back home the Toleman saga still wasn't over as, once again, they stepped up with an offer of a car for the last round of the European Formula Two Championship at Donington. This time I was to drive one of the previous year's March 782 chassis now powered – like their new ground-effect Ralts – by a Hart engine. Dougall had raced with just such a combination to a brilliant win earlier in the season, taking advantage of the opposition as they grappled to understand the new science, but once they got the Ralts sorted, Henton had worked his way into the lead of the championship while Rad's season rather fell apart.

Simply having to finish ahead of Swiss star Marc Surer to claim the title, Henton had qualified one place ahead of him in third. Dougall was back in 15th and I was 17th in a car that just didn't want to respond to any set-up changes we'd made to try and improve its rather wayward handling. After the race they found a cracked bulkhead was causing it to flex in the middle and adopt the handling characteristics of a supermarket shopping trolley.

While Rad was out early with a blown engine, I battled my way up to finish a respectable eighth in the awkward-handling March – one place ahead of some Irish guy called Eddie Jordan who would turn out to be a better team owner than driver! But the Toleman eyes were all on Henton who, under pressure from a closing Surer, was challenging Daly for a lead he didn't need to claim the title. When a brake problem caught him out with just three laps to go there was an audible gasp from the patriotic crowd as the local star's Ralt gyrated off the road.

While there was a great deal of sympathy for Brian, as it had obviously been a brake problem that had caught him out, there was still a feeling he hadn't needed to have been pushing so hard for the win. So when, a couple of weeks later, I was asked back to Donington to test his Ralt my hopes once again soared. Surely my chance had finally come for the next season? With sliding skirts being banned for 1980, and a design of their own being considered, Toleman wanted to try the car without them. Before that, though, I was allowed to set a benchmark time with the Ralt as it was – and my best was eight-hundredths *quicker* than Henton's third-place qualifying time. Just give me the right car and I'll do the job...

A topsy-turvy year of survival had come to a close with great hope but still nothing really concrete for the future. I'd been praised for my efforts in outdated machinery and proved I could be fast in the right car. And I'd had the dream of a Grand Prix drive snatched from my hands with no telling if another chance was ever going to come my way.

The BMW County Championship proved to be a great success, pitching touring car superstars like Andy Rouse against the likes of Le Mans winner Derek Bell and single-seater upstarts such as Nigel Mansell, a very young Martin Brundle, and me. The racing was often a little too close for comfort and on one occasion, at Oulton Park, Martin tried to go round the outside of me at Old Hall and found nothing but grass available on the exit. When he span back across the track it triggered a multi-car pile-up and the race had to be stopped. This inspired Mr Brundle Senior to seek me out in the paddock afterwards wishing to suggest that I was no more than a bl**dy stock car driver...

My best result of the year, though, would actually come not on the track, where my ever-improving tin-top skills saw me battling for race wins, but off the track at the BMW hospitality suite. Twenty-one-year-old Patsy Rowles was working in the company's marketing department, which meant she had to help out at the races, and her stunning good looks and flashing smile soon had me won over. The problem was how to win *her* over.

My first attempt got off to an embarrassing start. Earlier in the year I was sure she had had a green flash in her hair so I opened a conversation by asking her where it had gone, only to discover it had been a different girl who'd had that hair – so Patsy thought it was the other girl I was interested in and I felt about two feet tall. Fortunately BMW held a big barbeque party after the last race of the year at Thruxton and, fuelled with a touch of alcoholic confidence, I made a more successful approach. And after a brief courtship of 'only' nine years, she walked up the aisle to become Mrs Needell!

CHAPTER 9

SO NEAR YET SO FAR?

A new decade dawned. Surely the time had finally come for me to get the Toleman Formula Two drive that I had demonstrated I was worthy of – but life is never that simple in motor racing. Before we'd even got to the end of the first month of the year I'd learned that BP had offered the team a sponsorship deal, and with the money came two of their own rising stars: Stephen South and Derek Warwick. One step forwards had been swiftly followed by two steps back.

The only hope now was to find the sponsorship myself to buy a drive, but I was fast learning that sending out letters and following them up with phone calls was simply joining a pile of such offerings from every sport in the land in every marketing director's pending tray. Yes, you might strike lucky and approach a company whose managing director was a racing fan and thinking of sponsorship at that time, but it was a one in a million chance.

Beneath the glamorous world of Grand Prix racing very little of the sponsorship that keeps cars racing is strictly for commercial reasons. There is always a 'deal' somewhere in the arrangement which ensures that the front-line sponsor is being rewarded in some way other than just having their name plastered over a racing car. To find sponsors you need business acumen and that's not one of my strong points!

Yet all of a sudden, in the middle of February, out of the winter gloom came a call from Toleman's Alex Hawkridge. Could I be on a plane to Italy that night, ready to test their new Toleman TG280 Formula Two at Mugello the next day? I thought of suggesting that a plane wouldn't be necessary because I could fly myself, but I stifled the huge feeling of euphoria and hastily packed my bags.

Alex hadn't mentioned much about why the sudden call had been made, but I later discovered that South had apparently interrupted his Toleman testing in Italy to attend a test with the McLaren Grand Prix team at Paul Ricard alongside Alain Prost – possibly with regard to him replacing John Watson, who had had a lacklustre start to the new season in South America. However, he hadn't asked Toleman's permission to do the test and it hadn't gone down well.

Having made it to the hotel in the early hours of the morning and having not driven a racing car of any type for three months I was faced with one of the most demanding tracks in the world that I'd never driven on, in a car that I'd never driven, *and* using Pirelli's new radial racing tyres. I was about to undergo the most important test of my life. Adding to the pressure was the realisation at breakfast that most of the team didn't even know I was coming so sudden had South's departure been.

While Warwick pounded round in the morning I nervously awaited my turn. A seat was quickly made and I was soon burbling down the pit lane on a cold winter's day with a brand-new set of cold Pirellis. Until now the world of racing had been more than happy with conventional cross-ply tyres, but Pirelli were one of the market leaders for radials – which offer less rolling resistance and a softer ride – and they were keen to prove their worth on the track. Michelin had led the way a few years before with the Renault Grand Prix programme and Pirelli didn't want to be left behind.

To say the car felt nervous would be the understatement of my entire racing career. I thought it might be me. I relaxed my grip on the wheel to allow the car to breathe – were my own nerves being transmitted through the car? In just three corners I'd found the car fidgeting from side to side with no input on my behalf and then, half-way round my first lap, cruising into the normally flat-out Arrabbiata 2, the thing just swapped ends. It was an exact repeat of my first lap in the Durex Chevron, yet this time there had been no river to instigate it.

Fortunately it was another flash 360-degree spin and the car stayed on the tarmac, but my nerves were now in tatters. I persevered for a few laps to build some heat into the tyres but even so, down the long straight, the car was suddenly moving from side to side with no warning. I tried to appear calm when I stopped at the pit but my heart was pounding. This time, convinced they must have heard me spin as I was the only car on the track, I apologised for the error only to discover they had no idea. Who said honesty is the best policy?

It was by far my worst day in a racing car and, with Pirelli very much an important partner in developing the brand-new Toleman chassis, I knew I hadn't looked at all good, lapping well off Warwick's times. Yes, he'd already had several days adapting to the car and its tyres. No, I didn't know the track, nor had I driven anything for three months, but in motor racing it's 'on the day' that matters not the 'ifs or buts'.

Given another chance in the more confidence-inspiring surroundings of Silverstone a couple of weeks later I got much closer to Derek's times on a very busy track with changeable weather, but I still found it difficult to adapt to the radial tyre's handling characteristics. The softer sidewalls allowed the chassis to move laterally, even though the tyre wasn't actually sliding on the surface of the track, so the natural reaction was to try and correct that movement with the steering which, of course, simply made matters worse. It was a characteristic they would soon largely eradicate but it was one that took time to get used to – and time wasn't on my side.

Just five days after the Silverstone test I was booked on a plane to Tokyo for the only race I did have lined up for the year – another Formula Two outing at Suzuka – but this time I really didn't want to go. I wanted to be camped out on Toleman's doorstep, but I needed the money and I needed the race mileage.

I did have another good race and another fourth-place finish in the pouring rain, but the clouds above the circuit were nothing compared to the cloud of disappointment as the news reached Japan that Toleman had re-signed none other than Brian Henton. Pirelli had been understandably unimpressed by my performance and, allied to the fact that I only knew half the circuits, had 'gently' suggested someone with more experience should take the seat. For the second year running I felt like experimenting with a Voodoo doll wearing Henton's overalls.

Brian Henton went on to win the 1980 European Formula Two Championship, and partner Derek Warwick in Toleman's very own Grand Prix car the following year. South's courtship with McLaren saw him entered for the Long Beach Grand Prix – standing in for an injured Alain Prost – but the team was going through the doldrums at the time and while Watson qualified 21st Stephen didn't make the cut. He did, however, pick up a drive in the American CanAm sportscar series but, later in the year, a stuck throttle put him in the wall at Trois Rivières in Canada and he suffered a career-ending leg injury – another great British talent thus faded away.

Which brings us full circle to that moment a couple of weeks after returning crestfallen from Japan when I was lying in bed late in the night listening to the American Forces Network live commentary on that Grand Prix at Long Beach. From the tone of the commentator's voice I could tell Regazzoni's accident had been a big one and it was soon obvious that Clay had been injured. Even if it was only a broken ankle, they would need a replacement for the next race – and the team was sponsored by Unipart *and* they had offered me a drive the year before. If ever there was a 'Last Chance Saloon' this was it. Getting to sleep that night wasn't easy...

While the dream did finally come true on that Zolder grid, getting myself established with the team was always going to be an uphill task – especially in a one-car operation that had been built around a very experienced superstar. Ensign had a new American investor and Unipart's sponsorship wasn't massive so they couldn't dictate who drove for the team. Rising Dutch star Jan Lammers had qualified the equally unfancied ATS in a fantastic fourth place at Long Beach and yet his seat there was only temporary until their regular driver recovered from injury. Jan was the talk of the paddock, and once he was free the American was keen to have him in 'my' car.

I well remember Unipart's Mike Black, who had been in charge of the company's marketing exposure since the early Formula Three days, telling me that my trouble was that I was 'too honest'! It made me think of my Toleman test and of the many occasions when I'd apologised for not getting more out of a car – an aura of self-confidence, even if it is misplaced, can go a long way in bluffing your way through motorsport, but again that just wasn't me. I always tended to be very grateful for what I got and perhaps not aggressive or self-assertive enough out of the car when things didn't go my way.

Getting a team to believe in you when you don't have a string of good results to underline your talent is the hardest task. To make matters worse, I kept on complaining that the Ensign was understeering too much, that the steering had been tightening up over the crest after the chicane at Zolder, that it was unresponsive – but I kept being told 'Clay said it oversteered. Clay never complained of understeer. Clay said this, Clay said that...'

The next Formula One race on the calendar after the crushing disappointment at Monaco was what would turn out to be a non-championship affair in Spain and, for the preceding test, the team told me they needed someone with more experience to try the car, someone who would (I guess they hoped) confirm what Clay had said. Someone like... Brian Henton! Obviously they didn't have any faith in my feedback, but even when Brian politely told them he'd rather be racing the F2 Toleman because the car was so bad, I still didn't get my seat back. Instead, they turned to another old nemesis who had just starred in the Formula Two race round the streets of Pau, the same man who'd got 'my' drive at Ensign the previous year – Patrick Gaillard.

The team said they simply needed to get some sort of reference point from a driver whom they knew, and that there would be more opportunities later in the year when they planned to run a second car; by now Lammers's arrival was pretty much a done deal. I therefore dragged myself off to Spain to stand in the background and put on a brave face, backing up the team's party line to those who asked. How low can you go?

What should have been that year's Spanish Grand Prix turned into a 'them versus us' showdown as the battle for control over Formula One between FISA and FOCA reached its climax. The six 'manufacturer' cars from Ferrari, Renault and Alfa, who supported FISA, boycotted the event, thus reducing it to its non-championship status. Gaillard qualified 21st of the 22 cars that turned up for the race, so in effect he was 27th and wouldn't even have been on the grid at all, had it been a Grand Prix.

As I'd expected, Lammers was in the car for the next Grand Prix and, despite that stunning fourth in Long Beach, he then failed even to qualify for five of the next six Grands Prix in the Ensign. The only one he did make he qualified 24th and last in Germany – and he wouldn't even have made that if it hadn't been for the tragic death of Alfa's Patrick Depailler in testing the week before.

In the Ensign, then, I'd qualified as well as Regazzoni had at Long Beach and then – for the next six Grands Prix – better than the man who had qualified fourth in the same race in a different car – but none of that would get me my drive back. They did run a second car on a couple of occasions, but to add insult to injury they used the 'more experienced' Geoff Lees. He managed to scrape a 24th on the grid in Holland but then failed to qualify in Italy so yet again another driver had made no difference.

In an end-of-season interview the team's designer, Nigel Bennett, very kindly admitted that, looking back, my own feedback had actually been pointing them in the right direction – had they listened to it. They finally worked out that the aluminium monocoque chassis were quickly going 'soft', so when new and stiff they would more likely oversteer, as Clay had found, but once they softened they would... understeer. My feeling of the steering tightening over the Zolder crest had actually been due to the monocoque twisting so much it was seizing up the steering rack.

I'm convinced that if it had been a two-car set-up with an established team-mate, my times would have been close and my competitiveness proven. If I'd just had those races with Ensign in '79 I feel I could have held on to the drive in 1980 and then forged a decent career in Grand Prix racing. Who knows what might have happened if I'd got the Toleman drive? It just obviously wasn't meant to be.

It may have been one of the briefest Grand Prix careers on record, but I'm still immensely proud that I made it to the ultimate level of my sport without ever having to buy my way into a drive – apart from my brief spell at Safir in Formula Three. I'd got there on talent alone, from winning a car in a magazine competition to sitting on the Grand Prix grid in Belgium, and when you stand back and think that our sport has just 24 places at the top of a huge mountain the chances of getting one of them are very slim indeed.

I'm also strangely satisfied that I got there at a time when motorsport was still dangerous and sex was still safe! It sounds a silly thing to say, but for many of us the knowledge that we were driving a fine line between being fast and potentially having a big accident was all part of the sport's attraction. It heightened the experience and concentrated the mind, demanding a much finer margin of error – to be quick you had to be right on that line, but step over it and you paid a heavy price. With the massive tarmac run-offs of today, finding the limit on many corners presents little challenge; now, if you overstep the mark you simply recover on the run-off.

Of course the last thing anyone wants is someone being hurt doing the sport we love and, despite my era being much safer than it had been just a decade earlier thanks to Jackie Stewart's crusade, three drivers from that Zolder grid – Gilles Villeneuve, Elio de Angelis and Patrick Depailler – would all die at the wheel of Grand Prix cars, while Didier Pironi was so badly injured that he had to quit the sport. The dilemma is how to keep the challenge of that fine 'edge' without endangering the driver – but then without the danger you lose that 'edge'.

I enjoyed the fact that I drove at a time when the only driver aid was the mechanic who buckled you into the car. No power steering, no paddle-shift gear change, no telemetry feeding information to a bank of computers in the pits, not even a rev limiter to stop you blowing up the engine: it was all down to the driver. The deft arts of 'heel and toe' and 'short shifting' are long gone, as is the instant penalty of a missed gear that could so easily lose you a place or, even worse, blow your engine – the cockpit was a far harder and much busier place than it is now and consequently a much more rewarding one.

My faithful fans – Mum, Dad and Patsy – made it to Belgium to support me, but again it wasn't quite like it is nowadays as they drove there in Mum's new Datsun 120Y estate. They travelled overnight with my friend Chris Cordrey, who was helping make my sponsorship hunting a bit more professional, and with my then 12-year-old brother Chris squeezed in the back. It was quite some trip.

Unfortunately, with all the costs involved, Patsy was the only one to make it to Monaco. By now BMW had set up a new office in Bracknell to take over direct control of their UK sales from the previous Concessionaires company, so Patsy had found a new job with an advertising agency and was starting to do a bit of part-time modelling. Somehow she managed to blag a trip to Monaco to support me by getting a job helping Akai's promotion of their Williams sponsorship – not that I saw much of her – and, with Reutemann winning the race, I think she had a lot more fun than me!

So what to do now? I hung around the Grand Prix scene for a while and flew myself off to South Africa for the season's opener the next year, when the chance of a Tyrrell drive was in the offing, but it all came to nothing. I even approached Frank Williams with the idea of being a test driver, but he didn't really feel it was necessary as their race drivers did all the testing – I was a couple of years ahead of my time.

The BMW County Championship was running for a second year so that kept me racing but neither that, nor my Grand Prix efforts, earned me any money. Another trip to Japan, for a less rewarding ninth place, and a return to Malaysia to pick up second in the 'Selangor Grand Prix' pretty much comprised my only source of income – a grand total of £2,300 went into the coffers at a time when the average earnings were around the £6,000 mark. At this rate I certainly wasn't going to get rich as a racing driver.

CHAPTER 10

LE MANS AND A
200MPH CRASH

Having reached the top of the mountain the previous year, I soon found myself tumbling back down the other side at an alarming rate of knots. My first race in 1981 wasn't until the beginning of May, and even then it was just a ten-lap celebrity bash around Brands Hatch in Sunbeams. The following weekend, however, I made my World Endurance Championship debut at Silverstone in Ian Bracey's Ford DFV-powered Ibec P6 sports prototype. Having qualified eighth I ran as high as fifth in the early going but soon succumbed to an engine failure. The next race for the team would be something very special indeed, though – the Le Mans 24 Hours. I'd already made my first trip to Le Mans with the car the previous year, but had been prevented from making my first start in this celebrated event thanks to a further dose of French bureaucratic wrangling.

Ian Bracey was something of throwback to an earlier age of motor racing, a jovial Lloyds insurance broker with the blood group on his overalls reading 'A + Whisky'! In the fifties he might have been able to run a competitive racing team out of his private income, but times were changing fast. He'd been a very successful driver in his own right in smaller sportcars but he was now moving up – just as he was slowing down! Small in stature but rotund in shape, he was affectionately known as the 'Baked Bean'.

His *Ian Bracey Engineering Company* had commissioned former Hesketh Grand Prix designer Harvey Postlethwaite to build a Le Mans winner in an effort to restore British pride in an event that had only been won once by a British car since the fifties heyday of Jaguar and Aston Martin. Sadly he never really had the budget to do his dream justice and the car had retired from its Le Mans debut in 1978.

Two years later and the ever changing regulations of the forever fickle organisers had produced a qualifying concept that would be determined by the average speed of each car's drivers and, with 67 cars permitted to practise in six classes, the slowest two cars in each class wouldn't get to race. With just one five-hour session to set all the drivers' times and with the session starting wet and then drying out, any car problems would have dire consequences. As it was I only drove when it was wet, the Bean was way off the pace and, although co-driver Tony Trimmer set a respectable time in the dry, the 11th-fastest car overall somehow became a non-qualifier, despite team manager Gordon Horn's protests in his best French.

So it was that in the middle of 1980, in the space of just four weeks, I had failed to qualify for two of the most famous races in the world – not the sort of records I had in mind. However, while one failure saw the end of my first ambition, the other was very much the beginning of another dream. Although I didn't get to race on that first visit, the experience of driving round such a famous circuit had been just as exhilarating as my drive in Monte Carlo.

Indeed, simply arriving at the track for the first time on the Monday before the race had made me feel overwhelming emotion at being privileged to be following in the exact footsteps of so many of my own heroes. The paddock was much as it had always been – part tarmac, part gravel, part grass – with tall firs still standing in the middle to which the lesser teams attached makeshift awnings.

I walked up the steps at the back of the pits and the daunting grandstands opposite reared high above me, the terracing below it forever a reminder of the horrendous 1955 tragedy. There, still visible on the other side of the track, were the fading circles painted on the road where the drivers would await the traditional 'run-and-jump' starts which had been outlawed some ten years earlier with the arrival of the most basic of safety devices – seat belts! Opposite the roundels were the angled starting lines where the silent cars would sit awaiting their drivers. I soon lost myself in a daydream of all those great races that had gone before.

I'd seen such starts at Goodwood and they were occasions to be remembered for ever. Complete silence would fall as the starter prepared his flag then, as it dropped, the pitter-patter of soft-shoed feet filled the air before a rising crescendo of engines bursting into life and tyres squealing in protest as the cars surged out into the track, funnelling into the tightest of traffic jams as they fought for position towards the first corner...

The whole week that is Le Mans is an occasion that simply builds and builds, from the ritual of the scrutineering in the town centre on the Tuesday to the practice and qualifying sessions on Wednesday and Thursday, and then of course the race itself at the weekend. I walked the whole 8.47 miles on that first visit, blown away by the seemingly never-ending three-mile-long Mulsanne Straight and surprised by the sharpness of the famed 'kink' just before the end of it.

Wednesday night was my first time in the dark in a racing car and, with the Ibec being an open-topped sportscar, I remember glancing up at a starlit sky as I belted down that famous straight with more adrenaline pouring into my veins than ever before – oh was I living now! The long lap with every type of corner was such a refreshing change from the much shorter modern circuits. It took a few laps before I was comfortable enough to take the kink flat out. While the Ibec struggled to do much more than 190mph it was still a corner that grabbed all your attention. The amount of lock needed was as much as it takes just to lean your head slightly to the side and let your hands go with it.

Returning to the pits it was to 'those' pits and 'that' pit wall that all the greats had climbed in and out of. When work was being done on the car you could stay in it with your helmet off and chat to the spectators lining the little balconies just above you. Le Mans just had an atmosphere like no other and one sadly greatly reduced when those iconic concrete 'dug-outs' were pulled down to please the modern world in 1991.

With no radios in the cars, the pit signalling back then was done on a wall on the inside just after the Mulsanne Corner – the slowest on the circuit and about half-way round the lap. Communication from pits to signallers was via telephones that looked like they had come out of the First World War trenches as they had to be vigorously wound to make them ring. So once a lap – once every four minutes – you would be shown a board and probably given a wave of encouragement from your enthusiastic crew and then you were back on your own as you hammered off down the tunnel of huge pine trees towards the Indianapolis Corner... magic!

When we returned a year later we didn't really have much more joy with an engine that insisted on misfiring and a gearbox that was forever trying to do whatever you didn't want it to do. At least we qualified, albeit down in 27th place, but the frustration of knowing we had a top-ten car without being able to demonstrate it drove us to distraction. The race didn't go much better, with the team unable to cure our ills and, although we battled on for some 15 hours, we finally gave up before the gearbox seized solid.

While the Le Mans 24 Hours is one of those races that every driver wants to do one day, it remains one of the most dangerous and, for the likes of Patsy, sitting on the pit wall waiting every four minutes or so for the car to reappear, it can be a nerve-racking experience, albeit now greatly eased by the constant running of TV monitors. To make matters worse, during practice a friend had taken her out through the forests to watch the cars blast down the Mulsanne Straight in the dark; it wasn't a good idea.

In some places you could stand right by the guardrail watching headlights in the distance slowly getting brighter and brighter, with the sound of the car's engine growing louder and louder. Then, as it neared you, it seemed suddenly to accelerate towards you before blasting past with a wall of sound and a shock of disturbed air attacking your senses. In another instant you were left in an eerily still silence as the engine note quickly faded into the dark. Patsy never asked to go back again...

Tragically, there were two awful accidents that year which took the lives of a French marshal and Rondeau driver Jean-Louis Lafosse, with four other marshals also being injured. Both accidents were on the Mulsanne Straight and both were the result of failures on the car, something a driver can do little about. The problem was that, with the speeds so high, the impact folded back the Armco barrier and the car then got on top of it, ripping itself to pieces and sending debris flying in all directions. On each occasion all you knew in the pits was that an accident had happened and you could sense it was serious as pace cars and ambulances swept out of the pit lane with lights and sirens blazing. All you could do was strain your eyes to the left in search of your own car and phone the pit signallers for any news.

After the race Patsy and I began what would become a tradition of heading for somewhere on the Brittany coast for a cheap hotel and an expensive dinner of lobster washed down with chilled champagne. We couldn't afford an actual holiday, so this was our little treat and a great release after the pressures of the week before.

Mind you, the rest of 1981 turned into a bit of an *involuntary* holiday as very few drives came my way. My brother Michael managed to get me in a Touring Car race at Kyalami in South Africa, which got me out there for a week. Then there were a few more BMW County Championship outings, a one-off drive for AGS in a Formula Two race at Donington, and a return to Malaysia for more Formula Pacific... but that was it.

I knew now that if I was going to make any sort of career out of my sport then sportscars or saloon cars were going to have to be my future. However, motor racing can be a bit like a grown-up game of snakes and ladders – and I had quite definitely slipped down to the bottom of the next ladder. Fortunately, endurance sportscar racing was about to reinvent itself, with the 1982 season seeing the arrival of new Group A, B and C regulations for saloons, GT cars and sportscars to replace the old Group 1 to Group 6 system. For sportscars this meant the end of the old open-topped cars and a return to all-enveloping bodywork – and it was a concept that caught the imagination of both manufacturers and racing car specialists the world over.

One such enthusiast was Aston Martin fanatic Robin Hamilton, who'd already built himself a monstrous Aston Martin DBS V8 GT car which he'd raced at Le Mans in 1977 and '79. Inspired by the new rules, he constructed his own Nimrod chassis to be powered by the same Aston engine for the Group C regulations and launched his new machine at Goodwood in the late November of '81 with James Hunt doing the driving. The usual crowd of James Hunt 'wannabes' had also been invited and, as this was about the only decent drive I had a chance of getting, I was right at the front of the queue.

Once again it was a long, nervous winter's wait before any decisions were made, but finally I got the nod and signed up to drive alongside Geoff Lees and Bob Evans – who was more from Hunt's own era but brought a great deal of experience to the team. Even better news was that they were going to pay me! Not a fortune, I hasten to add, but with £2,000 on offer and a few other drives here and there my glamorous occupation might even get me half-way towards the average income.

On the minus side there was only the budget to do about half of the eight rounds of the new World Endurance Championship and once again my season didn't start until the Silverstone fixture in the middle of May. Little niggles plagued the practice sessions and then history repeated itself as we retired early with engine problems. With nine different manufacturers on the grid, however, the new formula had got off to a very promising start. Next stop Le Mans!

While the arrival of our most patriotic team might have got the Union flags waving more vigorously than ever from the massed ranks of the annual invasion of tens of thousands of British supporters, it was pretty soon obvious that the Aston Martin Nimrod was a long way off being a race winner. It was a very impressive first effort from a new manufacturer, but it was a massive 250kg *over* the 800kg limit. On top of that, despite trimming off as much wing angle as we dared, we could only manage 205mph down the Mulsanne Straight – 15mph shy of the front-running Porsches.

Of course this was just the beginning of a long journey, so we accepted our lot for the weekend and simply knuckled down to do the best we could. This translated into a lowly 26th on the grid! Still, the weather was glorious and Patsy and I had 'upgraded' to hotel accommodation for the first time, having spent the previous two years in rented houses that are commonplace for team personnel during the Le Mans week – quite often with the owners moving out into a caravan in their garden.

The race actually started quite well and, with fast trouble-free laps, Geoff worked his way to 17th by the end of the first hour. When he handed over to me, just before the two-hour mark, we were up to 11th. There was still an awfully long way to go, but dreams of a top-five finish were not unrealistic.

After an hour and 40 minutes in the car I was now nearing the end of my own double stint, the end of the first of the four 'Grand Prix' distances I would do during the 24 Hours, and we'd risen to seventh. With reliability not a strong point for many of the new Group C machines, we just needed to keep going. With two laps of my stint left, I was eight minutes away from a long cool drink and a change out of overalls soaked in sweat. No-one had yet thought of putting drinks bottles in cars!

Throttle wide open down the Mulsanne Straight, sitting on the left of the road preparing myself for the right-handed kink that comes up quite quickly after a little crest on what was, for the rest of the year, the Route Nationale 138, the trunk road heading south from Le Mans to Tours. Speed 205mph, relaxed, concentrated, contented, living the life. Suddenly there was a vibration behind me... deceleration... blown engine?... car turns sharp right... steel barrier straight ahead... full left lock... car snaps to the left... can't hold it... car spins to the left... this is going to hurt... going backwards... thump... the front of the car rears up underneath me... I'm going over the barrier. Miraculously the front crashes back down... the car ricochets off the barrier and spins like a top across the road... the door flies off... I pray that nobody slams into me, blinded by the fog of tyre smoke and flying debris... thump... I've hit the barrier on the other side of the road... surely this thing is going to stop soon? Marshals running toward me... petrol!... switch the fuel pumps off... switch the ignition off... undo seatbelts... I'm out... bloody hell, I'm actually walking away from it.

A helicopter hovered above the scene with a camera hanging out of the side and I remember that the race still had live TV coverage at this time. There was a television in Aston's hospitality box, where Patsy was watching the race, so I waved like mad to show I was fine. Even I was surprised I had no injuries, not even the slightest sign of shock, but then that's something few professional drivers suffer from as the mind and body are keyed up to such a high pitch that they are always expecting the unexpected.

It took a while to clear the wreckage and then hitch a lift back to the pits in the course car. Everyone wanted to know what had happened and I fended off the many questions with a casual 'something broke, I'm fine' while trying desperately to head for the team motorhome to find Patsy. She was still fighting back floods of tears. The accident hadn't appeared on the television and by the time the helicopter got to me she had already fled the hospitality box to get more information from the pits. She knew it was me who had crashed and she'd seen the rescue vehicles blasting out of the pit lane with their lights ablaze...

There were all the usual theories about the accident, from tyre failure to transmission seizure or broken suspension, but it turned out to be a simple little bracket supporting the rear bodywork that had failed. Unfortunately the bodywork hinged from the back so, as soon as it broke, the front opened up – causing the brief vibration; the wind got under it – causing the brief deceleration; and then the whole thing was ripped off the back of the car and with it went the big rear wing that was keeping the back of the car on the ground and, as it departed, it turned the car sharp right.

Having realised I'd been incredibly lucky to survive the crash in one piece my thoughts turned back to my Formula Two debut and those 'coincidental' 13s. Well, on the morning of the race we'd moved from pit box 14 to pit box 13. We started on the 13th row of the grid and the crash had happened on the 13th lap of that stint – but I'm still not superstitious! In fact, when I went back to the scene of the crash on the Monday morning I realised just how lucky I had actually been. The broad black skid marks still zigzagged across the road and that first impact had been a direct hit on a part of the guardrail that had a supporting post right behind it. The post was bent back at an angle of

45 degrees but it had still held firm and directed me back on the track – if I'd hit half-way between two posts I'd have almost certainly flattened the barrier and burst through to the trees on the other side. Well, the lobster and champagne went down particularly well that night! A full year later I was able to come back and re-live the opening scene of Steve McQueen's film as I really could see the faint trace of those skid marks leading to a shiny new piece of guardrail.

Unable to attract any new sponsors, Hamilton only did one more race with his Nimrod that year when he entered the car at Spa for Geoff and me. This time it was the engine's turn to fail once again. With no budget for '83 Robin set sail for America where his cars were also eligible for the IMSA GT Championship which started its season at the beginning of February with the Daytona 24 Hours. The promoters had sorted him out a deal to run American legends A.J. Foyt and reigning NASCAR Champion Darrell Waltrip in 'Pepsi Challenger' sponsorship colours, but he took me out with the team for the two weeks before the race to undertake some testing on the steeply banked track.

This would be my first ever trip to the United States, and arriving at the seaside resort of Daytona Beach in the middle of winter was a bit of a shock. 'Have a nice day'? How could you, in such a rundown and deserted place? Half the cars on the road were being held together by little more than rust, and the hotels felt damp and musty. I've been back several times since and it's improved out of all recognition, but in those days it was far, far removed from the glamorous 'Tinsel Town' I'd expected. Of course if I'd been there for the 'Spring Break' student invasion I might have had other thoughts...

The rust on the cars wasn't all due to the salt water being carried in on the sea breeze, because Daytona Beach is a beach you can actually drive on. It's where the likes of Sir Malcolm Campbell set world speed records until the mid-1930s and where, up until 1959, NASCAR ran races that went south on the coast road and then north on the beach. It's also where racing drivers go to see how far into the surf their hire cars will go – well it was, until the police got strict and closed it at night.

The Daytona International Speedway is, of course, the most famous
NASCAR track in America. Built to bring the 'good old boys' off the
beach, it lies a few miles inland and its daunting 2.5-mile oval with its
31-degree banking at either end makes the 12 degrees of America's
most famous oval at Indianapolis look almost flat. A road course was
opened in 1962 which takes the cars off the oval just after the start
line and then twists and turns around the infield before rejoining the
oval a few hundred yards after it left it. The first Daytona 24 Hour race
was held in 1966 and, like the Le Mans event of that year, it was won
by the new Ford GT40s. The Le Mans result had broken a string of six
straight wins for Ferrari, and the Italian marque would return to
Daytona the next year to gain revenge by scoring an emphatic 1-2-3
finish – after which their new 365 GTB/4 became known as the now
iconic 'Daytona'.

As it happened, 1983 was the last year that they ran the road course
without a chicane in the back straight to reduce speeds round the
Turn 3 and 4 banking so I was 'lucky' to get the experience. But what
an experience it was: down that back stretch at over 200mph, inches
from the wall, and then trying to stay flat on the throttle and just turn
into the banking. It took me about six laps to achieve that and even
then I felt I was hanging on by a thread. To see as far ahead as possible
you had to look right out of the top of the windscreen and at first you
couldn't help but keep on looking back at the wall to check if it was
getting any closer. Meanwhile the steering just got heavier and heavier
as the chassis pressed into the track, and you had to prepare yourself
for the 'bump' over the entrance tunnel in the middle of Turn 4 which
threatened to wrest the wheel out of your hands. It was totally
different from anything else I had experienced and I loved it!

Foyt was already 48 years old and had won everything in a glittering
career –Le Mans, Indianapolis (four times) and NASCAR's Daytona
500. He also had a reputation for being, well, slightly hot headed. He
was a man who would prepare and fix his own car, occasionally with
a large hammer if the mood took him that way, so when I was given
the task of explaining to him how to bed in a new type of brake pad I
approached the great man with some trepidation. It involved several

laps of slowly building up the heat and then deliberately overheating them before cooling them down again – but before I'd got half-way through the explanation he simply butted in and said, 'Well, boy, if it's that complicated, why don't you do them for me?'

Waltrip, on the other hand, was at the peak of his career as one of NASCAR's all-time greats. He'd just won the second of his championship titles and was another with a fearsome reputation – his nickname was 'Jaws'. He was someone who took no prisoners and, on the first night of practice, having climbed aboard, shut the door and *still* donned his goggles he went out and shoved someone up into the wall! I didn't think it necessary to point out that he didn't really need the goggles...

Sadly, the race was another disaster. The engine took a distinct dislike to the forces generated by the banking and managed to dislodge and eat its own sump baffles. I did, however, use the time at the track to make as many contacts as I could to get some more drives in America. Robin was only interested in drivers that brought money so I needed to look elsewhere. Rather than banging on the doors of team motorhomes to be greeted by a sea of strange faces, my tactic was to stalk important contacts and then move in at an appropriate time to introduce myself. One particular team manager proved distinctly elusive until I finally spotted him – in the toilets. Unfortunately he was sitting down in one of the bizarre doorless cubicles that the Americans had – discretion was definitely the better part of valour!

I did manage to sort myself a seat in the first Miami street race a few weeks later in a March Chevy, which gave me one of the roughest and wildest rides I've ever had in a racing car. Unfortunately the brakes locked on half-way round the first lap of the race, so that went down as another missed opportunity. By now, though, instead of going West I was starting to look East.

CHAPTER 11

TURNING JAPANESE

While 1982 had mostly been about my efforts to get a professional sportscar career off the ground, it actually ended with a return to the Macau Grand Prix to drive for the coincidentally named Japanese 'Le Mans Company'. This was the team that I had driven for in the Formula Two races over there and Macau was one of the few overseas races they contested.

Driving a Toyota-powered Ralt RT4 I qualified on the second row, alongside Roberto Moreno, with the two great Japanese stars of the day, Masahiro Hasemi and Kazuyoshi Hoshino, on the front row and the Teddy Yip duo of Geoff Lees and Roberto Guerrero right behind. As is so often the case there was a fair bit of chaos down at the tight first corner: it saw Hasemi out on the spot, Moreno off up the escape road and the rest of us reshuffled in the order Lees, Guerrero, me and Hoshino. Geoff had already won the event a couple of times before and was denied a third when his engine failed him. That left Roberto and me dicing for the lead with a recovering Moreno a minute or so behind – somehow I just felt this was going to be my day. The Colombian was hampered by a bent front wing and with just five of the 28 laps remaining I was working hard on a plan to make a move. Unfortunately I had my own small handicap as the car had started jumping out of third gear during the heavy braking at the end of the straight – the obvious place to make a move. It was easy enough to change down straight from fourth to second but it was still a niggling distraction.

Circuits don't get much better than Macau and, for the Formula Pacific cars that were having their last Grand Prix that year before a

I move up to slicks and wings with the Formula Ford 2000 Hawke DL14 and brother Michael takes over the magical Crosslé 25F – April 1976.

On the ragged edge in the Safir RJ05 Formula 3 through Snetterton's infamous Russell Corner – September 1976.

The most promising young British driver of 1976 meets the British 1976 World Champion, James Hunt.

Unipart Formula 3 debut at Silverstone – March 1977.

And Formula 2 debut at Donington – October 1977 in a Chevron B40.

Leaping after Nelson Piquet at Cadwell in June 1978...

...and joining him (in car 24) in the big crash at Brands in July 1978.

Sharing the grid with Alain Prost at Dijon – June 1978.

Formula 2 sensation in Toleman March-BMW 782 at Hockenheim in September 1978...

...until the engine explodes in a ball of flame, allowing Manfred Winkelhock to take 'my' third place.

Time to hand over my Unipart Triumph TR7 to Nigel Mansell and switch to my trusty Ford Capri.

Dream Formula One debut in Durex Chevron B41 at Zolder – April 1979.

My Japanese debut in a Formula 2 March-BMW 792 at Suzuka – May 1979.

Heading for the first corner of the Macau Grand Prix chasing the Ralts of Kevin Cogan and Bob Earl in my outdated March 76B – November 1979.

They're all behind me! Leading the field in the last ever BMW County Championship race at Thruxton – September 1980.

A Grand Prix driver at last! Making my debut at Zolder in the Ensign N180 – May 1980.

Qualifying 19th in the rain at Monte Carlo on the Thursday...

...but failing to qualify in the dry on Saturday.

*Trying to impress Rory
Byrne with my feedback
while testing the Toleman
TG280 at Silverstone –
February 1980.*

*Le Mans debut driving
the Ibec P6 – June 1981.*

*The Aston Martin
Nimrod at Spa –
September 1982.*

Daytona debut for the 24-hour race in the Pepsi
Challenger – February 1983.

Turning Japanese in 1983. Keeping fit with Geoff Lees
and driving the brutal Dome 83C.

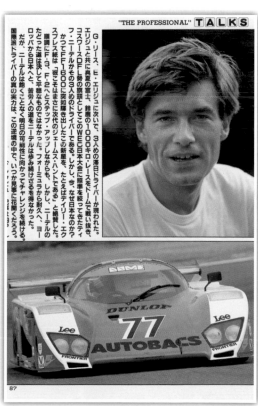

Preparing to finish second in the Selangor Grand Prix, November 1980, driving a Team Rothmans March 79B in Malaysia…

…and ready for the off at Macau, November 1982, in a Le Mans Company Ralt-Toyota RT4.

Japan 1984. Driving the Team Ikuzawa Ralt-Honda RT4, resplendent in its iconic JPS colours…

…and the Group C Dome-Toyota 84C.

switch to the less powerful F3 machines, every lap was heart in mouth excitement. From the tight Lisboa Bend – which is a bit like turning off a wide high street into a blind alley – you accelerate hard into San Francisco Hill which is nearly, but not quite, flat out. As at every corner the edge is defined simply by a steel guardrail or a craggy stone wall there is absolutely no room for error. Up the hill towards Maternity Bend it is exactly like the climb to the Casino Square in Monaco as you head for a blind crest, flat out in top gear. After Maternity a long left takes you in front of Teddy Yip's house and then, with a small lift in third gear, you are into the rollercoaster of the Solitude Esses, then the exhilarating plunge down Moorish Hill, the never-ending Donna Maria Bend, the full-lock Melco Hairpin before the two awesomely fast right-handers round the reservoir to fire you on to the start/finish straight with its two 'just' flat-out kinks to complete 3.8 miles of pure magic.

But there was no magic involved when I made the little 'lift' off the throttle to get the nose of the Ralt turned into the Solitude Esses on lap 24 of the Grand Prix and the gearbox spat itself out of third and into neutral. In a flash the deceleration that moves weight on to the front wheels to help them turn disappeared, the front drifted wide, got on the dirty part of the track and before I could say 'clang' I was bouncing off the barrier. It was only a glancing blow but the rear suspension was broken, and I had to crawl crab-like back to the pits, utterly deflated. The vertical drop from being on such a high to a shatteringly disappointed low is something you never get used to – and when you don't get a winning car that often it's a thousand times harder.

To make matters so much worse, on the same lap, having not checked his mirrors to see me drop away, Guerrero had himself pushed too hard and found the uncompromising walls... so Roberto Moreno cruised round to take the flag and go down in the history books as the winner of the 1982 Macau Grand Prix.

As it turned out, the day wasn't all bad. That evening, when Geoff and I were commiserating with each other over a large number of beers and whatever other concoctions we could lay our hands on, we

were approached by the heads of top Japanese preparation specialist
Nova Engineering. Not being fully coherent at the time, and with
their English none too fluent, it took us a while to take in the fact that
they were buying one of the first customer Porsche 956s – the likes of
which had just steamrollered the opposition to a 1-2-3 finish at Le
Mans – and they wanted the two drunks swaying in front of them to
drive it in the Japanese Endurance Championship. Now that's the
sort of job interview I can handle!

True to their word, I arrived back home to receive copious Telex
messages with detailed contracts for my forthcoming move to Japan.
For once, Christmas came with a deal sorted for the next season. Geoff
had fallen out of the equation as he had signed a Formula Two deal
with a rival Japanese operation and, in any case, they had now decided
they wanted one Japanese driver in the car. The money was good but
the prize money was even better and this would be the only Porsche
on the grid – sorted!

The Nova bosses had wanted to meet up with me when they came
to the Porsche factory for a January visit, but it coincided with my trip
to Daytona and it was while I was there that I began to pick up a
rumour that Porsche factory driver Vern Schuppan was going to be
racing in Japan. Strange? The news when I returned confirmed my
worst fears. The factory had somehow persuaded Nova that they
should have someone with 956 experience to drive their new car – my
collection of Voodoo dolls was growing fast. Of course I could have
sued for breach of contract, but you soon learn that it leads you
nowhere in motor racing and, in any case, you need to move on as
quickly as you can. To be fair, Nova had made many humble Japanese
apologies and they also introduced me to another drive in the Japanese
series with the Japanese Dome manufacturer, who were building their
own Group C car to be powered by the 3.9-litre Ford Cosworth DFL
version of the classic Grand Prix engine.

Having suggested my Swedish friend Eje Elgh as a co-driver I was
delighted when he was chosen and, along with Geoff, we became the
pioneers of what was to become a major influx of overseas drivers
looking to pursue their careers in a land where the racing was very

competitive and – unlike back in Europe – the teams were prepared to pay for our services. The era of the foreign 'gaijin' racing driver had begun and it remains healthy to this day.

With the Dome not ready for the opening rounds of the championship – where Vern cruised to his first two wins and first million or more yen in 'my' Porsche – I didn't head for Japan until the beginning of July, with a plan to stay living there till the end of the season. Patsy was going to come out later for a few weeks, so I looked forward to seeing what sort of hotel they had booked us into, as per the contract, only to find that they'd rented out two tiny little flats for the duration. While being quite normal accommodation for Tokyo dwellers, their size came as something of a shock. Their metal doors gave them the nickname of 'tin boxes' while the miniature bathrooms had tubs that were about four feet square. The bed filled most of the living room and that was it. Sitting watching the parched fairways of Royal Birkdale hosting the golf Open back in England's blistering summer, listening only to the Japanese commentary, I felt just a little homesick.

Geoff was already well established in a nice flat half an hour further out of town so, with the car still not ready for a couple of weeks, Eje and I began to try and fumble our way round town as best we could. Fortunately the team had supplied us with an attractive young translator and little Keiko Iwasawa would soon be busy getting her boys out of trouble. Supplied with a Honda Civic to get around in, one of our early discoveries was that you don't park in front of rubbish bins on collection day – assuming, that is, that you can read such signs. Explaining to Keiko that we couldn't drive anywhere because two of the tyres had had a spike stuck through them wasn't easy...

We next discovered that our international driving licences didn't seem to count for much while we were actually living in Tokyo. I'd been standing outside the tin boxes waiting for Eje to pick me up when I suddenly caught sight of his grinning face in the back of a police van. Much heavy muttering ensued before we were both transported to the local station to await the arrival of poor Keiko to sort it out.

The funniest 'crime' was a parking offence where a chain on a padlock had been inserted through our door mirror. When translated, the message upon it demanded we head to the nearest station where we could get it removed, but only after we had explained *why* we had parked there. There would be no fine or punishment – they just couldn't believe we could be so disobedient. I tell these stories to try and highlight just how different a world it was back then. Honour, tradition and discipline still remain strong in Japan but not to the level it was – loyalty to your family, your employer and your country was everything.

While the living accommodation might have fallen a bit below expectations, as on my previous visits we were royally entertained by our Japanese hosts at some of the most sumptuous restaurants in town, even if it sometimes meant the awkward discomfort of sitting on a tatami floor with bent legs and aching knees. We were soon to discover that the quality and variety of its food is one of Japan's greatest pleasures. Whatever the style, it will be prepared as it should be: whether it's the finest sushi or the simplest Italian spaghetti, they do it right. Down in the Roppongi district of Tokyo we could spend one night in the newly opened 'Hard Rock Café' – the fourth ever to be built – and then cross the car park to enjoy the very traditional 'Inakaya' restaurant the next evening. Back then Roppongi was in its prime as *the* classy nightlife centre for the few westerners like us to venture into. Nowadays the area has a much more seedy side to it, with a very multicultural feel that is all part of the way the world is moving. You can't turn the clocks back, but I much preferred it as it was!

There was no end of nightlife there, the tall buildings packed with floor after floor of clubs and bars, but Eje and I soon discovered that there were about three main venues, including the celebrity favourite 'Lexington Queen' where the westerners would gather – and we soon found out why. The use of foreign models was predominant in most advertising and the agencies had arranged for these clubs to offer them free entry, free food and free drink. The result was that we could sit having a beer and be entertained by a constant catwalk of beautiful models.

Watching the world go by has always been one of my favourite pastimes and I'm never bored by airport delays where you can observe every extreme of personality reacting in different ways. I love to try and imagine who they are and where they are headed. It never ceases to amuse me the way aeroplane passengers, on arrival, leap to their feet the instant the seat-belt signs are off and pull everything out of the lockers, only to spend the next five minutes hunched uncomfortably in the aisle before they can actually move anywhere.

Finding our way round Tokyo provided a whole new range of experiences, made all the more intriguing by the complete lack of any signs you could read or any people to whom you could talk to get help. There are no street names, only numbers for addresses, so landmarks become all important. We managed to find a tourist map with pictures of distinctive buildings at major intersections so, whenever we got lost, we would simply drive around until we saw a landmark that was featured. With my Boy Scout's initiative I soon became known as 'Tiff the Map'.

When at last the news came that our car was ready to test – and with its debut just a week away – we left the heat and humidity of Tokyo behind and took a 90-minute drive south-west to the town of Gotemba which lies under the shadow of the great Mount Fuji volcano and is home to the Fuji Speedway.

Built in the sixties, the Fuji track was supposed to be a full-on 2.5-mile oval to run NASCAR races, but they ran out of money after they'd built the first banked turn and soon compromised with a simpler road course. The banking was still used as the first corner, but after several horrendous accidents a short cut was made to create the basic shape that remains today. I say 'basic shape' because in 2005 the final fast corner was turned into a series of tight turns to attract the Grand Prix cars back, while even the original track where I was to test the new Dome DFL 83C would have chicanes introduced a couple of years later to slow the cars down. As it was, the 1983 layout was dauntingly fast.

The new Dome was a rough and hardly ready machine when we first drove it. My opening laps were greeted with a strong blast of red-hot air blowing all over my body as the team had left the sidepods from the cockpit to the engine bay completely open. I can only assume they thought the air would be dragged out the back, but it was an early indication into how much the Japanese needed to learn about this new generation of Group C racing cars.

One of my weaknesses as a driver is that I'm too easily distracted by small problems. This is a good thing when you are developing a car but a drawback when you want simply to concentrate on a quick lap time. Eje seemed totally unconcerned by such things and so, for the first time, I faced the uncomfortable situation of being slower than a team-mate in the same car. It's the one aspect of endurance racing that you can't hide from because your first competitor is actually your own co-driver.

Like so many early sportscar designers, Dome had built the car with a very low rear wing hanging off the back – great for straight-line speed but limited in effect. Aside from being roasted by the hot air delivered to the cockpit straight off the exhaust pipes, the handling was like taking a walk on the wild side. One thing Eje and I definitely agreed on was that the wing had to be stuck up into the airstream.

You soon learn that getting a car set up to your own liking makes a big difference. If your team-mate takes control you find yourself in a car that might not handle the way you like it and, as he goes faster, you go slower. You either have to make sure you are the number one in the team, or try to adapt your natural driving style to be more like his, or start to look for co-drivers who like the same sort of balance as you do.

To be fair, Eje and I blended well. We both liked the same sort of balance; it was just that I couldn't settle into this rough diamond of a machine as easily as he could and the Fuji Circuit was one of the most challenging I'd ever faced. The first corner was now a simple hairpin but after that there was an almost flat-out left-hander – something Vern didn't even consider as a corner in his Porsche – that led into the long '100R' right-hander that remains today. Exiting '100R' – the Japanese like to name corners by the measurement of their radius – a blind crest leads you into the braking area for the tight left behind the pits, after which there lay the most awesome series of almost flat-out right-handers with awkward cambers that led you back on to the long, long main straight with its 200mph plus top speed.

With everything being such a last-minute thing it probably wasn't surprising that gearbox problems prevented us from even starting the race – where guess who took his third straight win – so our actual debut would now not be until the next race at Suzuka, in five weeks. At least this was a track I knew, although I didn't think the Dome would be best suited to it.

In the meantime Patsy was heading over and Eje was heading home. We'd had enough of the tin boxes so we got the team to opt out of the deal and hand the rent straight to us. I'd managed to borrow a friend's flat for Patsy's visit and after that we'd just have to find something. Doing the tourist bit together was rather special. We'd already had our lobster and champagne at Le Mans but this was a proper holiday – well, almost! I had to attend a sponsor's sales conference and do a couple of days' testing, but most of the time we just enjoyed being tourists. Dome boss Minoru Hayashi was the perfect host for a tour of the magnificent temples in his home town of Kyoto, which remains beautifully preserved in contrast to the once war-ravaged Tokyo. We also headed for a short seaside trip to a hotel at the bottom of the Izu Peninsula – and then discovered it was a national holiday so half of Tokyo was down there too. Don't ever think traffic is bad until you try a busy day in Japan. We could have walked the 80 or so miles home faster than we drove.

While we had been enjoying ourselves, Eje had sorted the accommodation problem by finding a quiet little business hotel in the Aoyama region, just up from Roppongi, where the 'President Hotel' was about to begin its new life as the 'Racing Drivers' Hotel'. This would become a home from home for the 'gaijin' drivers for many years to come. Very simple in style, the coffee shop lay just inside the front door and would become the meeting place for what would be as many as a dozen drivers coming and going at one time. At reception the small staff all got to know us by name and we were greeted with enthusiastic smiles every time we returned.

The Suzuka race was a 1,000km event in the middle of August, the hottest and most humid month of the year – and 1983 was a particularly hot one. The circuit itself sits in a little valley that seems to shelter it from any wind, so if it rains it keeps raining, and if it's hot it just gets hotter. With a slow average speed around the tight circuit the race would last for nearly seven hours and finish in darkness, with our Dome able to make it on just four fuel stops – so each stint would be around an hour and 20 minutes. An hour and 20 minutes in a 50–60° centigrade cockpit with poor ventilation, no cool suits and not even a water bottle! Added to that was the fact that 'getting fit' in those days was something you simply did by racing more often, so we were far from being the supreme athletes that race today...

The new Group C cars were the first generation to have any real ground effect and they were cornering far faster than ever before. The great Porsche 917s and Ferrari 512s may have been just as hot, but they weren't generating the same G-forces. While the move towards having three drivers sharing a car at Le Mans to ease the stress had just begun, it was still a long way from becoming common in these 'short' sprint races.

By now the Dome was relatively well sorted, but at Suzuka we never really got on top of the rising tyre temperatures that pumped up their pressure. After just half a dozen laps it felt as though the rear tyres were more like party balloons. It became a long, long fight just to keep the car on the track – and fighting a bad car simply saps your energy even faster. The heat inside seems to rise up your legs until you feel they are inside an oven, the pedals begin to burn the soles of your feet to the extent that you don't want to brake anymore, your gloves are soaked with sweat, the deeper you breathe the drier your mouth gets. You end up driving in an almost trancelike state, simply trying to complete one lap at a time. These are times when you wonder what on earth you are doing there...

Eje had started the race so, luckily, I only had to do two stints to his three and with just five of the 166 laps left we were heading for third place and a hard-earned visit to the podium – and then the front suspension collapsed! Still Eje battled on. With sparks flying along behind him, he dragged the Dome to the finish in a state of complete exhaustion. It was certainly by far the hardest race of my life.

Another month of testing, and cruising Tokyo, and our final race of the year was at Fuji for Japan's round of the World Endurance Championship. By now our little Dome was beginning to become competitive, even if we did only qualify tenth with seven of the dominant Porsche 956s ahead of us. Mind you, there was still a little drama to come as first I had another 'Le Mans' moment, when the rear wing flew off in qualifying, and then, while I was driving in the race, the rear suspension broke. We made it to the end but were so far behind we were unclassified. With several almighty high-speed shunts it was also the end of that particular Fuji layout. Sadly, the chicanes were coming.

However, it was by no means the end of my Japanese adventures and over the next couple of years I would make sporadic outings for Team Ikuzawa – Tetsu Ikuzawa's eponymous team – both in a Group C Dome Toyota and his John Player Special Ralt Honda F2 car. Tetsu had been one of Japan's finest drivers and was the first to make a serious attempt to further his career in Europe in the late sixties and early seventies. He was a winner in Formula Three and highly competitive in Formula Two, but the Grand Prix dream never quite materialised.

With Eje signed to drive in another team, I persuaded Tetsu to enlist the services of fellow-Englishman James Weaver, a talented but much underfunded driver who had battled up through the ranks much like me. Once again we missed the early part of the year, so the Fuji race in July would be our debut.

After his spell in Europe Tetsu had become a bit of an Anglophile and we had to laugh when he booked his two English drivers into Gotemba's 'Chambers Lawn Tennis Club'. Like most of Japan's motorsport world his workshop was near the circuit and the first job was to get us fitted with seats – and with the new Dome being even smaller than the first that wasn't easy for two six-foot westerners. In the end we had to sit directly on the aluminium floor of the car and then create a two-part foam seat back. This was a perilous task on every occasion as two liquids combine to expand rapidly into a foam that goes hard in about five minutes, filling every little nook and cranny it can get into as it does so.

With its little four-cylinder, two-litre, turbocharged engine revving like mad to keep up with the more powerful Porsches, the team had made every effort to keep the car as light as possible and we were quick from the word go. In fact, we were so quick that I soon found myself at the front of the field and happily reeling off the laps – the easiest place to be in motor racing is in the lead!

There was, however, one small problem. With the engine in the back and the radiator in the front the hot water ran the length of the car in aluminium pipes which, to save weight, had been clamped to the aluminium floor without any insulation. Gradually the floor of the car was inheriting the 95° centigrade temperature of the water. Now, when you strap yourself into a racing car, you strap yourself in tight, so when my two little buttocks, which were pressed firmly against the floor, began to feel this growing heat I couldn't even lift them the tiniest fraction. Slowly my bottom was being barbequed! The only way to survive such pain in a racing car is to keep using the 'one lap at a time' mode. You've just done one so surely you can do one more...

Fortunately – or perhaps unfortunately – as I headed through the one fast corner that hadn't been neutered (the one on to the main straight), still in the lead, with 80 laps on the board, the rear left wheel broke in two. Travelling at some 150mph it was never going to be a soft impact with the concrete wall, but it was the happiest I'd ever been to have an accident. Before the wreckage had even come completely to a halt I'd burst out of the seat belts and pulled my sizzling behind off the floor. Out of the car in a flash, I skipped across the road to where I knew the medical centre was and raced through the door. Doctors and nurses looked concerned but could see no obvious injury until I dropped my overalls and leapt face down on the table, urging them to attend to my burnt buttocks. Apparently they were only first-degree burns, but if that wheel hadn't broken there would have been no way I could have got back into the car again. We would have had to retire officially due to a burnt bottom!

Staying on in Tokyo to race the Formula Two car, Tetsu put me up in a small flat he had near his home and it was there that I had the weirdest of experiences. Situated on the third floor of a big apartment block, its windows were level with one of Tokyo's many overhead roads. With no space to expand they had built these relief roads on columns directly above the road below and, with Tokyo being in an earthquake area, they sat them on flexible supports. These rubber mounts meant that if you came to a halt in a traffic jam the whole car moved up and down with the road.

In the middle of one night, deep in sleep, I had become aware that Tetsu's flat was also moving up and down in sympathy with the road. You could hear the traffic going by all the time and the foundations were obviously being affected. I was so convinced that my experience had been real that I told Tetsu about the problem the next morning. He laughed for a while before telling me that he too had been woken in the night – by a sizeable earthquake. I would experience one more of these spooky phenomena that same year when I was playing pool with James at our tennis club. Lining up a game-winning pot, I suddenly noticed the balls moving gently from side to side and my immediate thought was that James was somehow rocking the table to put me off...

It was great to get back into a single seater again after those hot, closed sportscar cockpits, but while the Ralt Honda had dominated in Europe, Tetsu's team hadn't been able to get the best out of it in Japan where it was the only one against a grid full of March 842s. By now the set-up of cars was becoming more and more critical and the days of a driver being able to drive around a bad-handling car were fast disappearing. The role of the race engineer was becoming ever more important.

I managed a solid sixth on that first outing at Fuji and hoped for better later in the year at Suzuka, having visited the Ralt factory and got a very complicated chassis set-up sheet to try and guide Tetsu's team. Mind you, trying to get my Japanese engineer to fully understand all the minute detail was another thing.

Testing went well, however, and I was looking forward to qualifying. Now the Japanese racing scene is dominated by the big tyre suppliers

Bridgestone, Dunlop and Yokohama, and qualifying tyres were very much the 'in' thing – but they would only last for one lap and you were only allowed one set. On the morning of qualifying, therefore, you'd get up, have breakfast at the Suzuka Circuit Hotel, wander down through the Disney-style Hondaland Amusement Park, climb into your racing car, crawl around one lap trying not to over-use your new tyres and then go completely ballistic for the next lap!

It was the greatest wake-up call you could have and I simply loved the challenge. Having never done such a qualifying lap at Suzuka before, though, I made the grave mistake of asking my 'gaijin' colleagues for some advice. You see, one of the great challenges of Suzuka is the left-handed '130R' that led to the then recently installed final chicane – something for which Eje was actually responsible, having triggered a massive multiple-car pile-up in a wet Formula Two race.

Now, in testing, this was yet another of those 'almost' flat in top corners, the sort of challenge that most real racing drivers live for, but I reckoned that with qualifying tyres it could be flat – and flat means no braking and not even a breath off the throttle. I thought it wasn't too stupid a thing to ask my mates, because we all used to help each other out a little as we fought to get on in this foreign land – but I was wrong! No problem, they all said...

So there I was, a brilliant lap behind me and beginning to think I might just surprise a few people. I was 13 corners down with two to go, the long straight out of the Spoon Curve climbing gently uphill and then flattening out as '130R' approached. I wedged the throttle hard against the bulkhead as the turn-in point neared at around 180mph and then fired it in towards the apex.

The initial turn was good, the tyres still had grip, but in the slight bump half-way to the apex, the back stepped out. I caught the slide with a flash of opposite lock and stayed glued to the throttle, but the car had 'walked' a foot to the right and the exit kerb was now in my path – and kerbs back then were kerbs you didn't cross! I tried to ease it back to the left but the back let go again and this time there was no room left to manoeuvre.

As the Ralt started to spin I de-clutched the engine and slammed on the brakes to try to keep the spin in a straight line, and somehow it stayed on the tarmac under a huge cloud of tyre smoke. I must have spun half-way to the chicane, but the car ended up pointing in the right direction with the engine still running so I completed the lap, bumping up and down on four very flat spotted tyres. From the back of the grid I managed to salvage eighth by the finish, but I never got a chance to go back and have another go. With no 'split times' or telemetry I still wonder what that lap time would have been – if only I'd just lifted a fraction off that throttle...

The final race on the Ikuzawa schedule that year was the World Championship round at Fuji where, once again, we were running strongly in the top ten when the engine went – so that was that. James and I stayed together for the following season and picked up a third and a fifth as our best finishes, and by the end of the year had developed the fastest Dome Toyota on the grid. However, good results at the final two races at Fuji were thwarted by typical Japanese monsoon weather.

The first of those races was the 1985 World Championship event and, as the pace car peeled off to start the race, so did all the visiting World Championship teams. In conditions that were even worse than those when Niki Lauda pulled in to hand the title to James Hunt back in 1976, the drivers had got together and decided discretion was definitely the better part of valour. For the Japanese teams, however, honour was at stake.

Fuji in the rain had to be one of the worst experiences in the world, as the old surface was etched with little dips and hollows that held varying depths of puddles – and the worst of them were in the braking area at the end of the 200mph straight. Not that we were doing 200mph, because it was impossible even to maintain full throttle in a straight line. Thanks to a tip from Geoff, who by now was also a Dome driver, the trick was actually to put the car into neutral as you began to brake. With so much aquaplaning you then had to 'float' your foot on the brake pedal and just press gently whenever you felt your wheels were actually in contact with the track. Even the slightest engine deceleration could be enough to lock the rear wheels, hence the neutral trick.

Driving blind into a huge wall of spray I was running in sixth – just in front of Geoff who was probably regretting giving away his little secret – but then water started to get in the electrics and it simply became a matter of survival. Driving with my heart permanently in my mouth, it was a huge relief when the fuel warning light finally flickered and I headed into the pits to hand over to James. However, the race had been reduced to a two-hour event so when I stopped they decided to leave me in as there was just half an hour left. It felt like half a day to me but finish we did, in a spluttering tenth place.

The Ikuzawa finale, also at Fuji, was in even worse conditions, leaving James and me very frustrated at being unable to show the true speed of the car we'd developed to work with a very low-downforce set-up – ideal for the dry but a nightmare in the rain. Even the top Japanese stars fell foul of the conditions, with both Hoshino and Hasemi clearing the guardrails in massive accidents from which they were fortunate to escape unharmed. After I'd survived several lurid moments and one massive pirouette down the main straight, Tetsu made the decision literally to throw in the towel, so we parked up long before the red flag called an end to the dismal proceedings.

With a contract to race for Lamborghini in the World Championship the next year my Japanese days seemed to be over, but when all that went pear shaped I soon returned to the East. First came a drive for the Le Mans Company, a March-Nissan R86V in the Suzuka 'sauna' – which retired early on – and then Costa Los's March-Porsche 84G which I had been racing in Europe, but that was never really on the pace.

After a very quiet 1987, I was back for another full season in Japan to partner Italian Le Mans winner Paolo Barilla in the latest Dome-Toyota 88C run by the works-backed 'Toyota Team TOM'S'. By now, however, the small two-litre engine was beginning to lag even further behind the ever improving Porsches – especially with the new 962 replacement for the 956 – and a new 3.2-litre V6 model would be introduced at the end of the year. After a promising start, when Paolo and I finished seventh behind five Porsches and our own team-mates, the team brought in the very talented young Japanese star Hitoshi Ogawa as a third driver for the longer races, and it rather became a case of 'two's company, three's a crowd'.

The Group C engine rules worked round a fuel-consumption formula – you could do what you wanted with the engine but you all had the same amount of petrol to use. While there were some races when it all became rather embarrassing, as the leaders started limping towards the finish trying not to run out of petrol, in general it worked very well – but to stay in touch with the Porsches our little Toyotas were using way too much fuel.

With Paolo being the number one he would start the race and, partly to put on a good show for Toyota, try and stay with the Porsches by using extra boost – and consequently too much fuel. When Hitoshi got in they had to give him the same deal so he didn't look slow in comparison to Paolo – and you can guess what happened when my turn came! 'Turn down the boost, drop the revs, save fuel.' I knew my position in the team but it wasn't much fun. Mind you, a fifth place in the 1,000km Suzuka August steam bath felt like a victory.

For the World Championship race at Fuji in October the team's sponsors had lined up Grand Prix star Stefan Johansson, so I was out completely. Still, I managed to pick up a drive in Fritz Gebhardt's Porsche 962 and enjoyed qualifying just 0.4 seconds behind them – not that either of us would feature strongly in the race.

I also had a couple of outings in a TOM'S Toyota Supra in the Japanese Touring Car Championship, sharing with Geoff, which added a bit of variety as we visited other tracks like Tsukuba and Sugo. Traversing backwards and forwards across such a fascinating country – and being paid to do so – was once again ticking all the boxes for the main reason I'd wanted to be a racing driver. Nobuhide Tachi, the 'T' of TOM'S, was my new boss and once again the hospitality was generous – even if it did include being dared to eat items such as raw octopus marinated in its own ink and, worst of worst, raw liver.

For 1989 I would once again be based in Europe, driving in the World Sports Prototype Championship, but it was back to Japan again for the following two years to drive for the private Alpha Racing Team owned by Tokyo property tycoon Nanikawa-san. This time, however I was finally in a Porsche 962 full time – the only problem was that by now the Toyotas and Nissans were dominating and no Porsche would ever win again in Japan. The story of my life – right place, wrong time!

Having said that, it was a good deal and we were treated royally. The drive was actually brokered by my old rival David Kennedy, who must somehow have forgiven me for screwing him up at Zandvoort (or was on a bigger percentage than I thought). And once again my suggestions for a team-mate had been taken on board, first by bringing in my '89 co-driver Derek Bell – complete with five Le Mans wins under his belt – and then, for the longer races, Anthony Reid, who was another talented young Brit struggling to get a professional drive.

The team manager was American Gary Cummings who had been working on Porsches for years and knew how to get the very best out of them – if only he could train his young Japanese crew how to do so. Watching him 'drilling' the team for pit stops was not to be missed. Having come from a military school and standing well over six feet tall he had a very strong presence – and a booming parade-ground voice which terrified the crew!

Our best result in Japan would only be a fifth at Fuji but, while we were usually on or near the Porsche pace, the dominant local marques had us beaten every time. The team continued into the 1991 season, but after just two races the collapsing property market in Japan forced the team to stop racing – and my love affair with Japan sadly came to an end with a seventh-place finish at Fuji.

On and off, I'd now been commuting to Japan over a period of about 12 years and had been a pioneer for the many 'gaijin' racing drivers who would follow. For many budding stars it became a waiting room where they could hone their skills and hope for a big drive in Europe to come up. Grand Prix stars like Jacques Villeneuve, Ralf Schumacher, Mika Salo and Eddie Irvine all spent a year or more plying their trade in the East.

At the peak of the sportscar season there could be as many as 20 of us in a race at Fuji, all heading for the President Hotel and a beer in Tokyo as soon as we finished. The hard shoulder of the two-lane motorway, which would be a 70-mile traffic jam on a Sunday night, soon became known as the 'Gaijin Lane' as we headed home as fast as we could.

The camaraderie of the Japanese scene was another part of what I'd wanted from my sport. My heroes used to share hire cars and drive from Grand Prix to Grand Prix together in the fifties and sixties, but the sport was fast becoming one where you hardly even conversed with your opponents, let alone socialised with them. In Japan we were all together in a foreign land – British, Swedish, Irish, Italian, German, Austrian, Australian, Brazilian drivers, all as one. The first to retire would go to the bar and then, as the six-hour race evolved, the next retirees would arrive to update the story until a full house had gathered. If it was one of 'our' days, the victors would then arrive – a completely happy time when we would often emerge from a club into the daylight of Monday morning, grab a quick burger at 'Mac-u-Donald-u-oes' and head straight for the airport and the flight home!

CHAPTER 12

TOP GEAR TV STAR

While the business of earning money as a racing driver was gathering momentum over in the Far East, back home in Europe opportunities to get paid to race remained few and far between so I had begun to widen my horizons.

In order to try and further promote my own racing career I had written a couple of stories for *Autosport* magazine – one about my first great adventure to Japan back in 1979 and then another in 1982 after I had first tested the Aston Martin Nimrod. They must have been reasonably well received because, after the Aston one, Simon Taylor invited me to become the magazine's regular track tester which not only paid me some money but also got me into all sorts of different teams' cars – teams that I would love to race for! Up until then, track testing had usually been done by the magazine journalists themselves, but with the cars becoming faster and faster Simon realised that it really needed a current racer to do them justice – not that my degree in civil engineering had best prepared me for any sort of literary career. My plan was simply to tell it as I felt it without any fancy prose, from getting into the cockpit to driving on the track, with the intention of trying to take my readers with me for the ride.

So it was that I began to get experience in a wide variety of not just racing cars but anything that had four wheels and went fast. In the first year alone, among other things, I drove three Formula Three cars, two Formula Two and one Formula One – just to keep things nice and symmetrical – as well as a Group A Jaguar XJS, a Group B Lancia Rally car and a Group C March Chevy.

The March story was actually part of another income strand as I had become a test driver for the Bicester company's sportscars, working with a very young boffin by the name of Adrian Newey whom I obviously trained well! I've always enjoyed the testing and development of cars – sometimes more than the hard slog of the races themselves. Working on providing feedback to an engineer who is then able to make alterations that make the car go faster can be very satisfying, even if only one change among dozens actually works. Testing also allowed me to drive at the circuit of my dreams: Goodwood.

While the track had been closed for racing since the mid-1960s it had remained open as a popular test venue, and I had first had the joy of driving where my heroes had been in my Unipart Formula Three days – including rolling my March 783 off the top of one of the old-fashioned earth banks. It was, and still is, a brilliantly flowing circuit with every type of corner you could want, and very fast, with just six corners per lap – but I'd rather do 160 laps around there than 80 round the modern 20-corner stop-go affairs of today.

At the other extreme, I also got talked into testing a Dragster – not quite one of the brutal 9,000 horsepower top fuel machines you see today but a scaled-down C-class machine with *only* 1,400hp. While it is without doubt one of the most impressive things to see two Dragsters launch off on their 300mph, quarter-mile missions, it's never been a sport that really appealed to me as 99 per cent of the driving input appears to be your launch reaction time. From then on you're pretty much a passenger praying nothing goes wrong – but the build-up to that launch certainly gets your pulse racing.

The 'Glacier Grenade' that I had been loaned had a track best of 8.21 seconds with a terminal speed of 176mph so I was quite happy to record a 9.23/154 on my one and only run and quietly retire from the sport. I was persuaded back many years later just to do a practice start in one of those top fuel monsters, and even that left me a nervous wreck...

Writing wasn't to be my only new job, however. On a trip to Mallory Park to watch a friend race I had been dragged into a commentary box to help out Andrew Marriot. With the late cancellation of that day's horse racing his 'two-race' feed for ATV Midlands had suddenly become an 'all-afternoon' live affair and he needed some help to fill the time. The use of an 'expert analyst' was still quite a rare thing then, but I thoroughly enjoyed the experience and thought it couldn't do any harm for my profile. Little did I think it would be the start of a whole new career!

As it was, it wasn't long before I had the BBC on the phone to see if I would be interested in joining Murray Walker in the commentary box for the various Formula Two and Formula Three races that they were covering live for 'Grandstand'. Of course James Hunt was Murray's man for the Grands Prix, in the greatest commentary pairing of all time, but I don't think he was too bothered about the smaller stuff. Working with Murray and the BBC team thus became an education in a whole new world and yet their team was pretty much like a racing team – except they drank more! Murray and I were the drivers while the producer, his stage managers and graphics team were the team manager and mechanics. Not that Murray was a drinker; indeed, he was always off to bed early, leaving me to be led astray...

Murray is just the nicest man I have ever met in motor racing – probably the nicest man I've ever met ever – and his love and enthusiasm for our sport were reflected in his commentary. He would learn everything about every driver in the race and, if the racing was exciting, he would talk as if his trousers were on fire. If it was a bit dull he would quieten down and accept it rather than following the modern trend of keeping on shouting in the hope that you can make it appear to be exciting.

A third new line of income – that would complete the skills required for the career for which I had, as yet, no plans – was that of being a 'precision driver' for corporate film work and, later on, a couple of TV commercials. I had got to know Alan More of Delta Films when he had been working for Akai in Monaco with Patsy – while I tried in vain to qualify the Ensign – and he suggested that I might be able to do some driving for him on some Audi films he had been commissioned to shoot.

Normally film companies would use stuntmen for such shoots and it was very much a closed-shop union affair but, while they were brilliant at crashing and smashing to order, they were not always so good at placing the car exactly where the director wanted for shot after shot, which is what Alan was after. By having me as a driver 'supplied by the client' we got around the union bit and went on to make several quite groundbreaking short films. With no 'health and safety' at all I drove through blazing cornfields, slalomed down ski runs alongside the British freestyle team and, on one memorable day, perfected the art of doing a 360-degree spin, straight at the camera, in the glamorous location of the Milton Keynes Bowl.

With my new-found diversity I had finally hauled my way above the average income and decided that, at the age of 33, it was probably about time to leave home. Gallivanting here and there it had seemed pointless to rent somewhere just for the sake of it, and with Patsy having a room in London I would spend a lot of my time there – even if that didn't always go down too well with her flatmates. I finally joined the mortgage world in the summer of 1985 and bought the cosy little two-up, two-down that is 244 Hersham Road, Hersham, Surrey, for the princely sum of £44,000. I managed to keep Patsy from packing her bags and moving in for a few weeks just to get a feeling of being in a 'bachelor pad' – eating junk food and watching too much TV – but it wasn't long before there were two toothbrushes in the mug.

One more 'career' that got going at about this time was that of being a driving instructor – not, I hasten to add, on the public roads but on manufacturers' 'track days'. BMW were the first to really do this, hiring circuits for the day and then lining up 20 or so of their latest models, with racing drivers on board, for their guests to drive. It wasn't always the most relaxing of days, sitting in the left-hand seat and trying to restrain your guest from doing their best Nigel Mansell impersonation, but the money was good. After BMW came similar jobs with the likes of British Leyland, Porsche, Volvo, Skoda, Daewoo, Citroën and Nissan – although by the time I got to the latter I had become 'host' and 'chief instructor' so I could avoid the dangerous stuff. Events like these continue to this day and provide much-needed income for the many young drivers trying to make their way up the ladder.

But it was in the spring of 1987 that the phone rang and my life would begin to turn in a direction that I had never even considered. Yes, I'd watched 'Top Gear' on the television – first presented by the likes of Angela Rippon and Noel Edmonds in the late seventies and now hosted by William Woollard – but it was a consumer programme looking at new road cars and checking how many suitcases you could get in the boot – interesting, but not really my sort of thing.

However, I now had programme producer Ken Pollock on the phone because they had been planning to do an item about the new Formula First single-seater racing car and their presenter, Chris Goffey, had broken his leg in a skating accident. Ken had read my track tests and heard me commentating, and he seemed confident that I could do the job, so off to Brands Hatch I went.

Formula First was another of Brands Hatch supremo John Webb's brilliant innovations. Formula Ford had become too expensive as an entry-level single-seater formula so he'd created this new, cheaper version. He even made arrangements for drivers to buy their cars with a hire-purchase agreement, which was how my brother Chris would make his own racing debut – and somehow my name was put down as his guarantor. Within a year there would be grids packed full of Formula First cars.

When I arrived I was greeted not only by Ken but by Chris Goffey as well, suitably attired in plaster and with crutches. The idea was that Chris would still present the item and I would simply be doing the driving for him and, as it turned out in the final edit, you wouldn't even see me without my helmet on in my debut item – a concept 'The Stig' would make famous some 15 years later! Unlike the Stig, though, I was allowed to talk, and when they found that I could drive right on the limit and describe exactly what was happening at the same time it almost seemed to be a eureka moment. How could I possibly do that?

Having watched so much on-board footage of motor racing, which often makes it look like anyone could just sit there and turn the wheel, I'd also made the conscious decision to make it 'look' exciting as well.

I'd decided that a bit of sliding about with some controlled oversteer would at least make it appear to be a bit more difficult. While this worked brilliantly on the television it didn't do my racing reputation any favours – because the 'quick' way is, of course, the neat and tidy route. And so the idea of 'Top Gear' having a tame racing driver had been born and they were now keen to get me presenting items of my own. For the first couple of years I would only do four or five pieces for each 12-programme series, but Ken was keen to use me more. There was a general feeling that the show needed a fresh direction and I was very much part of their plans.

In that first year I went off-road doing trials and Land Rover safaris but I also went on-road celebrating the history of the world's first true hot hatch – the Alfasud – and driving Beaulieu Museum's magnificent 1903 Gordon Bennett Napier. Mind you, whereas I had found it easy doing the talking while I was driving, doing it straight into a camera proved to be far more demanding – especially when you had to learn the lines and not simply react to whatever was going on.

With the image of the programme beginning to become a bit more racy, I managed to venture forth in a Formula Three car and the new Formula 3000. In 1989 we took a look at the up-and-coming names in the karting world and, having interviewed virtually every budding star there seemed to be, when someone suggested we ought to have a chat with a kid called Jenson Button we decided it was one interview too many...

It was around then that some lanky kid with a mop of curly hair suddenly turned up on the show. The programme was about to change forever. Jeremy Clarkson was invited to do a few items by Ken's fellow producer, Jon Bentley. They used to do alternate shows, so while Ken looked at the sportier side of motoring with me, Jon started to take a slightly more – how shall I put it – irreverent view of the world of motoring with Jeremy. It was a formula that saw the viewing figures begin to climb and climb, and it wasn't long before Jeremy suggested that one of his old mates, who knew everything there was to know about old classics and second-hand deals, should be brought on board as well. So Quentin Willson arrived on our screens.

While we might all have been part of the same team, few people realise that we rarely got together to meet each other as we were all off doing our own things. Filming an item is normally a one-day affair simply with you, the director, a cameraman and a soundman heading off somewhere to create a story. We'd all have to visit the Pebble Mill studios in Birmingham to finish off our items with some voiceover, but even that was spread out so there'd rarely be more than passing 'Hellos' in the corridor.

I remember one night in Birmingham, though, when both Jeremy and I were staying over, someone had suggested we meet for a drink. Quentin was invited along as well, but I think the two lads in their mid-30s had decided I was going to be a bit of an old bore. Jeremy had obviously got the short straw so he agreed to meet me in good old 'Bobby Brown's' down by the canal near our Hyatt 'home', but from the minute we first clashed beer bottles we both knew there would be no such divide.

As I began to become a recognised 'face' on television I was no longer able to do my precision driving jobs for the likes of Audi and BMW, although there was a job offer from Renault that I couldn't refuse as no-one would ever know it was me – I was to be Nigel Mansell for a week!

While the 1991 Grand Prix season had seen Mansell's Williams-Renault ending up as runner-up to the McLaren-Honda of World Champion Ayrton Senna, in the second half of the year the French-powered machine had become the faster of the two. A wheel-to-wheel duel down the Estoril straight typified the closeness of the two great drivers as Nigel battled with Ayrton, inches apart, in one of those moments that will never be forgotten – and it was a moment that Renault wanted to re-enact for a French television commercial.

Naturally, when I got the message that Williams had called, I assumed Nigel had quit and my moment had come! Instead, knowing that I was now both a racing driver and a film driver they just wanted me for the latter. With 'my' Williams-Renault FW14 bedecked in its regular Canon colours, complete with its 'Red 5' number, a second car was painted black to take the place of Senna's McLaren and driven by Johnny Robinson.

With a helmet my size painted in the famous Mansell colours I would be Nige for a week. Wander into the garage in the morning, a chat with the mechanics and then a few laps to warm up the car before they started fixing cameras all over the place. All our runs were done in bursts of two or three laps and the only filming was done down that start/finish straight – leaving us plenty of time to 'play' as we blasted round to do another run. Two boys with Grand Prix cars for toys – and we were getting paid.

At one stage I had a full Hollywood-style 35mm camera mounted on the sidepod of the car with a sort of periscope lens coming across in front of me and then filming the driver's view ahead – leaving me to peer through the tiny gap between the bottom of the lens and the top of the cockpit. To the great frustration of the crew the Portuguese weather wasn't at its best so we had to curtail the filming – and come back to do more a week later. Getting paid twice meant that that cloud really did have a silver lining!

While my professional life was all of a sudden moving on apace, so too was my private life. With money now coming in on a far more regular basis, Patsy and I had moved from the two-up, two-down semi in Hersham to a three-up, three-down semi at 12 Copse Road, Cobham. I'd always had a dream of being Weybridge's first 'home-grown' star, moving 'across the railway line' into the millionaires' row of St George's Hill and, while it was still a distant vision, I was getting fractionally closer.

After a 'brief' nine-year romance it was also now time to propose to the most wonderfully patient Patsy who, to my great delight, said 'Yes'. We got married on 17 December 1988 in St Andrew's Church in Cobham and she walked up the aisle looking as beautiful as anyone could ever be to the stirring sounds of Jeremiah Clarke's 'Trumpet Voluntary'. Our honeymoon was our first ever 'normal' holiday with three beautiful weeks in Thailand that made us determined to have many more.

As property prices began to soar beyond belief we realised we were never going to make it to St George's Hill, so we looked for the nearest area where we could afford a detached house and ended up on the edge of a hill in 'Sky House', just outside the delightful little West Sussex village of West Harting near Petersfield. We had moved about 30 miles down the A3 but gone back around 30 years in time and we loved it.

Just over the South Downs lay Goodwood, Chichester, Wittering and my birthplace, near Havant, so it all seemed a very fitting place to be. Both the A34 to the north and the A3 to London were soon due to have by-passes built around their respective bottlenecks of Newbury and Hindhead so there would be easy access wherever I wanted to head – if only those that feel a lesser spotted newt is more important than human misery hadn't intervened! As it is, traffic now happily flows round one while the hugely expensive tunnel under the other has yet to open...

The country air must have suited us because, not long after we moved in, the first of what would end up being three bouncing sons arrived on 23 January 1992 in the shape of Jack – and I would find that the joys of fatherhood were far, far greater than I had ever imagined. While the love for your Mum and Dad, your girlfriend or boyfriend, wife or husband is a strong bond, the love you feel for a daughter or son is a very different sort of feeling. The memory of the day that Patsy opened the door and, for the first time, little Jack tottered towards me, arms open, and mumbling 'Dada, Dada' still makes my heart feel like it wants to burst out of my chest.

By 1993 my world seemed finally to be on the up and up, with a new career in touring cars a good possibility. 'Top Gear' had taken off to such an extent that the team was pictured on the front cover of the *Radio Times*, and the first *Top Gear* magazine was launched in the October of that year with Jeremy, Quentin and myself as the lead columnists. The boys were on the move!

CHAPTER 13

THERE'S NOTHING LIKE
LE MANS

With the dream of Grand Prix stardom not quite coming true it would be the Le Mans 24 Hours that became the central part of my career, a race that would give me everything I probably ever wanted out of being a racing driver – not, perhaps, the great riches that I had once hoped for, but every experience I could have – and on occasions not have wished for! The fact that it has been running in virtually the same configuration since it began in 1923 gives it the history that satisfies my love for the sport. Most drivers these days have never been 'fans', like I was as a youngster. They've simply grown up racing in karts, not once queuing for hours to get a good view at a trackside fence and then waiting another hour or two before there was anything to watch.

The Le Mans 24 Hours, then, is a race that has real history, on a circuit where I knew every corner from the race reports that I had read; somewhere where all the greats had driven before always gave me that extra little buzz. Going to race at places like Monaco, Monza, Spa and Le Mans were always special occasions.

In many ways a 24 Hour race is the ultimate test of both car and driver. In this one race the car travels the same distance as a whole season of Grand Prix racing and each driver does the equivalent of five Grands Prix within that time period – and the speeds are high, very high! After my first three attempts had covered every experience of failure from not even qualifying to a mechanical retirement and then finally a 200mph crash, I headed back there in 1983 hoping finally to get my first finish at this gruelling event.

While waiting for my Dome to be built in Japan, the year had actually started off with my first trip to the legendary Monza Autodromo and a chance to race the mighty Porsche 956 that had previously slipped from my grasp. The car was Richard Lloyd's Canon-sponsored machine, one of the first customer cars, and it was an opportunity helped by my having tested it for one of my *Autosport* stories. When the team's driver, Jonathan Palmer, had a clashing Formula Two engagement, I was ready to go. Both the car and the circuit actually turned out to be slightly disappointing. The track of old had long been broken up with tight chicanes, and instead of being fast and flowing it had become very much stop and go. Yes, the average speed remained high on the long straights, but instead of discussing classic racing lines the conversation turned to 'how much kerb can you drive over'.

Still, in the early days of development and with the privateer customers like Richard having had little time to sort their new cars, the 956s tended to have long, soft brake pedals that didn't really inspire much confidence and made it difficult to heel and toe when changing down. Consequently the big braking areas that had become critical for a good lap time were hard to get consistent – and they were distinctly nerve racking at the same time. Mind you, the sheer thrill of driving this machine still left a strong impression. It was the first time I'd driven a turbocharged racing car and I had to get used to the lag that means there is a delay between opening the throttle and actually getting the power. The wonderful whistling sound as the turbochargers began to pick up speed gave plenty of warning, however!

Sharing the car for the race were Richard himself and my former Ensign nemesis, Jan Lammers, who would be Palmer's regular partner, but with the car proving to be such a handful he could only qualify it eighth and was a full six seconds down on the fastest Porsche. After a steady opening stint, Jan pitted to hand over to me and, as I headed out for my first ever race lap in one of these iconic machines, the front right wheel fell off…

We hadn't even changed the wheels during the pit stop so it had to be some sort of heat-soak issue, a problem that would affect several customer 956s in future races, although it never seemed to happen on the works cars. Whatever the cause, having managed to avoid flying off the road, I had to cruise slowly back to the pits to get another wheel. We got to the finish in sixth place but it had been a very difficult drive. For Richard Lloyd, though, it was the beginning of a process that would turn his car into one of the fastest Porsches in the field.

For Le Mans I'd picked up a drive in Steve O'Rourke's brand-new EMKA Aston Martin. Steve was, among other things, Pink Floyd's manager and EMKA was his production company. Having already raced at Le Mans a few times in GT cars he wanted to move up to Group C, so he commissioned motor racing's very own Michael Cane to build one for him.

Once again the shakedown 'test' would be in the traditional Silverstone 1,000km, one month before the big event. With the distributor breaking on the very first lap – fortunately near enough to the pits that I could coast in – and Steve then grinding to a halt with a broken wheel bearing just half a lap from the finish, it was a race full of dramas.

Partnering Steve, I was back in the same 'Pro-Am' situation as I had been with Ian Bracey and it's always a bit frustrating to have to have a co-driver who's quite a bit off the pace. However, this is very much a part of the endurance racing scene and a system for which many young drivers are very grateful as it gets them on to the grid along with the factory teams. Steve loved his racing and had the budget to do as he pleased, and I was more than happy to be part of his team.

The very experienced Nick Faure would help me keep up the pace, but the race was always going to be one of simply getting to the finish. After a variety of delays we duly took the flag in 17th place and received a huge cheer for being the first British car to finish – the first eight were all Porsche 956s.

My friend Phil Grellier – who had been our 'extra' mechanic on my Durex Formula One debut – had brought a bit of sponsorship to the EMKA team in the shape of chemical giants Dow Corning, for whom he worked, and their backing would see me installed in one of those iconic 956s for the 1984 race. David Sutherland had hired one of the

German 'Kremer Racing' machines and we would share it with Australian Rusty French. With little time in the car I was pretty chuffed to qualify it in ninth place and we ran strongly in the top ten, rising as high as fifth before a rear suspension failure pitched me off the road. Once again it was a problem several Porsche entries had encountered, with the suspension pick-up plate on the bottom of the gearbox working loose.

I only had a couple laps left to go in my stint and, running to the tight fuel regulations, you never want to pit early, so when I felt a bit of movement from the rear I kept going, thinking it was probably a tyre going off. As we would later find out, it was actually due to one of the two bolts that hold the plate in place dropping out. With no radio I couldn't discuss the problem, so I'd determined to get to the end of my stint. Unfortunately, as I changed direction from the fast right entering the Porsche Curves into the first left, the car just swapped ends – the second bolt had sheared under the strain...

With the barriers no more than a few feet off the road and travelling at well over 100mph I hit them big time. Amazingly, when all the crumpling and grinding noises finally stopped, I found that not only had I kept the engine running but I was also actually able to drive it forwards – albeit doing a bad impersonation of a crab! Luckily the pits were not too far away and, with some great work from the Kremer boys, it wasn't that long before we were back on our way. After the size of the impact I couldn't believe we were still in the race – and not only were we in it, but we went on to finish in a respectable ninth place.

The Kremer Team was one of the leading Porsche preparation specialists but, when I look at the way drivers maintain their fitness levels today, I always remember back to my first meeting with team boss Erwin Kremer in the Le Mans paddock. Over in Japan we had started to put drinks bottles in the car to help replenish lost fluid, but when I suggested this to Erwin he simply said: 'You are a professional driver. You will drive not drink!' They also had no catering for the drivers, so I did the whole race fortified by Croque-Monsieurs from the Paddock Café.

For the 1985 race I was back with Steve O'Rourke and his EMKA. This was not only now fully decked out in the striking turquoise and white colours of Dow Corning but also a substantially revised car. Having taken a year off, Steve had got Richard Owen to re-engineer the car and he had done marvels with a bit of wind-tunnel work. With Le Mans specifically in mind, he did away with the ground-effect venturi tunnels and turned it into a flat-bottomed car. He then replaced the low wing that hung out the back with a thin one, high up in the airstream, and created an air intake that better fed the big 5.3-litre Aston Martin V8 that had been starved of air.

The result was a light, nimble machine that was alive in my hands, went down the Mulsanne Straight 7mph faster than it had two years before, and lapped nine seconds quicker. The improvements enabled me to qualify the car 13th overall behind ten Porsches and the two factory Lancias. More to the point, though, I was the fastest non-turbo car and, while they could use extra boost in qualifying, in the race they would have to turn the boost down to manage the fuel consumption that the regulations demanded.

In glorious sunshine the first hour of that race had me living like I was walking on the moon. Film of the cavalry charge down the Mulsanne Straight makes for epic viewing, as a pack of about 20 Group C cars jostle for position over the gentle humps and hollows at well over 200mph. I was probably driving as well as I ever had, hugely supported by Michael Cane's small team who all believed in me and were urging me on. This was living!

True to expectations, the turbocharged cars didn't have the same straight-line speed in the race and, one by one, I began to pick them off. With less grip, I would have to hang on as best I could down the Porsche Curves and through the Dunlop Esses and then try for a perfect exit out of Arnage in order to get in the slipstream and slowly be sucked towards my next target down the three-mile-long straight.

The adrenaline rush of each move would never wane. As you close on a car ahead, the turbulence of their airstream starts to move your car around as you slowly edge nearer and nearer. You need to time the sling-shot just right. You know the kink is looming large and you need to get past and back to the left before you reach it. With the straight being a public road there is also the crest of it to cross, a tiny rise and fall, but at this speed it first resists your move and then sucks you over the top. Steering input has to be minimal.

After 45 minutes the signalling crew at Mulsanne were almost falling off the wall as they hung out a big 'P3' sign. Not sure of our own fuel consumption, we had decided to pit after 13 laps. After 12 laps I was up to third place and lapping at the same pace as the two leading Porsches of Klaus Ludwig and Jonathan Palmer, who would eventually go on to finish first and second.

It was at this point Michael Cane formulated a plan… Seeing me sitting there running just over 10 seconds behind the leaders, and with it taking nearly a minute to fill the regulation 100-litre tank, it had dawned on him that if we only half filled the EMKA we'd get out 20 seconds ahead. With neither Steve nor Nick Faure, who was with us again, able to run my pace this was a one-off chance to lead Le Mans.

Again, with no radios I had no idea of any of this as I shot back on to the track after what had, indeed, seemed a very short pit stop. There had been some shouts about only half filling, but no explanation. Frustratingly, we didn't get the official first place on the one-hour bulletin as one of the Porsches had eked out their fuel to manage 15 laps and still hadn't pitted at the time. But for the moment the number 66 EMKA Aston Martin led the race! For a while I was even pulling away from Ludwig, benefiting from a lighter car, and for five glorious laps our pit board proudly displayed the 'P1' sign. It was the first time an Aston Martin-engined car had led Le Mans since they won the race back in 1959 – and none have done it since. All too soon the 'P1' was sadly swapped for a 'PIT IN' and the fun was over, but it certainly felt good at the time!

Apart from a fractured fuel line the car ran pretty solidly just inside the top ten, but the problem would leave us to finish 11th in the end, once again the top-finishing British car, and we were mobbed by a sea of fans as we crossed the line just one place behind the works Porsche of Jacky Ickx and Jochen Mass and one ahead of the Dome Toyota

Patsy Rowles the young model in 1979...

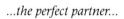

...the perfect partner...

...and the beautiful bride – December 1988.

First Le Mans finish – EMKA Aston Martin, 1983.

First top-ten finish at Le Mans – Kremer Porsche 956, 1984.

First laps leading Le Mans – EMKA Aston Martin, 1985.

*Being chased by Jim Crawford as
'the two speedfiends' entertain in
India – February 1985.*

*In a Thundersports Chevron B26
on the front row at the Cape Town
track of Killarney in South Africa –
December 1985.*

*More Thundersports at Brands Hatch
driving the Texas Chevron B26 in 1985...*

... and the CanAm March 847 in 1987.

Pressing on towards a podium finish with Jo Gartner at Silverstone – May 1986.

Brother Chris and his Formula First. The car for my 'Top Gear' debut – February 1987.

The Toyota boys at Le Mans. With my mate Eje Elgh...

...while the Toyota crew get busy with the Dome 87C – June 1987.

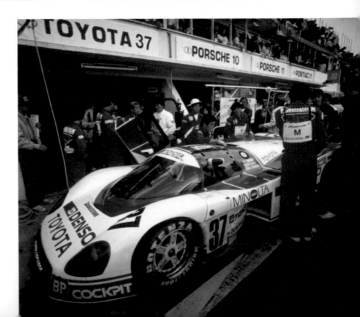

Anything goes! From a Dragster for Autosport in 1982...

...to TV stardom in a Rallycross Metro 6R4 at the Brands Grand Prix in 1988.

Back on the water in a Formula One Powerboat for 'Top Gear Waterworld'...

...and on the back of 1989 World Champion Steve Webster's sidecar outfit.

Saab racing in 1987, and fighting off the 911s in a Porsche 944 Turbo in 1988.

Le Mans legend Derek Bell and I join forces for Porsche Cars Great Britain and make our Porsche 962 debut at Silverstone in May 1988.

My Porsche nemesis Bob Wollek listens in as James Weaver tells me how it is!

The Richard Lloyd Racing Porsche 962 was the car for the 1989 World Sports Prototype Championship, but it got a little too hot at Le Mans.

The Alpha boys on parade at Le Mans 1990. From left, me, Anthony Reid and David Sears.

Pressing on in our Porsche 962.

The last time the famous balcony would be used – Patsy is at far right.

85C that I was racing in Japan. We were actually incredibly lucky that we hadn't ended the race in a fireball as the fuel line was leaking petrol right into the 'V' of the engine. When I pitted complaining of fuel starvation, as soon as the engine cover was removed, Michael suggested I vacate the cockpit very quickly because the distributor was actually sitting in a puddle of petrol...

In many ways that year was one of the most exhilarating of all my visits. During the night Steve had had trouble with his glasses misting up and poor Nick had gone down with a migraine so I did about five of the night hours and ended up doing something like 13 hours in total – the lobster and champagne once again tasted very good.

The following year, 1986, was a season of great disappointment. I'd signed a contract to race a factory-supported Lamborghini Group C car in the full World Endurance Championship, partnering Italian Grand Prix driver Mauro Baldi, and had turned down offers to stay in Japan. By the time I'd learned that there wasn't really enough money in place, and the whole thing fell apart, it was too late to fix up anything else and Patsy would have to go without her annual holiday.

We returned in '87 as part of the official factory-backed TOM'S Toyota Team, with their little 2.1-litre turbocharged engines bursting at the seams to stay in touch down the long straights. After the Lamborghini fiasco I was delighted to be asked back into the Toyota fold, but as it would only be for the one race I needed to impress! I was to share the second car with Japanese stars Masanori Sekiya and Kaoru Hoshino, while the lead car had Geoff Lees and Eje Elgh partnering former World Champion Alan Jones. By now Alan was in semi-retirement mode and on a nice little earner but he was still as competitive – and entertaining – as ever.

They'd only brought one car to the test weekend for Eje and Alan and me, and I got off to a good start by using my Le Mans experience to set the fastest time – albeit a fair bit off the pace as we simply weren't fast enough down the straight. In qualifying for the race Alan got his own back by lapping 0.44 seconds quicker, but we were only good enough for 14th and 16th on the grid.

Once again the early charge was a lot of fun as I latched on to Alan's tail. We circulated just outside the top ten for the first couple of hours before he ran out of fuel and, not long afterwards, we ran out of water. It wasn't exactly Toyota's finest hour, but I well remember one Japanese executive asking me, with a sense of incredulity, how I was able to run at the same pace as Mr Jones! He'd obviously seen the difference in our track records – not to mention wage packets – and thought it should be reflected in our relative pace. Such can be the frustrations of our sport…

Mind you, if I impressed Toyota in 1987 I decidedly did not in 1988. I was already having a difficult time playing 'Number Three' in Japan and we brought the same line-up of Barilla, Ogawa and myself to Le Mans – and the same team tactics. Like many drivers, I seem to operate that much better when I know my team believes in me: their confidence feeds my self-confidence, the mind is more relaxed and the driving simply flows.

First lap out of the pits in the race, after Paolo handed over the car in 18th place, I was heading down to the Esses in the early evening on my brand-new cold tyres when a Jaguar surprised me with a late lunge down the inside. In trying to give him room I promptly dropped the whole lot into the gravel trap. I hadn't hit anything, but by the time I'd been dragged out and limped back to the pits for a major clean-up much time had been lost.

Worse was still to come as I repeated the feat in the middle of the night on the tight left of Indianapolis, again on an out lap with cold tyres. Again, I didn't hit anything and it was only a half-spin, but the car got beached sideways on top of the exit kerb and then the marshals broke the rear wing trying to push it off. If I could have crawled into the proverbial hole I would have done so, and although we carried on with a few more minor problems, finishing 24th was no consolation. No amount of lobster or champagne could make me feel any better, but fortunately I had better Le Mans experiences to come.

CHAPTER 14

THE JOURNEYMAN
RACING DRIVER

While trying to build a full-time racing career in the World Endurance Championship there was still plenty of time to look at other areas of the sport. The Japanese seasons had fairly limited programmes and, at the same time, my *Autosport* track testing job – and later my 'Top Gear' position – would open plenty of doors for the odd race here and there, and bring me a wide range of racing that very few drivers have been as fortunate to experience. The Grand Prix superstars might hog the limelight and earn the big money but, as they say, variety is the spice of life.

The BMW County Championship had given me plenty of experience in tin-topped machines and in 1982 I did the first of six Snetterton 24 Hour races, brilliant amateur events where you could enter almost anything with no previous experience at all. Mind you, some of the driving did have to be seen to be believed, with cars suddenly appearing from the undergrowth in the middle of the night after various off-course excursions.

I finished third there in 1983 in Colin Blower's Porsche 911and we then spent four years conclusively proving that, despite often being the fastest thing on the track, a Mitsubishi Colt Starion Turbo simply couldn't run reliably for the full distance. Colin and I drove the 'old-fashioned way' with just the two of us sharing the duties – and we always finished – but always way down the field! Not for the first, or last, time I would say that 'it's better to have led and lost than never to have led at all'!

Much greater success came my way when my old Formula Ford 2000 sparring partner Richard Piper invited me to share in his

Thundersports programme from 1984 to '87. This was another great John Webb initiative that brought together every type of racing sportscar there was, both old and new, and stuck them all together on one grid for races that ran for less than an hour but with two drivers being mandatory. Richard had bought a 1974 Chevron B26 and stuck a Hart Formula Two engine in the back and, away from all the pressures of Group C racing, it was just a joy to drive. After three second places Richard decided we needed more power to beat the big CanAm machines that were starting to dominate, so he stuck a Cosworth DFV Grand Prix engine in the back and we went out and won!

The strain of it all was probably a bit too much for the 11-year-old chassis, as the win was followed by three retirements, so for the final year he joined the CanAm club with a brutal five-litre March-Chevrolet 847. It had apparently spent all its life as a spare car and I don't think it can ever have been raced because it had the heaviest steering I'd ever experienced. I'd actually tested one of the team's cars a couple of years earlier for an *Autosport* test and commented then that the 'the steering was surprisingly light...' so I don't know what had gone on in the meantime.

After retiring from our Brands debut with mechanical gremlins we took it to the ultra-fast Thruxton Circuit and, as the speed built up, the only way I could get a decent lap time was to use all my strength to turn into the long right of Goodwood and then wedge my left elbow into the side of the monocoque to hold the lock on at around 130mph. If that hadn't been scary enough I then had a front tyre explode exiting Church Corner doing 140mph – luckily I had just got the car straight! The flailing rubber destroyed the front of the bodywork and left Richard with no time to qualify himself for the race so I had to start right at the back of the 19-car field. Ninth at the end of the first lap, I handed the car over to Richard in the lead. With no experience of the car round the track it was now his turn to brace himself, and he held on for a memorable victory by a scant 0.02 seconds.

The team that supplied the car was Bob Fearnley's British RK Racing outfit which was running a very successful American programme for former Lotus Grand Prix driver Jim Crawford. They also had an arrangement to run cars in India for brewery tycoon Vijay Mallya, who now owns the Force India Grand Prix team. The events were the grandly named Bangalore and Madras Grands Prix where, in 1982 and '83, against precious little opposition, Bob had run Vijay in a full-on Formula One Ensign. Unfortunately the pressure of the family business had forced Vijay to step out of the cockpit, so Jim had done the winning for him in '84. However, they thought it would be good to provide a bit of opposition for 1985 – and my introduction via the *Autosport* test had put me in pole position.

Once again my dream job was taking me to parts of the globe that I might never have reached – although I still haven't made it to either Australia or New Zealand. Arriving in Bombay – now of course Mumbai – at five o'clock in the morning was not the most pleasant of first impressions as the streets were full of beggars and the homeless. It was certainly a different world! And then the flight to Bangalore the next day nearly brought my personal world to an early end as we aborted two attempts to make it down through the early morning mist – the second after the pilot was neatly lining up, not on the runway, but on the street lamps of the road alongside.

Bangalore turned out to be a pleasant relief from the chaos of Bombay, with poverty and decay replaced by prosperity and colour. Wherever you were, though, surviving on the roads was another story. The only rule seemed to be that whoever hooted their horn the most had right of way. Not allowed to drive ourselves, the rental cars come complete with drivers and so we were at their mercy.

Both the Bangalore and Madras tracks were old Second World War airstrips with rough concrete surfaces where we basically blasted up and down the runways and navigated the odd straw-bale chicane. Bob had brought out a couple of Formula Atlantic Chevrons for us to play in, but keeping them going in such harsh conditions wasn't easy.

Having agreed that we'd take one Grand Prix each – assuming we could coax our cars to the finish – the plan was to put on a display in our two black 'McDowell' machines. The local press certainly seemed to approve of our show. The reporter of the *Indian Express* was so excited that his report read like something from a Pathé News story at Brooklands.

'One witnessed some fierce driving. The two speedfiends went along bumping and boring. Thousands watched with bated breath as they sent their black beauties roaring around the T-shaped track. Jim just refused to be overtaken... now Tiff went hell to split... skewed through the turns as only he could... never for a moment could one say who would emerge the winner... the packed stands rooting and roaring... so fast and gutsy... he sent his machine scything in, risking life and limb.'

In fact the only people risking life and limb were the spectators who, walking from their local villages, kept pouring in all day long. Where the edge of the track was once a grass verge it soon became a wall of human beings. They even stood across the end of the runway, which had at least given us some sort of escape road: as we powered out of the turns on opposite lock they would step back a pace or two to give us more room!

So the Bangalore Grand Prix was mine and the Madras Grand Prix was Jim's and – with much use of our sponsor's products – a fun time was had by all as we were mobbed by the local fans. I doubt if many racing drivers can boast of having their feet kissed during a podium presentation!

Back in Bombay, the night before out flight home, Jim and I were honoured to be invited to Vijay's wedding reception at the Bombay Turf Club. All the trappings of the old colonial days were plain to see as we wandered the lush lawns under a starlit sky and marvelled at the most amazing display of fine jewellery – never before or since have I seen so many diamonds in one place.

Away from Japan, I did the Silverstone, Spa and Brands Hatch World Endurance rounds in the EMKA Aston Martin, but the lack of downforce that had helped it to be so competitive at Le Mans left it struggling for grip everywhere else. Not that we ever got to the finish of any of these races as the Aston engines proved to be more than a little fragile...

I also raced Chuck Graemiger's Cheetah Aston Martin in the

Hockenheim heatwave of '85 but, after more mechanical woe, I ended up spending more time trying to find my way back to the pits than I did driving in the race. Having broken down at the first chicane after just nine laps I set off into the tall pine forest to walk back but, with the sound of racing cars coming from both sides of me, at one stage I emerged from the deep dark woods to find I'd become so disorientated that I was walking the wrong way. It's not just in deserts that you can walk in circles...

That year would end with a very sad trip to South Africa. Great friend and racing rival Graham Duxbury had arranged a drive for me in their own Thundersports series. It should have been a trip that would have included a joyful catch-up with my brother Michael, but tragically it only coincided with the end of his battle with cancer. The dreaded disease had first occurred in one of his eyes and, with that removed and a false one in place, he had been given the all clear. He even resumed racing, married girlfriend Avril and had a son called Clifford whose first birthday came just before my trip. But at just 37 years old, the cancer returned and this time it attacked his liver.

The family knew the end was very near and, returning from racing in Japan, Patsy and I got to Johannesburg as soon as we could. High on painkillers he was by then talking very little, but when I went into his bedroom he sat up and greeted me with a great smile and a few words. Within a couple of days he'd passed away. My Mum and Dad were already there and it was almost as if he'd waited just that little bit longer to see me.

The race was actually down at the Killarney track in Cape Town, the town where Michael had first settled when he moved to the country and where he had become the track's Formula Ford champion in the Crosslé 25F he'd bought from me. This town has to be one of the most beautiful in the world, with its trademark Table Mountain overlooking stunning sandy bays, and it felt good to be where Michael had been having wonderful days of his own.

With so many people having great memories to tell me it was hard to concentrate on the racing, but once in the car you do as you always do – the concentration required simply blocks everything else out.

There was no Hollywood script to grant me a victory that I could have dedicated to his memory, only another mechanical retirement, but it is a great little track. This time not one where many of my heroes had raced, but one where Michael had raced...

It was, of course, much harder for Mum and Dad. Mum had been battling the ghastly disease herself and, although cleared at the time, she too would succumb just three years later. When Dad died in 1994 the Needell five had all too swiftly become two, but with Dad having three sons, Michael producing Clifford as well as Anthony from a previous relationship, me going on to have three boys and Christopher marrying Carol to create Sam and Charlie – and not a girl in sight – the lineage looks to spread much wider in the future. Quite where the Needell name comes from no-one seems to know, but a peerage registry just a few years ago could only locate some 18 Needell households in Britain, 70 in the United States and 12 in Germany – of which three were in Hockenheim!

It was going to be the big breakthrough year in 1986, that first full World Endurance season with the Lamborghini – even if the series had now been renamed the 'World Sports Prototype Championship'. But when the bubble burst it left me without a drive. Once again both Silverstone and Brands Hatch would have races, with Silverstone holding the traditional Le Mans build-up fixture in May, so when Kremer Racing were suddenly short of a driver I was free!

My co-driver would be rising Austrian star Jo Gartner who, after a brief burst of Grand Prix stardom, was forging his own sportscar career. He'd started the year off in style by winning the Sebring 12 Hours. Blindingly quick and instantly likeable, it was a pleasure to drive with him – even if I was once again in that awkward position of not quite having the time to get on his pace with the car set-up as it was.

Still, Jo put us fourth on the grid and we finished the Silverstone 1,000km one place better off, sharing the podium with the Derek Warwick/Eddie Cheever Jaguar and the Derek Bell/Hans Stuck factory Porsche. Jo's broad toothy smile reflected the satisfaction of a good result, while beating my mate James Weaver, driving the Richard Lloyd Porsche, into fourth was the icing on the cake.

Who could believe that just four weeks later my co-driver would become another Le Mans fatality when the Kremer car we had been driving suffered an unknown failure and turned Jo into the Mulsanne Straight barriers. For him, the barriers would not hold and he somersaulted into the trees, instantly suffering fatal injuries. He was just 32 years old. Mercifully, Jo remains the last to die on that notorious straight, indeed the last to die in a Le Mans race – not, I hasten to add, necessarily due to the introduction of the chicanes in 1990, as both he and Jean-Louis Lafosse were killed in accidents that occurred well before the first of those changes. It was more thanks to taller and better installed barriers that keep the cars within the track – a point well proven by Jonathan Palmer's huge accident four years later.

What the chicanes have done, however, is remove the danger of arriving at the famous Mulsanne 'kink' unaware you have a problem until you turn into it – at well over 200mph. How my good friend – and dentist – John 'Driller' Sheldon survived just such a moment is nothing short of a miracle. In the 1984 race his Nimrod Aston Martin, possibly suffering from a slowly deflating tyre, turned sharp right in the middle of the kink. Again, upon impact, the barrier folded back and tore the front off the car. Tragically a marshal was killed by the flying debris while the rest of the car, with John still strapped in, rebounded into the road in a ball of fire.

I must have been one of the first cars to arrive on the scene, slowing rapidly, warned not just by the yellow flags but by the huge plume of smoke. The wreckage lay all over the track, with the bulk of the car a huge red inferno sitting right in the middle from which I could feel the heat as I drove past. From what I could see I instantly assumed no-one could have survived, and I even had no idea what car it was. One long lap later, and now crawling past the wreckage, I could tell it was John's but of course had no way of knowing who was driving it at the time. Which of my friends had surely perished? Was it John, or Richard Attwood, or Mike Salmon?

With the pace cars taking over to control the race for the next hour, all I could do was cruise round waiting to use up the fuel until my next scheduled stop. No longer driving at racing speeds, your mind can now wander and you have to fight away thoughts of the full impact of what you have seen. Only when I finally made my pit stop did I discover that John had indeed been driving but, although badly burned, he had miraculously stood up from the wreckage and got himself out of the blazing inferno. Not only would he live to race again, but to drill teeth again!

Fortunately accidents like these are increasingly rare as both cars and barriers become stronger and safer, and there would only be one other such incident during the rest of my career. Not this time on the Mulsanne Straight, but almost as fast down the tree-lined avenue towards Indianapolis Corner. In the middle of the night it is completely dark down this stretch but, closely following another car, our powerful headlights cut a long path ahead as we once again built up towards 200mph.

Driving in the dark at such speeds is an exhilarating experience as the 'tunnel' of vision ahead of you accelerates the feeling of speed, with fluorescent marker boards and painted kerbs almost giving the surreal feeling of being in the most amazing 3D computer game. But when things go wrong you soon remember the speed is for real.

As we took the first kink of this narrow section yellow lights suddenly flashed brightly in the dark, warning us of danger ahead, but as our headlights searched forwards all they reflected was a wall of what I assumed to be tyre smoke just a hundred yards ahead. In a fraction of a second we had both dived into a dense fog. Convinced I was about to hit something, somewhere, very hard there was simply nothing I could do – and nothing the lights could see but a mass of debris floating in the air, illuminated by the red glow of the brake lights of the car in front of me – the blind leading the blind at 200mph! Yet the impact never came and suddenly we were both out the other side in clear air with not a sign of an accident at all.

It was only a lap later when we returned to the scene, now controlled by a pace car, that we saw blazing wreckage not *on* the track but a good 50 yards off it in the middle of the woods. Again the thoughts of 'who' and 'how' and 'whether they had survived' would float through my mind, but once again it was hard not to fear the worst. It turned out that Italian Fabio Magnani had speared off the course in his

Lancia-Ferrari LC2 after contact with another car just before the kink. At this point the barriers angled away from the track at an access point and they had simply served to launch him high into the trees, where the smaller branches progressively slowed his speed before dropping him upside down on the ground. Incredibly he was unharmed and had managed to crawl clear before the fire began, while our 'fog' had been a cloud of thousands of pine needles floating down through the air!

Back on the home front, with no drive at Le Mans, I began yet another different chapter, racing the most unlikely of machines – a Saab 900 Turbo. A new championship had been launched for these unlikely racing machines and the Butler boys, Richard and Simon, who ran their Dad's Kentish Saab dealership in Maidstone, had decided I was the man for the job.

Once again away from the stress, strain and many retirements of long-distance sportscar racing this was just good weekend fun and, over the next two years, some 14 starts would produce six wins, four seconds and a third and lead to me becoming a team-mate to none other than Damon Hill – and yes, I can claim 'I beat Damon Hill'! Meanwhile, another win in a production Porsche race at Donington in a 2.7 911 RSL for an *Autosport* magazine story was unknowingly opening yet another door...

There were other European Group C outings in '86, racing Costas Los's March-Porsche 84G at Brands, Jerez and Spa. In the Spanish race I was dead chuffed to qualify the two-year-old car in seventh, but even more delighted when the three Silk Cut Jaguars all fell off at the first corner and I laughed my way to third place in the early laps. That wouldn't last, but just finishing in the 40-degree heat was a victory!

The end of the year saw a much happier return to South Africa when I finally got to race the Lamborghini in a non-championship event at Kyalami. Unipart had once again been one of the sponsors of a car I was to drive, and I think a great deal of pressure was brought to ensure the car at least made its debut – even though it would also turn out to be its swansong.

The race consisted of two one-hour heats, so there was no need to bring a second driver – and I would be the only person ever to race the car. With a grid of just 20, the organisers opted for a novel American-style, single-car, single-lap qualifying session and I soon had all the locals rooting for me. Mine was the only non-turbo entry and the wailing tone of my 5.7-litre V12 powerplant could be heard round the whole lap – I even went for a bit of showboating oversteer out of the crested Leeukop Bend on to the long main straight and I swear I could hear the crowd hooting and hollering their approval! Once again it was a joy to have raced on such a classic Grand Prix track before it was neutered into the shape it is today...

Unfortunately in the high altitude of Johannesburg, while the Lamborghini sounded the best, it had no way to crank up the boost to compensate for the thin air so I was well off the pace. Yet two solid races saw me claim a respectable fifth-place overall finish.

Although my only sportscar race in 1987 had been the one outing at Le Mans with the TOM'S Toyota Team, my involvement with the Japanese outfit had led to my becoming a founding director of TOM'S GB, which John Wickham and I set up at its Norfolk base. Team boss Tachi-san was convinced Toyota would one day move into Formula One and, by setting up a European base, this was his first step towards his dream of running that Grand Prix programme. However, while his British set-up would go on to run Toyota's World Sportscar programme, in the end when Toyota did go Formula One racing they went with their former World Rally organisation in Germany – and the debate will always suggest that that is why they never won a race!

To get TOM'S GB going we ran a little front-wheel-drive Toyota Corolla in the Spa 24 Hours and the British rounds of the World Touring Car Championship. Always a contender for class honours, we didn't finish the 24 Hours but had a second and third in Britain, frustratingly beaten by Chris Hodgetts' dominant rear-wheel-drive Corolla.

Our rivalry was to become a partnership for a typical Hodgetts madcap idea when he invited me to share not one but *both* of his entries in the British Touring Car Championship's annual two-driver event to be held at Oulton Park. The plan – which worked to perfection

– was to run nose to tail for the first half of the race, pit together and then simply swap cars! There can't be many – if any – other drivers who have finished both first and second in the same race.

While I headed back to Japan for 1988, the TOM'S Corolla was entered in the British Touring Car Championship for Phil Dowsett and, with Hodgetts having moved on, he won the 1600cc class both that year and the next, and I partnered him to an easy win at Silverstone's European Championship Tourist Trophy race. I would race the car one more time – but I don't think we need to go into detail about my sizeable meeting with the wall in Macau...

Despite this unfortunate incident – look, it was a front-wheel-drive car and when you lock the brakes they won't turn into the corner – Tachi-san still wanted me to continue my Toyota involvement. By now, though, I was getting more and more involved with another manufacturer who I had flirted with for so long: Porsche.

CHAPTER 15

PORSCHE AT LAST

When you look back at the history of motorsport there are many manufacturers whose names are synonymous with success in endurance sportscar racing, from Bentley to Alfa Romeo, Jaguar to Aston Martin, Ferrari to Ford, Porsche to Mercedes Benz. They've all made their mark and won at Le Mans, but if there is one single *model* that deserves to be hailed as the greatest endurance racer of the twentieth century it has to be the Porsche 956/962. Two numbers but essentially the same car and one that was competitive for the entire nine years of the classic Group C era, it was the car that if you wanted to win, you wanted to drive! Making its debut at Silverstone in 1982 it was unbeaten in its first season when only the factory-prepared Rothmans cars were raced, and it would be beaten only on the odd occasion for the next five years.

From the second season onwards they offered identical cars to customers which they could race against the factory team on equal terms. Twelve such cars were sold in '83 for the grand price of £178,470 each; with a key to open the door and a key to start the engine, you were ready to go. The first 'customer' race was the Monza event, where I drove the Richard Lloyd car, and, as if to prove how good their customer cars were, the private Joest Racing entry beat the works cars to take victory.

I'd had my taste of this iconic machine – and even if it did spit a wheel off on my very first racing lap, I had to be impressed. The question was, how could I get a regular drive in one? I had come so close with that Japanese deal, but then for the next five years I would get only the occasional return to a Porsche cockpit. There were the

Kremer Racing drives at Le Mans and Silverstone plus the outing for Fritz Gebhardt at Fuji, but I wanted more. Yes, the Nimrod, the Dome, the EMKA and the Toyotas were great cars to drive, but it was almost always a Porsche that was winning.

My chance would eventually come thanks to the increasing involvement of Porsche Cars Great Britain with the brand's motorsport pedigree. With Derek Bell winning Le Mans for Porsche in 1981, '82, '86 and '87 it wasn't exactly a bad time to wave the flag and, with Derek already on their books, their PR guru Jeremy Snook was quick to spot that an association with a racing driver who was also now appearing on a certain BBC car show wouldn't be a bad idea. We'd already worked together on Porsche driving days where the likes of Derek, Richard Attwood, Tony Dron, Colin Blower and I would assemble to try and impart some of our skills to Porsche customers. The day would often end with them driving home with 'square' tyres after we'd tried to teach them the anti-locking art of cadence braking in the days before the arrival of ABS!

In the mid-eighties the grand Porsche plan had been that the new front-engined 944 model would eventually take over from the quirky 911 as the world's most popular Porsche – little did they know how wrong they would be. Nevertheless, Jeremy's first involvement for me in 1988 was to enter me in the domestic Porsche series in a 944 Turbo to put all those ageing 911s in their place. It seemed like a simple task – after all, I'd blown away all these 'club' racers in my one 911 outing at Donington a couple of years earlier – so how hard could it be? The answer: about as tense as it could get! I found myself not just in a 911 war but a tyre war as well, as my BF Goodrich-backed machine fought off the Pirelli marauders.

It was simply brilliant racing with the likes of Mike Jordan and Chris Millard providing some of the fiercest opposition I have ever faced. With four wins and three thirds from eight races, honours would end up pretty even – but I would never underestimate the competitiveness of the national scene again.

Jeremy also fixed me a drive in the German 944 Turbo Championship at the Avus Circuit in Berlin – well, I say circuit, but I really mean motorway. This weirdest of tracks started life in 1921 as a six-mile blast down an autobahn, round a hairpin, a six-mile blast back and round another hairpin! Admittedly it was intended more as an automotive test track, but in 1937, in an attempt to make it the world's fastest racetrack, they built a 43-degree banked, brick-surfaced 'wall of death' at the start/finish end – with no fence at the top at all. As a result, Hermann Lang's average speed winning the race in his Mercedes was 160mph – four decades before such numbers would be achieved at America's Indianapolis Speedway.

After the war the long straights were cut in half, but even the shorter five-mile track held little attraction and the only Grand Prix held there was when Tony Brooks won in a Ferrari in 1959. Tragically that same weekend saw the death of the great French star Jean Behra in a supporting race when his Porsche sportscar went over the top of the banking.

The great brick edifice was finally pulled down in 1967 and the circuit I would race on had a long, flat horseshoe corner in its place and two coned-off chicanes slowing the speeds before the ends of the straights were reached. It rained for my race and I spent most of my time staring into a ball of spray using only the gantries over the top of the road to give me an idea of where I was – and doing that in a pack of 944s travelling at 170mph. Stupid to say the least...

The most interesting part of the whole trip was that I actually got to visit Berlin a year *before* the wall came down and saw for myself the shocking futility of cutting a city into two. West Berlin, as it was then, was almost like a small country rather than the oppressive dark city I had somehow imagined it would be, with the bright, tree-lined 'Curse first and then dam' (well, how else do you pronounce Kurfurstendamn?) reminding me of the Champs Elysées in Paris.

The best part of the year, however, was when Jeremy put Derek and me together to drive the Richard Lloyd Porsche at the Silverstone round of the World Sportscar Championship in May – and now the RLR Porsche 962 was one the best cars in the field. The great Rothmans era had come to an end and, apart from a works entry at Le Mans, Derek was without a drive while Richard was without a sponsor, so help provided by Porsche Cars Great Britain was much appreciated.

My old Unipart Formula Three team manager Dave Price was now running the team so, with the sort of confidence-inspiring team talk I had so enjoyed – 'Come on you w***er, give it the berries!' – once again ringing in my ears, I relished the opportunity to escape the in-team tension that was so affecting my driving that year with the Toyota Team over in Japan. Of course, as my luck would have it, now I had finally made it into a top Porsche 962 the era of the Silk Cut Jaguars and factory Mercedes was in full swing. Over the next three seasons, until the end of the Group C era, there would be just one more victory for this great racing car – but there was still the honour of being 'best of the rest'.

I didn't quite do that to out-qualify Bob Wollek in the leading Joest entry, but I was just 0.34 seconds slower to line up right behind him, fifth on the grid and ahead of Jan Lammers in the second of the Jaguars. In these cars the Grand Prix track of old was simply brilliant and demonstrated why I still clamour for simpler circuits. Silverstone was then just less than three miles in length, with only five corners to worry about – make that nine if it was wet – yet each corner was very different and posed its own individual challenge. With an average speed of nearly 140mph it was certainly fast, but it also meant that an error in any one of the corners would cost you dearly all the way down the next straight. You might even get overtaken!

Club Corner still remains strongest in my memory. Having survived the long, long, semi-blind crested swoop of Stowe Corner it was a slight downhill run to Club with just about enough time to take a deep breath and think about how *little* you were going to brake. Preferably geared so you wouldn't have to go up to fifth and then back down again, you could concentrate on braking as late and as neatly as you could and then, with a very deep turn in, arc the car round to a late apex. At the exit lay a rough kerb that, if you ran over the top of it, would leave you at the mercy of luck as to whether you caught the ensuing moment or plunged into an earth bank at 140mph. For a good lap you simply had to be inch perfect and to me that is how it should be.

Of course the Grand Prix cars began to outgrow the circuit and Copse, Stowe and Club would become flat-out; instead of changing the circuit, I would have demanded they changed the cars! A classic case today is that Spa's Eau Rouge is easily flat for all the Formula One cars so, to keep the challenge there, why not simply make that corner the benchmark and reduce the grip until it isn't flat?

In the Silverstone race Derek and I did, however, manage to win our 'class', finishing fourth overall and beating the Joest cars, with just the two Mercedes and one Jaguar ahead of us – not that the record books will show it, as we were later deemed to have a fuel tank that could hold 2.5 litres more than it should have. We were thrown out of the results!

Having had the taster I now desperately wanted more, but I had to wait for the following season when Porsche Cars Great Britain put together a deal to run the Richard Lloyd car for Derek and me in the 1989 World Sports Prototype Championship. Finally, a full season in a top-flight car – and with a Porsche 944 Turbo as my 'company car' I was living the life...

Having ended the previous season's championship with the traditional Fuji finale in Japan, the calendar was turned upside down for the first round of the year with an immediate return to Japan, but this time to the Suzuka Circuit. It was a new track to many but a familiar part of my second home, so I arrived full of optimism.

By now, Richard Lloyd Racing was one of several teams to build their own versions of the Porsche 962, using most of the running gear of a factory-built car but with their own monocoque chassis and bodywork. Peter Stevens was the aerodynamicist – the man who shaped the fabulous McLaren F1 road car – and our '89 car certainly looked the fastest thing in a straight line without even turning a wheel. When Derek Bell went out and stuck it on provisional pole position in the first, soaking wet, qualifying session it stunned the European contingent and, better still, shocked my former Japanese employees. This was going to be a year to enjoy – well, it was until it dried out for the second session and we qualified 22nd. Hero to zero had never been so painful.

With little more than a shakedown test before we'd shipped the car we knew it wouldn't be perfect, but we didn't think it would be that bad. From the word go we struggled for rear-end grip, and in the race it just got worse and worse as the rear tyres struggled to keep up. From an era of Porsche domination the front of the field was now the realm of Mercedes, Jaguars, Toyotas and Nissans. It was the start of probably two of the greatest years of endurance racing – and we had set off on the back foot!

At least the cause of our problems was revealed once we'd got home, because when the team stripped down the gearbox they discovered that the limited slip differential had been assembled the wrong way round. Instead of being free while decelerating and then stiffening up on acceleration it worked the opposite way. While not taking anything away from Derek's skills, this had obviously been of benefit in the wet but decidedly not so in the dry.

Unfortunately the revamped calendar also meant there would be no round at Silverstone this year so the next championship race at Dijon would take its place as the forerunner to Le Mans. There was, however, a round of the German-based Supercup sprint series filling the vacant date at Silverstone so, as it was on our doorstep, the car was entered with just me doing the driving for the two short heats and a one-hour final.

Once again that man Bob Wollek in the Joest Racing Porsche was the man to beat in a field that lacked any other front-running World Championship entries and unfortunately he had the edge on me all weekend. From pole he led me all the way in the first heat and, despite getting ahead of him at the start of the second, he was back in front when it mattered and again in the final. I had pushed him all the way, though, and it was still a good morale-boosting result for the team before we headed for Dijon.

Driving there in the 944 Turbo with Patsy – and planning a slow return that would take in more than one lobster and champagne dinner – at long last we could both enjoy the opportunities my racing career had to offer – and we tried to make the most of them. Armed with a map and a *Relais & Château* guidebook, we intended to make the most of the season.

After Japan it was my turn to use the qualifying tyres and, with the boost cranked up to provide getting on for 1,000 horsepower, it was the sort of wild ride I'll never forget. The 962 was far from the most classic handling of racing machines but it was a magnificent workhorse. The suspension was usually set up with as much castor on the front as possible to help the car turn in to the corners – and that meant as heavy a steering load as you could handle. With no power assistance these cars were hard work but among the most brutal and adrenaline-pumping machines ever raced.

With a few improvements after Silverstone the car was on the money for Dijon qualifying and I finally got one over Bob Wollek and took the Porsche class pole position – one spot ahead of him and fourth overall behind two Mercedes and the Toyota of Johnny Dumfries. With both the Jaguars and the factory Nissans also behind me, I walked the paddock ten feet tall. Moments like this during a career when I struggled to get the best drives going made them all the more special. Once again I felt like shouting 'Look, give me the car and a team that believes in me and I'm as quick as anyone!'

The race didn't go quite as well as qualifying as, even with the diff the right way round, our rear grip soon dropped away. We had the same Goodyear tyres as Wollek and, while he moved forwards partnered by Frank Jelinski to what would turn out to be that final Porsche victory, we struggled to stay in touch. A fourth-place finish was on the cards before Derek had to pit twice for a door that kept opening itself, and while fifth was still good it didn't feel good enough.

Next stop was Le Mans and the circuit where our slippery looking RLR Porsche was intended to be blindingly quick down the long Mulsanne Straight – but it wasn't! If ever a team had looked depressed it was ours. The wind-tunnel figures indicated that minute adjustments of the rear wing would have significant results, but we could put it full up or full down and it made no difference as we hit a top speed brick wall at 212mph – *thirty* miles an hour slower than the front runners. Wollek qualified top Porsche in fifth place; we were down in 21st!

James Weaver had joined us for the race and it was great to be working with him again. We faced up to our predicament with a truly British sense of 'whatever will be will be' humour and determined to make the most of what was obviously going to be a very hard race. RLR were running a second car which saw Damon Hill also return as one of my team-mates and once again I can say, 'Yes, I was faster than Damon Hill!' Back then, three years before his call to Williams Grand Prix stardom, he was just another young British driver short of sponsorship to further his single-seater career and looking around for any alternatives. Fun to be with, he and his wife Georgie always did their best to avoid the 'I am Graham's son' story and I was so pleased when he went on to become a most deserving World Champion.

The weather for the race was hot and, to try to make up for our lamentable straight-line speed, for which we could find no cure, we simply had to hustle as much as we could in the corners. We were beset, though, by niggling problems like a puncture, wheel vibrations, a loose windscreen – and a wheel falling off while Derek was driving down the Mulsanne Straight! That was the final straw for Derek and, after we'd hauled our way up to a respectable seventh place with just three hours to go, he headed off to a nice Sunday lunch to soak up memories of his five previous wins and left James and me to drag 'the brick' to the finish line. If only we could have been so lucky…

A 'stint' at Le Mans is normally about 14 laps long, determined by how quickly you get through your 100 litres of fuel – but you needed to average near that 14 laps on that fuel or you'd run out of your car's allocation before the end. To help you manage this you had a gauge that you zeroed after you'd been refuelled, which then showed how much you'd used in that stint, and there was also a warning light that would flash on when the tank had just 10 litres left – which was good for about a lap and a half at full speed.

To help you manage your consumption, Porsche had worked out what the gauge should read when you reached the Mulsanne Corner half-way round each lap. You could drive as hard as you wanted round the rest of the lap but, wherever you were, flashing down the Mulsanne Straight at over 200mph, when the gauge hit that number you had to knock it into neutral and coast to the corner. Simple but very effective – until it got dark and then we couldn't read the numbers that were stuck on the steering wheel...

At around one o'clock in the afternoon, I was sitting on the pit wall as James ticked off the laps of another stint. My hot, tired, aching muscles were wishing for a long soak in a hot bath. I was watching for the red Porsche to appear out of the chicane for the 11th time so I could begin to think about screwing my earplugs back in, donning the fireproof balaclava and helmet, and preparing myself for another hour in the oven – but instead of driving past, James came stuttering up the pit lane.

The fuel lamp was shining brightly inside the cockpit as he stopped at the pit; he was almost out of fuel a full two laps early. Without thinking, my helmet was on and I was clambering into the car. The tyres were changed and the fuel was going in. The meter read '83' as I punched the reset button just in time for the order to restart the engine and get back on track. It was all done in less than a minute and the stop had gone like clockwork, but why had James pitted so early?

My first concern was simply to concentrate on getting the tyres up to temperature and not doing what I'd done last year, falling off at the first corner. The next priority was to pull the belts tight once I hit the Mulsanne Straight for the first time and then have a good look around the gauges to check they were all reading what they should read. Finally, I had time to collect my thoughts, sitting in my hot little office fast approaching its 212mph brick wall. Now, if the fuel light was on, over 90 litres must have left the tank – but that gauge said 83, so the engine reckoned it had only had 83 litres but the tank has lost more than 90 litres. Obviously the answer was that they couldn't have filled it properly at the previous stop.

Down to Indianapolis, round Arnage, I felt the car 'wander' left and right as I straight-lined the heavily cambered public road that leads you to the Porsche Curves: into the very fast right, the long left, a short straight, another left, then a long, long right that feeds into the deceptive left 'flick' at the bottom of the hill. You need maximum concentration before the short straight that leads to the Ford Chicanes and the start of another lap.

I checked the mirrors… big red ball… checked the mirrors again and the big red ball was going at the same speed as me. I was on fire! I now knew where the missing fuel had gone. The car had sprung a leak and the missing couple of gallons had just ignited. Somehow my mind was still operating with amazing clarity. Concentrating 100 per cent and pumped full of adrenaline, despite having had virtually no real sleep for over 30 hours and having already driven the equivalent of four Grands Prix during that time, this was no time to panic.

There was no fire or smoke in the cockpit but I knew that as soon as I stopped that big red ball was going to catch up with me and things were going to get very hot, very quickly. Of course the car had its own on-board fire extinguisher, but I reckoned that was best kept for when I stopped   but where should I stop? My first thought was to dive into the pit entry just ahead, but I quickly realised that taking a blazing car into a narrow lane full of fuel tanks wasn't such a clever idea, so I headed on through the Ford Chicanes and into the view of the main grandstands and the pits. Immediately the voice of team manager Ian Dawson was on the radio. 'Tiff, you're on fire, stop and get out!' Tell me something new, I thought.

By now I'd been trying to remember where I'd seen the biggest fire engine parked up and reckoned there was one at the end of the pit straight, so I cracked my seat belts open – didn't want them snagging – got the door *just* open to make sure that was okay as well, and then gracefully flambéed my way past the packed grandstand, to provide them with a nice after-lunch dessert, with my finger hovering over the extinguisher button. When I stopped the whole car seemed to be enveloped by the flames – I hadn't reckoned on the wind that was coming from behind me – so having set off the extinguisher I was greeted by a wall of flame coming in at me as I burst out of the door. Fortunately I was through it and away in an instant and no personal harm was done, except for the fact that I got a bollocking from Richard a week later for not closing the door on the way out, to minimise cockpit damage!

Our next outing would be on the magnificent Brands Hatch Grand Prix track. With the cornering speed of cars rising all the time, and with little scope to increase the limited run-off space at the Kent venue, this would be the last high-profile World Championship event to be held there and, in hot humid conditions in front of a huge crowd, it would be a brilliant finale.

In 1991 the FIA would introduce new sportscar rules that favoured 3.5-litre normally aspirated engines, cynically designed to encourage manufacturers that were involved in the Group C championship to build engines that would also be suitable for Formula One, which already had just such a regulation. The hand of Bernie Ecclestone was reaching out! It was a plan from which sportscar racing has still fully to recover – and there were those at the time who felt that perhaps it had become *too* successful for its own good.

Whatever the conspiracy theories, no-one can doubt that the last three years of the original formula saw some of the greatest sportscar racing ever, with Porsche's old dominance now challenged by factory efforts from Mercedes, Jaguar, Aston Martin, Toyota and Nissan. The field at Brands saw 25 Group C cars supported by 11 of the less powerful C2 machines filling a capacity grid, with Jan Lammers on pole for Jaguar and Mauro Baldi alongside for Mercedes. The quickest Porsche was, yes, Bob Wollek in sixth with me right behind him in seventh and delighted to be one spot ahead of the TOM'S Toyota of Johnny Dumfries. The first hour of the race turned into a mad flat-out sprint with some of the best racing ever seen at the circuit.

Charging towards Paddock Hill Bend the huge pack of sportscars filled the narrow top straight for the rolling start – and by the end of the lap I was the leading Porsche, in fourth place. It wasn't to last, but I handed over to Derek still in sixth and fending off John Nielsen's Jaguar. Unfortunately a pace-car error would soon put us a lap down, and then we started to struggle with a very soft brake pedal. Assuming it was just the heat of the day and the demanding nature of the track, we battled on – pumping the pedal with the left foot to build up pressure as the braking zones approached. Little did anyone know that, deep in the middle of the new front uprights installed after Le Mans, the airflow to the brakes was blocked off. With pad wear far higher than expected, I ran out completely with 20 laps still to go...

First a fire and then brake failure: two of a driver's worst fears and I suffered them in consecutive races. My moment of reckoning happened entering Clearways for the 96th time and no amount of pedal pumping had any effect. All I could do was thump down a couple of gears and try to short cut the corner by heading across the grass at the apex. Going way too fast it was a pointless exercise as the car swapped ends and headed backwards into the tyre wall at well over 100mph. James Weaver had already parked the other RLR car in almost exactly the same spot and Richard was none too pleased with his two young chargers. At least I was eventually exonerated, but James was left delving deep into the famous racing driver's 'Book of Excuses' and finally settled on heat exhaustion due to a badly ventilated cockpit – it is *never* a driver's fault!

Unfortunately we went to the next race, at the new Nürburgring, with the front uprights unchanged and the Brands Hatch heat still to blame. By now we were experimenting with the new carbon brakes which, in their early days, were very temperamental things – too cold and they hardly worked at all, too hot and the discs would soon turn to dust. Their stopping power was awesome, but getting them to work consistently was a nightmare.

It was Derek's turn to qualify and start the race but, having tried the carbons, he was forced to change back to steel due to our excessive temperatures and, with little time left to sort the car for the circuit, we qualified 11th, and fifth-fastest Porsche. The race was a long battle with the brakes still not cured and that, and our old problem of overheating rear tyres, consigned us to a depressed 15th-place finish.

Back in Britain for the next round at Donington, and with the brake problem sorted, I qualified the car ninth, missing the Porsche pole by 0.134 seconds yet still only being third best as Oscar Larrauri squeezed his Brun car between me and Wollek. Hosting its first ever World Championship event, the stop/start nature of the circuit proved tough on brakes and fuel consumption. However, taking the Craner Curves flat out in qualifying and reaching 170mph before braking for the Old Hairpin was an experience to remember! Unfortunately we still hadn't really got to the bottom of our rear-tyre wear problem and, using too much fuel to at least try and stay in touch saw us eventually limping home in 11th place. In an extremely competitive championship we were beginning to feel the strain of being a small private team trying to compete against the big manufacturer-supported outfits.

The wonderful Spa-Francorchamps Circuit in Belgium was next up, but after a typical pot-luck wet/dry qualifying session left us tenth on the grid, a rare engine failure ruined our day before it ever really got going.

Our last chance to shine, then, would be at the season's finale in Mexico City, yet another exotic location to which my sport would take me. Sitting in its own little cloud of smog, nearly 7,500 feet about sea level, it's just over a quarter of the way to the top of Mount Everest, so the first thing you have to get used to is simply breathing. With armed guards outside almost every shop it's not the most relaxing place to be, either, and joining the mad throng weaving up and down the roads makes driving in Paris seem like a doddle. Ancient American gas-guzzlers seemingly held together only by rust are a sight to be seen.

The Autodromo Hermanos Rodriguez was another historic venue where I was delighted to get a chance to race. Translated simply as 'Rodriguez Brothers Racetrack', it is named after the two Mexican greats who both died pursuing the sport they so loved. The younger, Ricardo, was aged just 20 when he was killed during qualifying for the non-championship Grand Prix at this very circuit back in 1962 – the year it opened – while Pedro would survive to win two Grands Prix and become *the* superstar of the sportscar world in his iconic Gulf Porsche 917 before himself perishing behind the wheel of a Ferrari 512M in an Interserie race at the Norisring in Germany nine years later.

The first World Championship event, held in 1963, was won by Jim

Clark and the date remained on the calendar until 1970 when crowd problems led to it being dropped from the championship until the mid-eighties. Nigel Mansell would win the last Grand Prix to be held there, in 1992. Very bumpy, it was a punishing track for both car and driver but a great challenge to both with its long start/finish straight, a series of increasingly fast Esses and then the daunting final Peraltada Curve – an awesome fourth-gear, never-ending, 180-degree turn that led on to the straight.

Derek started the car ninth and had worked his way up to fifth before I took over for one of the toughest stints I had ever driven. Naturally weakened by the lack of oxygen in the thin air and faced with the bumpy nature of the track, amplified by the heavy steering of the Porsche, it was a mightily physical affair.

Exiting the hairpin of Turn 6 on the far side of the circuit you began a series of four right/left Esses that simply got faster and faster. None were flat out and all were corners that demanded full concentration. With arm muscles aching for relief there was then a good straight down to the magnificent Peraltada Curve to give some respite – but that long, long, slightly banked corner was the toughest of them all. Bumps on the way in threatened to pitch you straight into the wall and then the G-force built and built as you tried to maximise your exit speed. The high-speed nature of the corner brought the ground-effect downforce of the car to its maximum and added yet further to the weight of the steering – and the biggest bump was yet to come! Just before you left the long apex there was one that wanted to wrench the steering from your grip every time you hit it.

Fast, physical and highly rewarding are what motor racing tracks should be and this one certainly had it all. It's even more rewarding when you have a good race – and we ran inside the top six all the way. I even had a moment of glory in the lead during the second round of pit stops, which was a nice little gift on my 37th birthday! We would end up finishing a hot and exhausted fourth, frustratingly close to ending the year on the podium but delighted nevertheless.

After the race my Thundersports mate Richard Piper (who had also

finished fourth in what was the last race for the C2 cars) and his wife
Ina joined Patsy and me for a stylish week of relaxation at the Las
Hadas resort in Manzanillo. This had been the setting for Dudley
Moore and Bo Derek's canoodling in the film *10*. While memories of
Dudley hopping and skipping on the hot sand still make me laugh,
our own 'Sunset Cruise' fuelled with very strong margaritas will never
be forgotten.

CHAPTER 16

MY FINEST 24 HOURS

Porsche Cars Great Britain had no budget to run their own car in the 1990 championship but they would support Jonathan Palmer's switch from the Grand Prix world to a seat in the now factory-supported Joest team, while my own Porsche career was set to continue in Japan with the Alpha team. Indeed, the next World Championship round, to open the season, was back at the Japanese Suzuka Circuit where I was having my second race for Alpha, partnered once again by Derek Bell. A full grid of 34 Group C cars assembled for the race and it was a fabulous sight – it wasn't surprising that the Grand Prix promoters were beginning to look on with not a little jealousy.

Among the growing number of factory entries I wasn't too disappointed to qualify 14th – but I was delighted to qualify one place ahead of Jonathan and two ahead of my old RLR car! Running a conservative race we would end up eighth, three places in front of the Joest Porsche and, without knowing it at the time, I would earn myself a factory drive at the next round in Monza.

Palmer was supposed to be partnered by Hans Stuck for the year, but clashing calendars had got in the way and Jonathan would end up sharing his car with no fewer than six different drivers over the nine-race series – and the second of them would be me. With Jeremy Snook still rooting for me in the background, pushing my name forwards to the Porsche hierarchy, another 'big' day dawned. But it didn't go well...

Having already mentioned that I'd found, unfortunately, that I was the type of guy who needs to feel appreciated in order to perform at his best, things didn't get off to an ideal start when I received a decidedly frosty welcome from the German team. I think they felt I had been slightly imposed on them and had had their own ideas on who should partner Jonathan – and it wasn't me. To make matters worse, I hadn't been back to Monza since my rather awkward debut in a Porsche 956 some seven years earlier *and* the Joest cars were running on the most radial of radial tyres: Michelins. By now all racing tyres used radial technology, but most still included a fair amount of bias banding to give the sidewall a bit more stability than the Michelins. My Toleman nightmare had returned to haunt me!

I found myself on a kerb-hopping track that I just couldn't seem to get on with, fitted with tyres that didn't seem to suit my style, and – with Jonathan desperately trying to sort the car so that at least he could be quick – I got precious few laps to acclimatise. Falling off at the second chicane in practice did little to build either my confidence in the car or the team's confidence in me, but at least we survived the race. Jonathan had qualified seventh and then lost the best part of a lap when the engine mysteriously cut out, but we did manage to salvage eighth by the finish and then headed for the comfort of my Silverstone 'home' with me still in the seat but very much feeling 'on trial' for the next round. Incidentally, a young kid by the name of Michael Schumacher was trying to make his World Championship debut there with Mercedes.

Again, on the few laps that I did get in practice, I managed to loop the bloody thing up the road, getting on the power just a little too early out of Becketts and wiping the nose off the car. More thunderous looks from the Germans and the 'Island Monkey' – as our English nickname goes – was feeling distinctly ill at ease! Once again the handling characteristics of radial tyres weren't for me – brilliant for traction and braking but 'sensitive' in the corners.

Fortunately there was still the race to come and Jonathan had qualified an excellent fifth. However, to keep up with the leaders would use too much fuel and he soon dropped back to run in eighth, one place ahead of team-mate Wollek. Running to a strict fuel consumption meant lifting off early for corners and then braking late to keep the momentum going – not the most fun at times, but a discipline you had to accept and learn. Having settled into my stint I finally began to feel the car nearing my comfort zone, as I got more laps under my belt, and I held the gap ahead of Wollek's co-driver, Frank Jelinski, for the duration while saving enough fuel for Jonathan to have a bit of a charge at the end. Sadly that wasn't to be because a driveshaft broke when he left the pit at the next stop and, while our team-mates ended up fourth, we failed to finish.

Derek Bell was to partner Jonathan in the next round at Spa, in preparation for a return to the works team at Le Mans, but, in any case, I already had the feeling I wasn't going to be asked back. It proved to be so – but not before I had had my finest hour in that year's Le Mans 24 Hours and shown the Joest team just how good a bunch of monkeys can be!

We'd entered my Japanese Alpha Team Porsche in the great event and, with Derek heading for the works team, enlisted another underfunded yet talented British star, David Sears. He had just joined the 'gaijin' drivers in Japan, racing a SARD Toyota, and took his place alongside me and my other Japanese Championship co-driver, Anthony Reid. Before packing everything away to be sent to Europe our team manager, Gary Cummings, had virtually rebuilt the entire car himself, overseeing every little detail, using his vast experience as a mechanic on these machines in the past and making a few improvements of his own. On top of that we'd also been doing our homework...

The 1990 season was to be the first year when the legendary three-mile Mulsanne Straight was to be split into three by two chicanes. It got us thinking whether or not the traditional, low-downforce, long-tail bodywork would still be the one to have. Porsche insisted it was – possibly encouraged by the fact that it made all the teams buy the optional nose and tail at great expense just for this one race – but we weren't so sure. We still had the long tail delivered, but we had realised that the long straight at our local Fuji Speedway was pretty much the same length as each of the three new parts of the Mulsanne so we decided to test the theory out – not, as most had done, in a wind tunnel or on a computer, but for real!

At first it was hard to get used to the lack of grip the low-downforce set-up offered round the rest of the circuit, but the extra straight-line speed was very encouraging – after all the easiest thing for a racing driver to be is fast down a straight. Yes, the lap time was slightly slower, but then there were more twisty bits round the rest of Fuji than there are at Le Mans, so that had to be considered. However, with the normal short tail fitted, confidence around the corners was instantly restored – but it felt so slow down the straight. What we then did was to take off as much downforce as we could, with the higher rear wing now set at its minimum angle, and trade some of that cornering grip in order to claw back a bit more straight-line speed.

Our final touch was to replace the Porsche main plane of the rear wing with an even lower downforce, low-drag section supplied by my old Ibec team manager Gordon Horn. By the end of the test, with the top speed now not that much slower but the handling still a lot better, we were convinced the short-tail set-up we finished with was the way to go. We would be one of just two customer Porsche teams to pack both options for the trip.

At Le Mans we actually began practice with the long tail fitted like everyone else, but once we'd swapped to our own 'low-drag' short tail, we never went back. Yes, we would struggle to overtake on the straights, but Le Mans had now become a circuit where extra downforce reaped dividends not just through the new chicanes but around the whole of the circuit. The downside was that the changes meant Le Mans was about to become a much more physically demanding circuit: with the cornering speeds increasing so did the energy-sapping G-forces and the later and more violent braking. The chicanes themselves were well laid out, but anyone going off the track on the way into them would shower the exit with gravel – gravel that would then puncture tyres and create the very danger the chicanes were supposed to alleviate.

Having qualified a very pleasing tenth on the first day of practice we went about the traditional routine of putting the race engine in for the second day and simply accepted the fact that we would be pushed down the field by the factory cars going for glory with extra boost runs on qualifying tyres. We weren't too disappointed when we dropped to 20th, but our Japanese owner, Nanikawa-san, wasn't best pleased after the promise of day one. The pressure was on to make a positive start!

Not that I needed much encouragement, as starting at Le Mans is just one of the greatest things you can get to do on this planet. After the morning warm-up to check the cars, the build-up goes on all day as the clock slowly moves round to the 4pm off. Team briefings, toolkit training – as only the driver can work on the car away from the pits – and the great drivers' parade are just some of the things that take up the time. Union flags wave wildly whenever a British driver is introduced and there's massive support for the factory Silk Cut Jaguars – not to mention the Hawaiian Tropic girls.

Finally it's time to get strapped in – and the wonderful moment when Steve McQueen closes the door in the *Le Mans* film is exactly as it is. At last you are left in your own little world and all the outside noise is locked away. Yes, the race is 24 hours long and, *of course* you won't doing anything silly, but you are a racing driver and the first stint at Le Mans is the best race of them all.

With no fitness guru, team masseur or sports dietician on hand our plan was to run single stints flat out until the cool of the night when we would consider doing doubles. We knew we would have to drive hard with the extra downforce, and my theory was that doing a macho double and finishing completely knackered would take much more to recover from than ending just one stint still reasonably fresh.

As the massive rolling start weaved through the Ford Chicanes I remembered the old trick of pulling down my visor to protect my eyes from the inevitable blast of grit through the air vents, caused by the cars using parts of the track other than the regular racing line. And so the journey began...

In conditions hotter than they had been all weekend, the extra downforce was even more appreciated by the hard-worked Yokohama tyres and the car was running beautifully. Fast through the corners, it felt like I spent the whole opening stint bottled up behind cars in the twisty bits and then having to be brave on the brakes to pick them off one by one. Gradually we gained places – one of them when Bob Wollek pitted after just six laps to have the wing raised on his Joest car as the rear grip from his Michelins was so bad.

I was back in the car as the three-hour mark was reached, and even we couldn't believe we were up to ninth in one of the most competitive Le Mans fields ever assembled. In front of us were the four Jaguars, two of the Nissans and just the one Porsche, belonging to the highly professional Brun team, fractionally ahead in seventh (and the only other front-running Porsche to opt for the short tail). All we had to do now was keep going and an unbelievable top-ten finish could be ours. We were mixing it with the big boys. Surely it couldn't last.

Yet last it did. The car that Gary had built and the Japanese crew that Gary had trained kept working like clockwork. Bolstered by a group of four fellow-American mercenaries, whom he'd worked with many times in the past, Gary's team might have been small but it had plenty of experience – and to add a bit of local interest the Beaumesnil family were manning the Mulsanne pit-signalling post while a French chef from Paris kept us well fed.

On into the night we went and by the time dawn came we were still doing the single stints, driving flat-out but never exhausting ourselves. You could easily change drivers in the time it took to refuel and you just had to accept that sometimes you'd go out on new tyres and sometimes on old. None of us felt like being the first to volunteer to do a double and, to be honest, none of us thought it would be of any benefit. It did mean that you were only ever out of the car for about an hour and 50 minutes, at the most, but I'd never been one for sleeping much during the race in any case.

Having finished a stint I'd pick up my previous set of overalls and fireproof undies from the tumble dryer, which simply kept on tumbling for the whole 24 hours, then change into these dry clothes and dump the sweaty ones back in the dryer. Still buzzing, there would be time for a coffee and a snack and then a brief lie-down to chill out for a while – usually with Radio Le Mans quietly cackling away in the background, keeping me in touch with the race.

Never out of the top ten from that third hour onwards, we had risen to sixth by eight o'clock in the morning with eight hours to go, still pinching ourselves that this was really happening. Now there were only two Jaguars and one Nissan ahead of us but also *two* Porsches – the Brun car had been joined by the Joest entry for Hans Stuck, Frank Jelinski and... Derek Bell! While that was a minor killjoy, our main focus for the next seven hours was waging a constant see-saw battle with the Japanese-entered Nissan of Hoshino, Hasemi and Suzuki. All of a sudden the overall position became irrelevant. If we could at least be the leading Japanese entry that would be a huge victory in itself.

By two o'clock in the afternoon the heat was becoming overwhelming. We were still going flat out, responding to pit boards showing the gap ahead of the Nissan. My head was bursting with a headache, doubtless induced by dehydration, but there could be no letting up. To add to the strain Anthony had got a tiny piece of glass in his eye, when something smashed into the screen, while David finally owned up to having fallen off a skateboard the week before and had been hiding a damaged elbow. We were beginning to struggle...

The car didn't miss a beat, however, and the bodywork never had to come off at all. Gary's preparation had been second to none and all the Porsche needed was from expected wear and tear: new front discs, three sets of front brake pads and two for the rear. Add a lot of fuel and a little oil and that was that. Their only worry was the crack on the windscreen that threatened to need replacing, but a bit of an epoxy bodge-up held it together.

Obsessed with this one Nissan, the fact that the Joest car had dropped back with a turbo problem and the American-entered Nissan had gone out with a fuel leak almost seemed irrelevant. No-one really seemed to notice that we were now running fourth overall in the Le Mans 24 Hours with just two hours to go...

With no more than 90 minutes left to run the Nissan finally cracked. Hobbled by gearbox problems, it fell away. Finally we had clear air behind us and, for the first time in the entire race, began to ease back our pace. The adrenaline of the chase had masked the effort we had all put in and suddenly the exhaustion was felt by everyone. Three laps behind the third-placed Jaguar and two ahead of the Joest Porsche, fingers crossed we could cruise to an unbelievable fourth-place finish in the greatest race of them all.

Honoured with doing the final stint, it was hard to hold back the emotion as I entered the back of the little 'dug-out' pit boxes that were being used for the last time before the bulldozers would make way for the great commercial world of the future, the clinical garages and air-conditioned hospitality rooms. Standing on that famous pit counter, which was about to be gone for ever, where all my heroes had been, the moment was one to savour. A mass of Union flags was waving wildly on the spectator banking opposite us as our patriotic supporters not only awaited a great victory for Jaguar but also much appreciated the British underdogs in their little black Porsche.

When the car came in for that final pit stop, the crew went through the same routine. There was still time for tired minds to make a mistake – and until that engine fires up for the final time you're never sure you'll make it. But then, with a huge lump in my throat, I could hear the roar of the crowd as I edged out of that narrow pit lane…

Union flags were waving all around the circuit: it's a race that the British just love to attend. And I knew that what we had all achieved that weekend would probably add up to my finest racing moment. I realised that I'd now never get that drive in a potential race winner – I'd always been in underdog teams with flashes of promise and moments of glory to remember – but this one was for Gary and me. I'd picked the drivers, he'd provided the car, and we'd worked on a plan that would deliver the best result possible. I loved the fact that it was an all-British driving line-up, but it had also been a Japanese man's dream, an American engineering triumph and an odd mix of Japanese and French support.

Every time I reached the Mulsanne Corner there were the Beaumesnils, cheering and waving, but rounding the corner with just 15 minutes to go there was pandemonium on the wall. Everyone was in an agitated state. I could see them leaping up and down, but at the same time they were trying to change the read-out on our board. We had an onboard radio but it only really worked near the pits, and when I came into view Gary was on it instantly – but for once he was so animated and so loud and distorted that I couldn't work out what he was trying to say.

When I got back to Mulsanne it was obvious – the Beaumesnils were leaping up and down with a huge 'P3' on the board! I must have been the only person in the whole of France who hadn't spotted that the Brun Porsche had pulled off the road just after the corner, with a crestfallen Jesús Pareja walking away. The cruellest of blows had robbed them of second place. They had been faster than us all weekend and had completed one more lap than we would but, at Le Mans, if you don't drive your car across the line after 24 hours you don't finish. No-one likes to inherit a win or a podium position, but it is very much a hard fact of life in motor racing – and for the many you lose, you know there will always be the few that you win. If anyone deserved to benefit from someone else's misfortune that weekend I felt it was surely our team.

The final two laps were a blur. Tears were in my eyes, just as they are as I write about that moment. I'd caught the two Jaguars who were now in a formation cruise to the finish. I was trying to run alongside them, but for some reason Hans Stuck kept trying to gatecrash the party, perhaps still unable to believe that the little private Porsche team from Japan was finishing ahead of his works-backed Joest machine. I might not have reached the heights of the sport that I'd yearned for, or achieved the great results that others have so deserved – and, as my mate Jeremy Clarkson loves to say, my career amounts to the fact that I 'finished third in a big race once' – but oh what a race it had been! Ahead were two factory Jaguars while behind us came a factory Porsche, a factory Nissan and a factory Toyota.

As I pulled into the pits there were bear hugs all around, with grins as wide as any winners' smiles have ever been. Anthony and David looked as shattered as I felt, but we each knew what an amazing job we had all done, keeping up that same pace for single stint after single stint. I'd wanted to drag a tearful Nanikawa-san up on to the podium until I lost him in the crowd, but Patsy was alongside me as we climbed the steps for our moment of glory on the famous old balcony that the victorious Jaguar crews had just vacated. This year she would get her champagne early!

At the time we didn't know we were also making our own little bit of history. This would not only be the last time that that famous pit balcony would be used, but we were also the last Porsche 956/962 drivers to earn a podium position at Le Mans – the 21st crew since Jacky Ickx and Derek Bell topped a 1-2-3 finish at the car's first outing in 1982. It would be first, second and third for the next four years as well: first and second in '87; second and third in '88; and third in '89 and '90. It was a truly remarkable machine.

Yet my days behind the wheel of this iconic racing car weren't quite over. I still had the Japanese Endurance Championship to contest and, although the World Championship rules would favour the new breed of 3.5-litre cars from 1991 onwards – and even have the first ten places on the Le Mans grid reserved for them – the older machines were still welcome, even if the rules rendered them less competitive.

They were, however, still right on the pace in the American IMSA Championship, which had its own GTP engine rules, and I was delighted to head back to the great Daytona Speedway for their season-opening 24-hour race in 1991 and once again partner James Weaver, driving his Dyson Racing 962. James was fast becoming an established star on the American scene and he was in the early days of an association with Rob Dyson's team that would last an incredible 20 years.

With American racer John Paul Junior completing our driver line-up, we qualified a rather circumspect tenth in very un-Florida-like pouring rain but, with the top dozen very evenly matched, the race turned into the typical Daytona battle of attrition. With almost equal hours of day and night, and the pounding strain of the 31-degree banking, this is one tough race.

With a field that included two factory Jaguars, three factory Nissans, two factory Toyotas and six Porsche 962s – with one each crewed by members of American dynasties from the Andretti and Unser families – it was an all-star line-up. The Florida sun returned for the start but there was more rain to come – in which John Paul was simply awesome – and plenty of mechanical woe for all the hard-pressed mechanics to work on. However, we were in the mix from the word go.

The huge NASCAR totem pole displays the race order, so when driving at Daytona you can actually check your position for yourself as you come off the Turn 4 banking and head into the tri-oval in front of the pits. During one memorable stint in the middle of the night, there was number 16 shining brightly on top of the pole – my number!

Having just wrested third place from Raul Boesel in one of the works Jaguars, with a move that was straight out of *Days of Thunder*, I actually led the Daytona 24 Hours for the rest of that stint, when the two leading Nissans that were on a different fuel strategy pitted. I'd been slowly edging up on Boesel for several laps and, having closed right on to his gearbox, with a faster exit from the chicane and on to the Turn 3 banking, I finally had the momentum to get past him.

Raul had been holding a central line on the banking while I always preferred to stay as high as possible – partly to minimise how 'out of shape' the car could get before slamming the wall if anything broke. On this occasion I stayed in his wheel tracks to maximise the slipstream. Up ahead we were catching a slower car, so I pulled out from behind Raul and began to edge past on his outside – at almost the same time that he decided to overtake the slower car on the same side. I'd assumed he'd seen me coming and would choose to go underneath the backmarker, but I had assumed wrong and here he was moving up towards me, while the gap between him and that wall was getting ever closer. I probably should have aborted the move, but once a racing driver always a racing driver and, at around 200mph, with a kiss from the Jaguar and a kiss from the concrete, I emerged from the other side with my heart in my mouth – Tom Cruise eat your heart out!

Unfortunately our Porsche wasn't to last the day and we were out with a blown engine as the Sunday dawned – just when the hard work had been done. But, once again, it had been better to have led and lost than never led at all.

After Daytona came my final two drives in Japan and then yet another last-minute call to Silverstone, this time to drive Franz Konrad's 962 in the World Championship round. We didn't last long, as more engine troubles intervened, but it had been such a pleasure driving with the ever-excitable Austrian whose whole team ethos appeared to be first and foremost to enjoy the weekend whatever the outcome.

For Le Mans I once again picked up a drive with Kremer Racing, but Mexican Tomas Lopez fired the 962 off the road before I even got a chance to drive it in the race. My final outing with this great car would come a year later with one of the Porsche's greatest ever drivers, Derek Bell. He'd arranged for his son Justin and himself to drive the ADA Engineering 962, and I was honoured at being invited to be a part of the family for the weekend. No longer a competitive proposition, we were none the less delighted to take it to a 12th-place finish, simply soaking up everything we loved about driving this superb car in such a wonderful race.

It wasn't quite my final goodbye to the 962, however, because as the World Sportscar regulations wandered this way and that after the inevitable collapse of the 3.5-litre Group C formula, new regulations saw new versions appear. First, there were thinly disguised road cars that qualified for new 'grand touring' regulations – with the Dauer 962 winning Le Mans in 1994 – and then, when open-topped sports prototypes came back into fashion, Kremer produced their K8 Spyder model which was essentially a 962 with the roof cut off. Another last-minute call from Franz Konrad saw me get to drive one at Daytona in 1995.

This was a race where the exotic Ferrari 333SPs were expected to dominate, faced only with American-based cars like Dyson's Riley & Scott with Ford power, or Spice chassis with Chevy or Oldsmobile engines. The great days of the factory entries were long gone. Lined up against them there were plenty of muscular GT cars and two of the Kremer K8s. We were by no means the fastest, but the legendary Porsche reliability made us the tortoise chasing the hares, and by the time dawn came we were running first and third!

Kremer's own entry was the one in the lead, as we'd suffered a front hub problem on the Konrad car which had set us back, but I was in the car when the sun gently began to rise and really enjoying a solid stint round this most unique of racing tracks. Driving well within my limits, with the lap times dropping as they always do in the cold morning air, life felt good – until, with no warning at all, I once again became a 200mph passenger...

Coming off the Turn 4 banking, checking my position on the totem pole and just about to lap a slower car as we neared the pit entry, the rear right tyre simply exploded and the flailing tread smashed through the engine cover and tore off my rear wing. The car immediately snapped sharp left and, to my great fortune but not his, the only thing that stopped me spinning into the pit lane – and anyone that might have been working there – was the weird and wonderful Chevy Cannibal of Briton Graham Bryant who was, at that precise moment, directly alongside me.

Bouncing off the Chevy, the K8 now slewed this way and that into the long 18-degree tri-oval banking where the start and finish line is and, after one firm connection with the concrete, slithered down on to the beautifully manicured grass that lies below and ground to a flaming halt. Fortunately the fire was a brief burst of oil, as the tyre had also ripped one of the turbochargers off the side of the engine – and that would be the last time I climbed out of a Porsche 962 seat.

The Kremer Racing K8 went on to score a famous victory and it was now *my* bad fortune that it would be someone else's good luck to inherit a podium position. And a sprightly 70-year-old megastar by the name of Paul Newman was that lucky man!

CHAPTER 17

IT'S SHOWBIZ TIME

By the time I returned from Daytona, in the spring of 1995, my 17th series of 'Top Gear' was about to hit the screens, but now my involvement had become a whole lot more than just being an occasional presenter on a specialist television show. With a team that, along with Jeremy Clarkson, Quentin Willson, Chris Goffey and myself, now included the ever-jovial rally man Tony Mason, biker boy Steve Berry and the glamorous Michele Newman, we were attracting attention from all quarters. The viewing figures were soaring towards six million – and we'd also moved into live entertainment.

It had all begun at the London Motor Show at the end of 1993 when Jeremy and Quentin had appeared on the stand of the newly launched *Top Gear* magazine and got involved in a bit of banter with the audience. This had quickly had all the aisles around the stand jammed with fans and started a tradition that would grow and grow over the years.

Alternating between Birmingham and London, I joined the act and it quickly developed into a full-blown stage show with competitions, music and dancing girls adding to the glitz. Of course trying to share the floor with the two 'wordsmiths' often left the 'racing driver' struggling to get a word in – and things would normally end with me being the butt of their jokes. Little did I care, though, because this was fun!

I would occasionally come up with a new funny line, but then at the next show it would usually get nicked by one of the other two before I had a chance to use it. On top of that, they would constantly set challenges to get certain song lyrics included in the general chat, and while theirs fell off the cuff, I had to work hard on mine. Doing four or five shows a day was quite stressful, and we didn't make life any easier for ourselves by starting most days with awful hangovers! Trapped in the dreaded Metropole Hotel, isolated in the middle of the vast National Exhibition Centre near Birmingham, drinking the night away was the only real escape. There was one memorable occasion, though, when Quentin – who was off booze at the time – took us out for the night.

It had started with a Ford party at the nearby Belfry golf club, but when the bar closed we thought we should head for Birmingham while there was still an hour's drinking time left. Jeremy and I decided it would be safer to sit in the back, where we alternated between howls of laughter and screams of terror as Quentin guided the 'Benz' towards our destination. Never had we travelled so fast through the tunnels of that town. Later we would move the Birmingham base to our regular Hyatt home, preferring to commute to the NEC rather than stay there, but now we had a whole town to play in. It was the same story in London, where the legendary Nam Long 'Flaming Ferrari' cocktail would kick-start yet another evening out – and hangover to follow!

The shows themselves would get progressively more outrageous as Jeremy honed his now celebrated observational skills. Describing Birmingham as a 'rugby player's bath with the plug pulled out – empty in the middle with a ring of scum round the outside' a week before we arrived one year didn't help, and references to the Korean penchant for eating dogs when one of its car manufacturers' stands was next to our stage soon had complaints heading our way.

By now, in nearly a hundred items for the show, I had brought to the screen a great variety of experiences that included rallycrossing a Metro 6R4, driving a Le Mans-winning Jaguar, winning a round of the British Touring Car Championship in a Ford Sierra Cosworth, hanging on the back of a World Champion's motorcycle sidecar, and winning my first ever rally, with Tony Mason as my co-driver. But the story I still seem to be best remembered for, even now, is my test of the McLaren F1 Supercar.

Aired in the spring series of 1994, this was not the sort of fast-cut, instant-action, five-minute blast that is the fashion today but an in-depth piece nearly ten minutes in length that, for the first half, took you through the concept, the manufacturing and the usability of this awesome machine. It wasn't until I was some five-and-a-half minutes in that I finally said 'This is what you've been waiting for me to do' – and opened the throttle!

With so many viewers commenting that they genuinely believed I was shocked by the sudden acceleration, my acting ego received a huge boost, but I really was mightily impressed with this wonderful car. The fact that the cameras stayed running for a full two laps of Goodwood Circuit is a credit to the director of the piece, Ken Pollock, and it was something every fan appreciated. Indeed, it must never be forgotten that you don't get a great item without a good backroom team, good cameramen, good soundmen, good editors and, perhaps most of all, good directors like Dennis Jarvis, David Wheeler, David Leighton, Chris Richards and Ewan Keil. It's always a team effort and I'm forever grateful to all those people who have helped propel my image on to the screen.

It was later that same year that 'Top Gear', or Chrysler to be more specific, gave me one of the greatest experiences of my life – a flight on Concorde. A trip to Chicago to test their new Neon road car and join in a celebrity race supporting the Indycar meeting at the Belle Isle street track had been offered, but the timetable clashed with some track-day work. Already committed, the only way to get there on time was on the most beautiful, most graceful, most awe-inspiring passenger jet ever built – and its Delta wings were developed thanks to my family connections at Fairey Aviation, whose Delta 2 plane had been the first to break the 1,000mph barrier.

Having rushed from Silverstone to Heathrow it all began with my first experience of the First Class Lounge – canapés and champagne flowed in all directions, and this was just the beginning. I was looking forward to landing in New York an hour and a half before I'd left! The flight was almost full but the seat beside me wasn't, so double helpings of caviar awaited me – and more champagne, of course.

Just taxiing to the end of the runway was cool enough, but once we'd lined up there, with engines roaring, the adrenaline was pumping. I hadn't expected the strong smell of kerosene that wafted through the ventilation, but it didn't seem to matter, because the throttles opened and we surged forwards. We were off... except suddenly we weren't! Half-way down the runway the engines were throttled back and we were heading back to the terminal. Perhaps that kerosene smell wasn't normal? Had I just had the shortest Concorde experience ever? Would I be doomed to transfer to a jumbo jet and a late arrival? Fortunately the answer to all those questions was a resounding 'No!' The captain informed us that there had been a potentiometer problem, or some such thing, and after a brief fiddle back at the terminal I was soon on my way to the best three-hour lunch I'd ever had.

Cruising at an altitude of 60,000 feet, way above the riff-raff of everyday transatlantic flights, having slowly but surely crept up to Mach Two – twice the speed of sound – I made sure I checked out all the wine choices, white and red, and was just on my second cognac when the call came to fasten seat belts for landing. Unfortunately there was plenty of time to catch a jumbo jet for the return journey...

By now the 'Top Gear' portfolio had been enlarged even further, with the launch of 'Top Gear Motorsport' in November 1994, and more and more of my time was now being soaked up not just driving but reporting on a wide variety of racing and rallying cars from across the world – and getting to drive some of the greatest machines from years gone by.

In terms of personal satisfaction, three cars stand out from the rest as they are among the most iconic cars in the whole history of motor racing – Stirling Moss's 1955 Targa Florio-winning Mercedes-Benz 300 SLR; Jim Clark's Lotus 49 in its original sponsor-free green and yellow colours; and Alain Prost's Ferrari 641/2 that scored the famous marque's 100th Grand Prix victory in France in 1990.

I drove the Mercedes on the short Hockenheim track and could only imagine, on that safe modern circuit, what it would have been like to average 100mph for 1,000 miles on narrow public roads crammed full of spectators. But that's what Moss as good as did, stopping only for fuel in a ten-hour epic. With only 300 horsepower, by modern standards it's not exactly over-powered, but with old-fashioned drum brakes to slow you, once you'd wound it up to the 170mph that Moss did, you needed the reactions of a maestro like him not to get into serious trouble. All I wanted to do was bring it back in one piece, with my biggest concern being a gearbox that had its change 'upside down' – so, while normally you pull the gear lever straight back to go up a gear, on the SLR that would do the opposite and over-rev the engine.

Of course the downside to all these wonderful opportunities that I was getting was that I couldn't just sit back and concentrate on enjoying the drive. I had to talk coherently at the same time, bringing out words with meaning and not just ooohs and aaahs of excitement!

I'd already driven Clark's 1962 Lotus 25, struggling to shoehorn my six-foot frame and size 11 feet into a car that was designed around his much smaller dimensions, but just to look where he had looked was enough for me – pure magic. However, it was the move from the 1.5-litre formula to the big three litres in 1966 that was more my generation, and the Lotus 49 was, of course, the car that changed the Formula One landscape. With its Ford Cosworth DFV bolted directly to its monocoque it was a truly revolutionary design, so neat and simple, yet so effective.

The car I drove was actually Graham Hill's 1967 version, which now sits in the Beaulieu Museum, and I drove it exactly where Graham had had his first drive, at Snetterton Circuit near Lotus's Hethel home. With no seat belts and wearing an open-face helmet with goggles I had the full experience – and just wanted more and more...

The Ferrari 641/2 drive came as part of a *Top Gear* magazine story and was, as the front cover proudly announced, very much a world exclusive, with me in the F1 car going head to head with Jeremy in the Ferrari F50, which was built in the spirit of the Grand Prix car. I'd already driven an ex-Gilles Villeneuve 1979 Ferrari 312T3 for my last *Autosport* track test, which was almost as special, and a 1994 Jordan

Grand Prix car for *Top Gear* magazine, so this journalism stuff was working wonders!

The 641/2 was the model that took Prost to four of his five wins in that 1990 season, and it was also the one that Ayrton Senna rammed into, in order to ensure the World Championship went to him and not the Frenchman. 'My' 641/2 was one of several chassis used over the season, but this is a car of such importance that it now holds pride of place in Ferrari's own museum. Once, when visiting with a group of enthusiasts, I told a tour guide that I had driven it and she gave me a look that suggested she thought I'd had a grappa or two too many. This car is that special.

I only got to drive it on the Padua test track, which is pretty much a runway with a loop at each end, but I was still able to blast it up to 160mph, marvelling at the simplicity of the paddle-shift gearchange which Ferrari had been the first to use a season earlier. With the V12 wailing away behind me, days didn't get much better than this.

Mind you, while going head to head with Jeremy in Ferraris was the stuff of dreams, there were many days we shared that were simply brilliant fun. Few seem to forget me throwing Quentin and him around in a Ford Puma and, while it never made the screen, I did play a little trick on Jeremy when we were filming his Christmas video entitled 'Head to Head'.

One of the segments included a duel between me in a BMW M5 and him in a Jaguar XJR, and we were filming a part of it on the Millbrook Proving Ground's two-mile banked bowl. The top lane of this perfect circle has 22-degree banking which, whatever car you are in, allows you to take your hands off the wheel at 100mph and it will steer itself round. Go slower and it drops down the banking, faster and it climbs up. So, with Jeremy right behind me, I put the BMW on cruise control at exactly 100mph and then climbed over into the back seat and made rude signs at him – just for once I think he actually was speechless!

Meanwhile the show business side of things was also expanding, as Jeremy and I were brought in to present the live-action arena of the Autosport Show at the NEC. At least we were now on equal terms: he could do the gags while I was the one who knew about all the action. While we might have inhaled copious amounts of exhaust fumes and tyre smoke, as we held centre stage amid a maelstrom of motorsport, it was all brilliant fun. One year we had a 'doughnut' finale that wowed me every time, even though I saw it four or five times a day, and it would leave the crowd on their feet hollering for more. Showbiz, when it goes well, can be pretty addictive!

The first year we appeared was 1995, and on that occasion my grand entrance was as a passenger in a rally car. A year later it was in a McLaren F1 and then, as we began to add a lot more 'show business', I arrived abseiling down a rope from the ceiling wearing a full James Bond tuxedo outfit. With more dancing girls than we could count and clothes flying everywhere, half the time we struggled to remember our lines. Jeremy, of course, was the baddy and soon began to introduce me as 'the dope on a rope'!

For '98 Samantha Janus brought even more show to the show business side of things as the presenter line-up briefly expanded to three but, by the following year, Jeremy had gone and I had to be consoled by having the lovely Melanie Sykes *and* all the dancing girls to look after me. Oh how I missed Jeremy!

The most ambitious shows of all, though, were a couple of Top Gear Live extravaganzas that took over the whole of Silverstone as a type of moving motor show. At the first attempt, in 1996, Jeremy, Quentin and I hosted different areas of the project, with the motor manufacturers involved giving drives and rides to as many as they could on the circuit itself.

In '98 the car experience followed similar lines but this time the boys were joined by the lovely Vicki Butler-Henderson, who had added her driving skills and racy personality to the line-up of the 'Top Gear' team a year earlier, and we got together to present an action-packed show in the centre of the circuit. Full of powersliding cars, machine guns and explosions, along with the usual banter, our show was a great success – even if it wasn't a financial one! Little did we think that Top Gear Live would reappear some ten years later and set out on a world tour.

But 1998 wasn't over yet, and as if 'Top Gear', 'Top Gear Motorsport',

Top Gear Live, Top Gear Magazine at the Motor Show *and* the Autosport Show weren't enough, yet another offshoot, 'Top Gear Waterworld', was launched. Yes, I was about to go back to my roots and get my feet wet again.

I went to Sweden to be scared stiff by World Offshore Champion Steve Curtis in a Bat Boat, to the Isle of Man to drive *through* the waves in a revolutionary wave-piercing design for the SAS, to Bangor in the north of Ireland to win an OCR offshore powerboat race – as a navigator – and to the Rother Valley to drive a Formula One catamaran.

The Formula One experience came courtesy of Andy Elliot, the man – or boy as he was back then – who had bought my little Junior Runabout exactly 30 years earlier – long before we'd both battled our way up to the Grand Prix ranks in our chosen sports. I'd always marvelled at the way these 150mph machines appeared to float above the water – and also been amazed at how quickly they could fly up into a back flip and then disintegrate when they hit the water.

This was, possibly all too literally, like jumping in the deep end. Before I could drive it I had to do a 'Dunk Test' in a mocked-up cockpit that they lowered into the lake – not a problem if there hadn't been a huge panic when the seat belt jammed on the expert checking out the rig. I'd already done a test for going in an offshore powerboat, but that is done in a nice big helicopter-sized cage that slowly rolls into a warm, fresh swimming pool. This was very different.

Strapped into a tight cockpit, with a steering wheel that has to be removed, it turned over very quickly and I was instantly upside down in a cold murky lake. Once the belts were released I was fine, having done some scuba diving, but it is very easy to become disorientated and it's something that some drivers dread having to do.

Once back on top of the water and sitting in the cockpit of Andy's boat, a boat that weighed just 260kg and had a 350 horsepower outboard engine bolted on the back, I began to feel a little more apprehensive. These catamarans are known as 'three pointers', with the idea that the boat sits on the very back point of its two hulls with just the bottom half of the propeller being the third point as it slices into the water in between them. This magical balancing act is performed by using two toggle switches. One raises the whole engine up and down while the other alters the angle it enters the water – increase the angle and you lift the nose, increase it too far and all you see is the sky.

Totally out of my comfort zone, my 'points' remained a good three or four feet long, but I had enough time in the boat to get a feel for the skills required to race these machines. Of course there are no brakes, but as soon as you come off the throttle the boat sits down and the water drags you back. Turn in to the hairpin corners and the two hulls literally act as rails, with the top drivers able to pull some serious G. Out of the turn you can slam the throttle wide, tilt the engine out and the acceleration is incredible as the hulls free themselves from the drag of the water and the boat tries its best to become a plane. Able to reach 62mph in less than four seconds, you're talking supercar performance.

It wasn't the only new sport that I'd get an inside view of that year either, as earlier I'd headed to the United States and the Charlotte Motor Speedway in North Carolina – NASCAR country! With 90 per cent of the teams based in a 50-mile radius, this really is NASCAR's home. I was there not just to meet and interview the greatest driver of all time, Richard Petty, but to try one of his cars for myself round the 1.5-mile, 24-degree banked oval with its average speed of 190mph.

Like most Europeans, it had always looked to me to be a rather crude and undemanding form of motorsport, simply turning left all the time in a car that had its technology stuck in the 1950s – fast maybe, but sophisticated not! Well, I was in for a real eye opener. To be quick round these banked tracks you have to have a very specific car set-up and you need to understand the way it works in order to get the best out of it.

First, the car is actually set to turn left on its own – so down the straights you are constantly turning slightly right. When it comes to the corners you have to gently release the steering and let the car drop into the banked turn. Meanwhile, with a differential that is set free on the over-run but quickly tightens up under load, you can't jump off the throttle like you would normally because the car would most probably swiftly swap ends. Instead, you have to gently roll off it as the car turns in.

Down at the apex you are now adding a bit of left lock with the throttle fully closed and it's soon time to start cracking open the 'gas pedal' and feeding the rear tyres with oodles of torque and power – and gently does it is usually the order of the day if you don't want to be biting the concrete! Led around by a Petty Experience instructor, we gradually built up speed, and by the time we got to the 175mph mark my respect for these 'good old boys' had grown immeasurably.

A trip to film the running of the 50th Daytona 500 many years later led to my becoming an addicted fan of this extremely American sport. The build-up to the races provides great drama on its own, from the Christian prayers to the singing of the National Anthem, with the arrival of some sort of awesome military aircraft timed exactly as it ends. When the traditional grid of 43 cars then rolls into Turn 1, the spectacle is something to be seen.

To enjoy it fully you need to have a favourite to follow – not necessarily by the driver's name but by the car's number. At the track you can listen in to all their radio communications and almost become part of the team. For the Needell family it's the '42 car' of 'Juan Pablo Montoya' that grabs our attention – and when he gets himself in the 'catbird seat' anything can happen!

I ended up back in America that year to meet another of the country's great speed-hungry legends, for a 'Top Gear' special about the world land speed record entitled 'Blood, Salt and Tears'. If there was one man who had to be interviewed it was Craig Breedlove, and to track him down we needed to head to his home in the sleepy little town of Rio Vista, east of the San Francisco Bay area.

Breedlove had set his first record way back in 1963 when his jet-engined 'Spirit of America' set a new mark of 407mph across the salt lakes of Bonneville. It brought the record back to America for the first time in 32 years and made him an instant hero. Now, 35 years later, at the age of 61, he wanted to rescue it once again from Britain's 'ThrustSSC' – but the speed he had to beat now was a supersonic 763mph!

Taking us into the workshop behind his small town-centre home, he showed us the machine he intended to use to break a mark set by the massive ten-ton ThrustSSC that bristled with modern technology. It was just a simple tubular frame, housing a whacking great jet engine in the back with Craig sitting in a tiny cockpit right at the front! With one huge twin-wheel at the front, right behind his cockpit, and two on outriggers at the back, it had all the handling characteristics of a three-wheeled Reliant Robin. Just two years earlier, when trying to break the previous Thrust2 mark of 634mph, it had indeed been blown on to its side after Craig had set off for a run: he'd thought the cross-wind report had said 1.5mph and not the 15mph that it actually was. Somehow, at 675mph, it didn't turn into a barrel roll of destruction but instead sat on its side, carving a massive arc across the dry lake bed, with Craig's head just inside a cockpit canopy that was scraping along the salt surface. He ended up some three or four miles off the course. Yet still he wanted to come back for more! Having spent time with the soft-spoken Californian you could see the fire in his eyes whenever he talked of going for a record, but in a way I'm happy that he never found the sponsorship to allow him to have one more go.

There are enough dangers around without even going to such extremes, though, as a test for 'Top Gear 'of the race-bred million-dollar Mercedes-Benz AMG CLK-GTR the week before I left for America nearly proved. This was the thinly disguised road-going version that allowed the model to race in International GT competitions. It was way too wild for the roads…

Still, I wasn't complaining as we set off to test it over in Germany. With a couple of mechanics from AMG to help guide us around, we were based in a little village from where, with cameras installed, I would head out for a few miles doing my on-board chat and then turn around to come back and have what I'd done checked over. As usual, it took a few attempts to get the sound, picture and my words all in harmony. Turning round had been a nightmare as all I could find was a little farm road to back into – a laborious task with very little lock and virtually no rearward vision. However, with what I thought was finally the perfect take, I headed back towards the village and began to notice how much attention this outrageous supercar was getting.

Drivers coming the other way were flashing their lights and waving, so naturally I waved to them. Back at the village the attention being paid to my car also seemed to be increasing, as even the pedestrians were jumping up and down with excitement. Only when I arrived where the team were waiting and saw the AMG mechanics running towards me with fire extinguishers did I realise something was wrong – the back of the car was ablaze. I'd been cruising through the German countryside with a flame-thrower belching out of the back! It was lucky in a way that I hadn't noticed, because if I had there would have been a million-dollar pile of ash in a farm road entrance.

As if my work schedule hadn't been exciting enough, things weren't exactly quiet on the home front either. In February 1996 Patsy and I had been overjoyed by the arrival of a brother for Jack, and when Harry was born our family seemed complete. However, another trip to America, in April 1998, for Patsy's 40th birthday took us to New York for a few days – the city that never sleeps – and nine months later little George made it three Needell boys. He shouldn't have arrived until the first week of January and we'd treated ourselves to a nice relaxing Christmas, being spoiled at the Bath Spa Hotel, but the Boxing Day panto must have provided too much excitement because he decided to arrive in the early hours of the next morning.

So ended what must be the most eventful year of my life. Still racing – and still winning – with TV stardom and showbiz galore, things could hardly be better. But big changes were on the horizon...

CHAPTER 18

RALLYING, TOURING CARS – AND NIGEL!

With the collapse of Group C sportscar racing, my golden era behind the wheel of those 700 horsepower racing machines had sadly come to an end. By the time the Le Mans prototype class had become properly established, towards the end of the 1990s, my name was well off the professional drivers' radar – not that I wasn't still racing, and winning! While 1992 might have seen my racing kit spend more time in the cupboard than in the car, this was the dawning of an era when diversification would be the name of my game. While the fact that I was now a 40-year-old TV presenter might have put off a few of the more serious teams, there were still plenty that realised a quick driver with a TV audience brought its advantages.

Winning my first ever rally in the Ford RS2000 Rallye Sport section of that year's Tour of Cornwall wasn't exactly a bad start to the season, especially as a couple of young rally stars of the future were second and third. Co-driven by my 'Top Gear' colleague Tony Mason, who had sat alongside such greats as Roger Clark, this was a part of my sport at which I'd always wanted to have a go – and I wasn't disappointed. My second rally later that year, though, was a slightly tougher proposition.

Invited by Ford to take part in one of their production class Group N Sierra Cosworths, I lined up among the 157 entries that would climb the start ramp for the British round of the World Rally Championship – the Lombard RAC Rally. From a club event to a major international was a huge step, and the co-driver given the daunting task of trying to guide me to the end of 350 miles of treacherous forest tracks was the bubbly blonde Swedish star, Tina Thörner. Tina had navigated Scottish rally driver Louise Aitken-Walker to their Ladies'

World Championship a couple of years earlier, and the car I was to drive was supposed to be for her, but with a baby on the way she decided it wasn't perhaps the best idea to take part. I'd picked up drives before due to people getting injured, but pregnancy was a new one!

Back then these events would take up a very full two weeks of your life. There were eight days of recceing stages that stretched from the start in Chester down to the Midlands, across to Wales and then up through the Lake District (and the infamous Kielder Forest), to the lowlands of Scotland before heading back to Chester – and that was before you even started the actual rally. It was more than double the distance they do today, but also less than half of what they'd done 20 years earlier…

With snow and ice on the ground in some places, I was struggling even to keep the recce car on the road at just 30mph, so my confidence wasn't exactly high. All I could do was pray for a big thaw. For eight days we were up before dawn, driving mile upon country mile from stage to stage, then jolting down each stage with Tina trying to explain to me what all the pace notes were about. And understanding them was one thing, but believing in them was quite another!

When the thaw did come it was replaced by rain, mud and slush – especially where the forestry workers had been piling their logs – so I still had little idea how much grip I would have when I arrived at each corner. After a brief excursion into the trees on only the third stage, Tina's use of a rather Scottish sounding 'Nor Nor Nor!' to slow me down became a frequent shout down the intercom, followed on the many occasions, when a visit to the ditch seemed imminent, by a louder 'Oj Oj Oj!' as she expected the worst.

On one occasion she simply burst out laughing because I was going as fast in the slow corners as I was in the quick ones. I was only really happy to have a go when I could see the corner I was about to tackle – simply believing that I should steer slightly right *and* stay flat in top gear over a blind crest because of something she had written down on a bit of paper in front of her just didn't seem to register as a good idea!

The fact that we got to the finish at all was to Tina's immense credit, and that we were 30th overall out of the 101 finishers and seventh in our Group N class didn't seem too bad a result for a rallying novice. The shock to me, though, was that I was seven seconds a mile off the pace. Used to lap times split by tenths of a second this seemed totally useless, until you understand just how much goes on in each mile of a forest stage. When Martin Brundle tried it a few years later and was in the same zone I felt much better.

In the spring of the following year I found myself driving an original Mini Cooper in the Charringtons RAC Historic Rally over beautiful, dry Yorkshire Moor stages. With journalist Ian Bond alongside and no pace notes permitted it was down to poor old Ian to try to decipher whatever he could, reading off the map. With me constantly screaming 'What's next?' while keeping the little engine revving madly on full throttle, and my left foot hovering over the brake, I was now an instant Scandinavian master – well, at least that's what I was trying to be! With the dry conditions at last giving some constant grip we somehow ended up having a great battle with a couple of Lotus Cortinas for eighth place and the honour of being the first non-Porsche 911 to finish – but then, with just one stage to go, the flywheel fell off the end of the crankshaft.

With my rallying confidence fully restored I now went in search of more opportunities, and was most grateful for an offer from Vauxhall to drive one of their Astras in the Formula Two class of the Scottish Rally – a round of the British Championship that was about to launch Richard Burns to international stardom. Although the Astra was front-wheel drive and not exactly the Mark 1 Escort of my dreams, the Charringtons event had got me working on this left-foot braking malarkey. In the Mini I would right-foot brake initially so the left foot could operate the clutch for the down change and then, at the end of the braking, move both feet one pedal to the right, so if a corner tightened unexpectedly my left foot was instantly on the brake. The difference with the Astra was that it had a 'dog box' transmission which allows you to change gear without using the clutch – so once you've left the starting line, you can left-foot brake all the time. The great thing about this, in a front-wheel-drive car is that you set the balance of the brakes to the rear so, if the nose of the car starts to run wide and understeer, you can squeeze the brakes to step the back out *and* keep accelerating at the same time.

Once fully into the swing of this, and again on consistent, dry stages, I was loving it. With a completely unflappable John Meadows calmly reading the notes beside me, on one stage I managed to reduce my deficit to just two seconds per mile and felt I was almost becoming a real rally driver. With the left-foot braking you could set the car sideways as you entered the corner, with very little steering input, and then once pointed at the exit simply fire it straight out. Of course, with this new-found enthusiasm errors were likely to happen, and on a couple of occasions I'd dropped the Astra into a ditch on the exit of corners but, urged on by John, simply kept on the power and dragged it out. Unfortunately, once again on the penultimate stage, the ditch I entered had a solid concrete culvert across its path...

Undeterred, I still wanted more but I would have to wait another three years before Skoda offered me a chance, back in the British round of the World Championship, which by now had become the '1996 Network Q RAC Rally'. Again it was a front-wheel-drive Formula Two machine, and the car I was to drive was the Skoda Felicia which had been campaigned in the British Championship that year by Steve Wedgbury. After a season frustrated by problems with both the power steering and the brakes it had been sent back to the factory to be sorted for the RAC, so hopefully all would be well.

Once again the week before the event was spent touring half of Britain, with Brian Hardie as my brave volunteer in the passenger seat. Having marvelled at some of the most flowing rally stages I had ever seen in consistently dry conditions, I couldn't wait to be let loose. Yes, there was a bit of snow up near Scotland, but that would surely add to the fun. However, by the time of the Oulton Park shakedown test, the week before the event, my car had still to reappear from the depths of the Czech Republic or wherever it had been sent. I had to borrow the factory test car and it felt brilliant. Dabs of left-foot braking,

snips of the handbrake, the car twitching this way and that under my
control, I was going to enjoy this...

Having been delivered just in time for scrutineering, I got to drive
my rally car on the night before the event and I immediately knew we
were in trouble: the handbrake couldn't even lock the rear wheels.
One of the car's main problems obviously hadn't been cured. Okay, we
could fiddle with it during the rally, but it wasn't a good start – and
when I woke up the next morning it was worse. The thickest and
hardest frost probably since the ice age had descended on Britain and
with it a gentle dusting of snow. When Brian turned up wearing dainty
little driving boots I suggested that perhaps crampons would be better,
but that's what he had and that's what he was going to wear.

With no handbrake and no real braking on the rear at all, the
conditions couldn't have been worse. My newly honed left-foot
braking skills were now of little use as they merely aggravated the
understeer instead of reducing it and, without a handbrake, hairpins
would be embarrassing. Not surprisingly it didn't take me long to find
a ditch. With Brian slipping all over the place in his pretty racing
boots, it was only thanks to the two spectators who happened to be in
our part of the forest that we ever got to the end of day one – and with
cars crashing out all over the place that was quite some achievement
on its own.

The next two days were simply a matter of survival. We were not
allowed studded tyres, so grip was almost impossible to find. Rally
legend Stig Blomqvist in one of the factory Skodas was making it look
ridiculously easy up at the front of the field, embarrassing most of the
more powerful four-wheel-drive machinery and eventually finishing
an astonishing third overall. Using his experience, he spent most of
the time half off the road, searching for the best grip he could find –
but further back down the massive 182-car field the less skilled drivers
were facing roads that were becoming more and more polished. Even
the hardened regulars who queued up around me awaiting the starts
of the stages hated this one. No-one was enjoying it and, for the first
time ever, I felt scared behind the wheel of a car; I had so little control.
Over the many miles of stages in the dark it was even worse, and on

a couple of occasions we simply shot off into the scenery with only luck dictating whether it was into a massive tree or off the edge of a huge drop...

Spectators would gather round hairpin corners at the bottom of hills and when you inevitably ended up in a ditch in front of them, as that was the only way to stop, these smiling and laughing souls would gladly lift you out and get you back on your way. Me, I just wanted to be left in the ditch!

My over-riding memory, which really summed up the event, was when we were struggling up a hill at about 2mph, desperately searching for grip – yes, this is on a World Championship motorsport event – and some glaring headlights were slowly catching us. Edging to one side to give them room I was greeted by the sight of Rachael Simmonite overtaking me *on foot* pulling her sister's Ford Escort up the hill with a rope...

Martin Brundle met something bigger than his Escort Cosworth in a ditch early on the third morning and went no further, but I somehow slithered my way to the finish, ecstatic simply to have survived. Out of just 82 who made it to the end, less than half that had started, I was the happiest ever 52nd-placed finisher. It gave me even more respect for the rally stars of the day because it really is a sport where experience is vital if you are ever going to gauge how much grip lies ahead.

Fortunately I did have a chance to get my confidence back in 1998, contesting a round of another one-make series for the smallest car with the longest name – the four-wheel-drive Daihatsu Cuore Avanzato. Running as part of the McRae Stages event around Lanark, once again in nice dry conditions and urged on by Cliff Simmons, the whole idea of pace notes really began to work – and with the little Avanzato unable to gather speed too quickly I had more time to pay attention to them.

Up until then I had been like a beginner learning a foreign language. I'd hear a call like 'Right one over crest – 50 – left six into right nine' and I'd have to translate it into 'Gentle right-hander over a crest, then 50 yards to a pretty sharp left-hander which leads almost immediately into a very sharp right-hander'. Now, though, I'd made the breakthrough that language students talk about, when they actually start to think in the foreign language instead of having to translate it back and forth. Cliff was beginning to call further and further ahead of where the car was, and the picture of what was coming up was instantly in my mind. When you reach that point it provides an incredible buzz. You're hurtling into the unknown, no longing easing off the throttle because you're not quite sure, because now you have an exact picture of what's coming up. Nerves are calmer, the tension in your body eases and you go with the flow. Up against the usual bunch of ambitious hotshots, I managed to hold my own after a slow start and made it to the finish in fourth place, overjoyed by fastest time on one of the stages

Sadly, though, that would be the end of my rallying career. I did eventually get into a Mark I Escort and won my class at a Silverstone Historic Rallysprint – and I still think rally cars should switch to a rear-wheel drive, silhouette formula, not only to reduce the speeds but also because it would make it so much more fun to watch! However, it wasn't really in rallying that I was looking to further my career in the early nineties. Instead, it was in the new two-litre Touring Car Championship that was getting a lot of attention from manufacturers – and there were well-paid professional drives in the offing.

Up until 1990 Touring Cars had always been a four-class system, and if the winner of the smallest class had more points than the winner of the biggest class they were the overall champion. Now, however, it had become a one-class affair, and with more freedom in the regulations virtually any 4.5-metre long, four-door saloon could be made into a winner, so plenty of manufacturers were showing some interest.

During 1992 I had been running Nissan's track days for them and, as they were running two cars in the championship, they were my first port of call. I persuaded them to run me in a third car for the championship finale of that year – naturally bringing my TV cameras along for the ride!

In wet practice I struggled to get used to the front-wheel-drive

Primera eGT, but I was happy enough to be only a fifth of a second behind team leader Keith O'dor – even if that meant we lined up 11th and 13th on the 23-car grid, with champion elect Tim Harvey's BMW sandwiched between us. When Keith's engine blew I would be the lead Nissan, in tenth at the finish, in a race made famous when Steve Soper torpedoed John Cleland in a move that handed the championship to his BMW team-mate. Afterwards my TV job got me a drive in both that championship-winning car, the race-winning Toyota Carina and a Vauxhall Cavalier – and oh how I wanted a ride in one of those rear-wheel-drive BMWs. They were just so easy to drive...

But, nice though the BMWs were, rear-wheel-drive cars were handicapped with extra weight and the front-wheel-drive machines were more often quicker over a single lap. In any case, my connections were at Nissan. However, while I originally thought the TV work could only be a plus, I was now being faced for the first time with a general feeling that now I was a telly star I couldn't be a committed, full-time racing driver any more. What I saw as my 'bonus' was becoming a 'barrier'...

So it was that in '93 the second Nissan seat went to all-round touring car star and top bloke, Win Percy. Being eight years older than me I could hardly claim my age was a barrier, plus Win had been a British Champion in the 1980s and won races in almost everything he drove, so there could hardly be any complaints – just jealousy and another Voodoo doll! I was offered a third car in selected events, however, so I still had my chance to shine.

My entry would run a Japanese-tuned version of the Primera engine to help speed up the development of the car, which up until then had been undertaken by the Janspeed team that ran them. Not the fastest in a straight line, the Primera handled brilliantly but it needed more power.

After one race in an outdated spare car and another in an unsorted new one, my season didn't really get under way until the seventh round of the championship at Pembrey, deep down in Wales – and when I qualified seventh with Keith and Win back in tenth and twelfth it caused quite a stir! Holding that position in the race and

feeling quite comfortable, a misfire suddenly started and I was soon
pit bound to have it fixed. But it had been a promising start.

The next race was the big one, supporting the British Grand Prix
around the high-speed swoops of Silverstone where the Primera's
handling could come into its own. In the test the week before I was
again the fastest of the Nissans and we were right on the pace, setting
the car up to be as neutral as possible; I was almost flat out through
the fast Bridge Corner. With orders to my engineer to leave it exactly
as it was, I looked forward to qualifying. Only four new tyres were
allowed so you'd basically get two runs with the fresh rubber on the
front wheels. However, the balance just didn't seem to be there on the
day and I nearly had an almighty accident when the rear stepped out
going through Bridge. What was going on?

'So the extra toe-out on the rear didn't make it any better, then?'
(He'd changed the set-up.) 'Don't get so uptight, we'll put it back how
it was for tomorrow.' And then it rained! Sitting proudly on pole
position was Keith while I sat fuming, less than a second slower but
way back in 13th on the massive 29-car grid where eight different
manufacturers were represented. This was the Super Touring Formula
in its heyday.

To make matters worse, I made a bad start and got stuck behind
Tim Harvey in his Renault 19. This car was like a rocket down the
straight and a rickshaw round the corners. Seeing Keith and Win
battling up at the front caused my frustration to build: I needed to get
up there and join them. Tim was sorted out with a little tap up the
inside at Stowe – it's the touring car way – but it brought little relief
as I shortly found my way on to the boot lid of Tim's team-mate, Alain
Menu, who left not the smallest of gaps!

As the laps wound down, Keith and Win were heading for an
historic Nissan 1-2 while Alain and I were waging war over the
dubious honour of who would end up seventh. But racing drivers are
always racing drivers and, knowing I was much quicker over a lap, my
point had to be made. Alain was equally determined that the TV tart
wasn't going to get by! I made my final suicidal bid with just two
corners to go and almost got away with it, but I broke a steering arm

in the rather robust move. Frustration had got the better of me. Unfortunately I'd made the move in front of all the corporate boxes, including Renault's. Now, unbeknown to me, after our little contretemps Tim had had another off and rolled his Renault into a ball – and the rumour had got back that that was due to me as well, so the protests started flying.

One of the occupational hazards of touring car racing is that you often have to wait behind for the 'headmaster's report' to decide whose fault everything was in the many clashes that happen in almost every race – and this time the fine came my way. Having said that, it did all calm down a bit once it was understood that I hadn't binned Tim and, to his credit, Alain phoned me the next day to let me know he had been no party to the protest and fully understood my frustrations. Of course that was also the race where Julian Bailey put his team-mate Will Hoy on his roof when they were running 1-2 in their Toyotas, so in many ways it was just another typical day in the touring car world...

The next round was up at the Scottish circuit of Knockhill where our engine's lack of torque left us for dead. Still, I qualified second of the Nissans and Keith and I finished a resounding 1-2 – except it was 11th and 12th! Given one more opportunity at Brands Hatch before my budget ran out, I qualified seventh and was once again fastest of the Nissans – but then had to retire early with more electric gremlins. So, no results to speak of, but surely I'd shown the speed was there and would be one of the favourites for a drive next year...

Before that, though, there was one more touring car race that was on my schedule: a big one-off event for a £12,000 winner-takes-all race called the 'TOCA Shoot-out' – and someone had invited Nigel Mansell along to join in the fun! Nissan weren't entering, but *Top Gear* magazine wanted to have a presence and fixed for me to drive a second Ecurie Ecosse Vauxhall Cavalier run by Ray Mallock as team-mate to David Leslie. Our Nige had just won the American Indycar Championship, the year after he'd become World Champion, and Ford had invited him along for a hero's return to drive one of their Mondeos, a car that had just taken Paul Radisich to victory in the World Touring

Car showdown in Monza. With Mansell Mania reignited, a huge crowd turned up with their Union flags and 'Red 5' T-shirts to cheer their hero on. A great race was in prospect.

To add an element of extra drama to the event, TOCA had done away with the usual qualifying system for the grid and lined the cars up based on previous form – but in reverse order! Suddenly my lack of results was an asset. I would share the third row of the Donington grid with Matt Neal. Derek Warwick sat right behind me in a Toyota, with Nigel back on the sixth row in his fast Ford, just ahead of Leslie, Radisich and BMW star Steve Soper.

Almost inevitably the race turned into a battle for survival, with cars going off all over the place and the pace car making regular appearances to bunch the field back up again. Nigel had surged forwards at first but then dropped right back, struggling with a misfire. Somehow the problem went away and, with another pace car allowing him to close back up, the scene was set for a sprint to the finish.

With the cream finally rising to the top, the order now had a more settled look to it, with Radisich in front, then Leslie, me and Soper – but Nigel was looming large in his mirrors. Revelling in the fact that I now had a car that could hold its own on the straights, I was beginning to think this could be my day. So far Steve was playing it fair, although I knew a tap would be coming sooner or later, and Paul and David weren't getting away, so if they were to clash I would be ready...

Then the white BMW in my mirrors swapped to a blue Ford and I could hear the crowd roaring their hero on from inside my car. With good straight-line speed I still thought I had things covered and, with a comfortable gap past the pits, I opted for the normal racing line at Redgate, never imagining Mansell would make a move from so far back – but he did! I saw him coming and had to give him room at the apex, but if he hadn't used me as an extra brake, I don't think he would have made the corner. As it was, I was rudely shoved on to the grass on the exit and had the extra frustration of seeing Steve sail past me as well, as I lost momentum trying to get back on the track.

Diving down the Craner Curves towards the Old Hairpin we reappeared in front of the huge crowds gathered on the banks of this

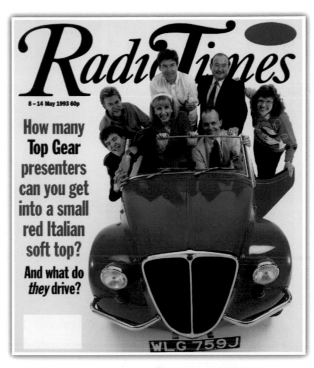

Is it me or is it Nigel Mansell?
Filming a Renault commercial –
December 1991.

'Top Gear' makes the cover of
Radio Times *– May 1993.*

Driving in my dreams. Moss's 1955
Mille Miglia winning Mercedes-
Benz 300SLR and Graham Hill's
1967 Lotus 49.

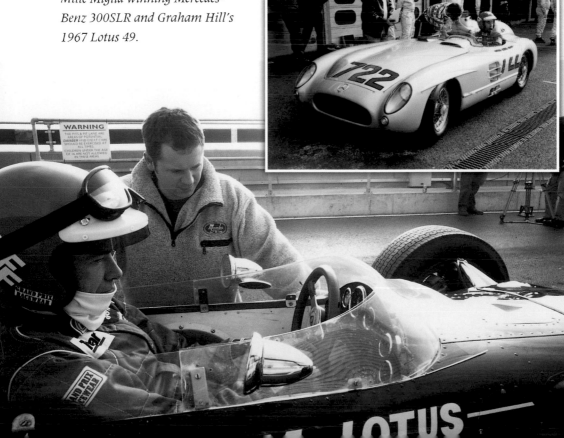

The wildest car I ever raced. The Jaguar XJR15 at Monaco – May 1991.

Forza Ferrari! On the cover of Top Gear *magazine in Alain Prost's 1990 Ferrari 641/2 alongside Jeremy in the new F50 – June 1996.*

Last Le Mans in the legendary Porsche 962 with Derek Bell and his son Justin – June 1992.

It's all about to kick off at Donington! Nigel Mansell looms large in my mirrors while Steve Soper keeps a watching brief – October 1993.

Trying my hand at rallying. Splashing through the Lombard RAC Rally, with Tina Thörner in a Group N Ford Sierra Cosworth – November 1992.

Sideways in a Mini! Ian Bond hangs on in the passenger seat as I sort things out on the Charringtons RAC Historic Rally – March 1993.

And surviving in the snow with Brian Hardie in our Skoda Felicia on the treacherous Network Q RAC Rally – November 1996.

Presenting the Lister Storm to the Toon Army at Newcastle United – January 1996.

Pit stop action at Brands Hatch as I take over from Geoff Lees – September 1996.

My last Le Mans. Driving the GTL Lister Storm – June 1997.

Flame throwing towards a hat
trick of British GT wins in a
Lister Storm...

... and spraying the champagne
on the podium with Dave Clark –
October 2000.

'Fifth Gear' is go! With Vicki
Butler-Henderson, Adrian Simpson
and Quentin Willson – April 2002.

Back in a Grand Prix car! Blasting a Williams-BMW FW26 round Rockingham for the 'Fifth Gear' cameras – May 2005.

Hamming it up on stage with James May and Jeremy Clarkson...

...and taking my rocket-powered mobility scooter for a test drive – MPH 06.

Back at Spa in July 2006 driving Tom Alexander's GT3 Aston Martin DBRS9, and about to go for a roll in the hay with John Barrowman for 'Fifth Gear' – July 2009.

Glorious Goodwood! Leading the Sussex Trophy field into Madgwick, driving Chris Lunn's 1958 Lister Jaguar.

Taking a guest for a ride at Thruxton in a BMW M3 – what a way to earn a living!

Patsy and me dressed up for the Goodwood Ball and with the boys on holiday.

Jack, Harry and George. Growing up fast, from 2000 to 2009.

natural amphitheatre. Once again the roar was audible as a mass of waving flags celebrated Nigel's move up to third. Into the Old Hairpin we went, despite its name one of the fastest corners on the track, and Mansell's Mondeo suddenly snapped sideways at the apex. It's a nasty trick these front-wheel-drive cars had: they had to be set up as near to oversteer as you dared, but when they let go, they let go big time!

With the Mondeo looking to spear off into the infield, Steve dived past on his left and I went to follow him, but Nigel had done what comes naturally to a rear-wheel-drive racer: he'd lifted off the throttle and piled on the opposite lock. The front tyres regained their grip and the Ford snapped back to the left – now heading straight for the gap between Steve's BMW and my Vauxhall...

Seeing him coming, I braked to try and avoid him but still slammed into the back of his car as he sliced between us. As he exited stage left I sorted out my own little drama, mainly concerned by the fact that my bonnet was badly crumpled and my race had been ruined – unaware that the impact had helped direct Nigel straight towards the solid brick bridge parapet on the outside of the corner. Only when red flags starting flying all over the place did I begin to consider that maybe Nigel had taken quite a big hit. We all came to a halt on the grid to regroup and waited for news but, in the meantime, my main concern was getting my battered Vauxhall ready for some more action. After all, there was still £12,000 to be won!

From the state of my car it was pretty obvious that I had played a part in Nigel's downfall, and some of the more vociferous members of the public decided to find me guilty without a trial and began to show their disapproval. A quick chat with the commentator to give my side of the story seemed to prevent the lynch mob from descending on my car and, fortunately, it soon emerged that although badly battered and shaken Nigel was more or less okay. And so we lined up again for a six-lap sprint for the cash.

Sadly, my Cavalier was now one of the walking wounded. My only consolation would be that David Leslie carried the *Top Gear* magazine logos to victory ahead of Radisich and Soper as I fell back to finish sixth. If I'd known what Nigel was going to say afterwards, though, when he virtually blamed me for the whole accident, I might not have braked so hard to avoid him!

Several years later we would meet once more on the touring car battlefield when I returned for a one-off TV outing in a Nissan Primera at Brands Hatch, towards the end of 1998. Nigel was contesting the full season in a Mondeo – but by then it was no longer the fastest car in the field and we would once again end up disputing the same piece of tarmac. I'd qualified down in 17th for the day's Feature Race – three places ahead of Mansell's Ford – and Nigel was already in a grumpy mood, having ended up in the Graham Hill Bend tyre wall on the opening lap of the earlier Sprint Race – not his fault, of course.

Having not made the best of starts – these front-wheel-drive machines were notoriously tricky to get off the line – I spent the first few laps busily doing my utmost to find a way past the battling Peugeots of Tim Harvey and Paul Radisich. And then the blue Ford once again loomed large in my mirrors. Heading up to Druids, I was trying to prise open a gap on the inside of Radisich but got the traditional chop and had to brake hard to avoid contact... boom! My head shot backwards from the force of an impact behind me: Nigel had planted his Mondeo firmly in my boot! With a full-on dose of whiplash and a temporary loss of my senses, I gathered it all together and continued on, while my assailant headed for the pits and some front-end remedial work. Unfortunately I was now, once again, one of the walking wounded as the impact had hit me so hard it had distorted the rear suspension pick-up points of my Nissan.

After the race I suggested to him that he'd at last got his own back, only to be accused of once again causing the accident, this time by deliberately brake-testing him. For the second time he had ruined one of my rare opportunities to get a good result, and instead of the expected 'Sorry, mate' you'd get from most drivers, once again, apparently, it had all been my fault. He may be one of the greatest racing drivers Britain has ever produced, but there are times...

To round off 1993, *Top Gear* magazine did a feature where eight of the top touring car stars brought road-going versions of their race cars to the Silverstone Grand Prix circuit to see how their lap times compared, and I went along to represent Alfa Romeo and Volvo. They were all around 30 seconds off the two-minute mark of the racing models, but with a 12-second spread from fastest (Soper's BMW) to slowest (me in the Volvo) as opposed to the 1.5 seconds for the racing versions!

With time to spare at the end of the day someone thought it would be a good idea if we then all did just one flying lap in one of the Silverstone Racing School's Peugeot 309 GTis – and guess who was quickest? Yes, me! Lots of excuses about damp tracks and lightening fuel loads were being bandied about, but after Paul Radisich looked to have set the time to claim the bragging rights, I pipped him by a fifth of a second.

Surely, now, that Nissan drive for 1994 was as good as mine... but no! Nissan Europe are based in Belgium and when Belgian star Eric van de Poele took the unfancied Primera to fifth place in the world showdown at Monza he became their overnight sensation and the drive was his. By now I was running short of Voodoo dolls...

Once again I was offered a limited programme in a third car, with the Primeras now wearing the bright red colours of their Old Spice sponsors, but after Eric and Keith O'dor began the year with massive car-destroying accidents, once again it wouldn't be until the seventh round that I joined the series at Oulton Park – and then immediately qualified between Keith and Eric. By now, however, the Primeras were not only slow in a straight line but also struggling to keep up round the corners. At the big British Grand Prix support event at Silverstone we qualified 12th, 13th and 19th, with me once again closest to team leader O'dor, but we all ended up in a massive multi-car first-corner tangle. Parking our battered Primeras in the Copse gravel trap did, though, enable us to hop across the track and join the guests at Nissan's lavish hospitality centre in time for a beer before we watched the restart.

Eric was gone after Silverstone, disillusioned with the whole affair, so it was left to Keith and me to do the best we could for the rest of the year – and my ninth at Brands Hatch would end up being the team's only top-ten finish after I joined them. Keith was always the quicker of the two of us, and my sole motivation was to get as close to him as I could. With Janspeed being his father's team I'm sure he quite rightly tried to get all the best bits put on his car, but there was no doubt he was blindingly quick in a front-wheel-drive touring car.

When Nissan, not surprisingly, withdrew from the series at the end of the year Keith was out of a drive, but he was back in a Primera for the German series of 1996 and beginning to make a name for himself in the world arena. After a breakthrough victory in the first of two races at the Avus Circuit, he was lying third in the second race when some sort of car failure pitched him off the road at high speed and then back in front of the oncoming traffic. Hit hard in the driver's door, he would suffer injuries that proved fatal and robbed us not just of a great driver but also a very gentle and kind man.

With the British Touring Car Championship over for the year, my 1994 season would come to an end with two uplifting trips overseas to restore a bit of much needed self-confidence. First it was back to South Africa for a Touring Car Challenge in a Ray Mallock-prepared Nissan Sentra that was rewarded with a third and a fourth, and then home for just a day before getting back on a plane for a 'Top Gear' mission out east, to drive in the first ever international race in mainland China – a GT race round the streets of Zhuhai in the Guangdong Province.

Invited to join my new best Austrian friend, Franz Konrad, in his Porsche 911 Bi-turbo, it was a fascinating trip that ended with us climbing on to the second step of the podium behind the factory-built 911 Turbo S Le Mans driven by the French all-star cast of Jean-Pierre Jarier, Jacques Laffite and... Bob Wollek. Yes, my Group C nemesis was still getting in my way!

Round the tight, bumpy, wall-lined street circuit, the 500 horsepower Porsche was quite a handful and demanded maximum concentration for my 90-minute stint. Exhausted and elated by the finish, it had reminded me of everything I had been missing, teetering round tracks in front-wheel-drive boxes doing half-hour sprints. I needed to get back to rear-wheel drive and oodles of horsepower, but how?

CHAPTER 19

BACK TO LE MANS WITH
BLACK AND WHITE STRIPES

While the outing in China had reignited my passion for all things powerful and rear-wheel drive, the endurance racing world was still going through an awkward transition from Group C sportscars to open-topped prototypes and GT cars. I'd had a taster of racing production-based GT machinery when I contested the one-make JaguarSport Intercontinental Challenge for the £500,000 Jaguar XJR15s back in 1991. The cars were built and run by Tom Walkinshaw Racing and the series consisted of just three races, with the last round at Spa offering a winner-takes-all million-dollar purse. Most of the 16-car field were private entries, and I had been asked to drive the car owned by investment specialist David Warnock and his business partner, but there were half a dozen or so factory entries for drivers to represent different continents of the world – and their cars always seemed to be a little bit quicker in a straight line than mine!

The series kicked off around the narrow confines of Monte Carlo where these 450 horsepower machines with very limited aerodynamic downforce and a great big six-litre V12 in the back proved a real handful. To make matters worse, the first qualifying session was held in damp, drizzly conditions. To say this car was the hardest thing to drive that I ever raced is probably an understatement – they were just plain nasty! Snappy oversteer was their favourite trick, and they would use up the grip from the tyres very quickly. They felt very heavy and cumbersome round Monaco and, unable to take the curve through the tunnel flat out, they certainly kept the heartbeat raised.

I managed to qualify a respectable seventh on the grid, one place behind guess who? Bob Wollek! Bob was in a factory car representing

Europe along with works Jaguar driver Derek Warwick, who was the class of the field in pole position. With the second session run in pouring rain times didn't improve, so the first opportunity to run on a completely dry track was in the race itself. At last I would finally get to compete around this most famous of tracks, having failed to make the grid on both my previous visits. It really was a case of third time lucky. I made quite good progress at first, moving up to fifth in the opening laps, but then I started to have a problem with the engine not responding to the throttle out of slow corners and began to fade. Mind you, it wasn't just the engine that was fading as, like the rest of the field, I was soon struggling with tyres that had simply run out of grip – and with a lack of cockpit ventilation, the driver was overheating badly as well! I made it to the end in seventh, hotter than hot and gasping for a drink.

The Silverstone race supporting the British Grand Prix turned into a complete crashfest. Warwick, who had won at Monaco, was on pole again, but I was way back in tenth. According to the team there was nothing wrong with my engine, and I got the impression they thought I'd been inventing the problem – having an engineer that doesn't believe in his driver is one of the greatest frustrations of our sport.

When Warwick started playing pinball with Cor Euser and David Brabham in their half-million-pound cars on the opening laps it set the tone for the whole of the race. By the sixth lap I'd worked my way up to third place but in so doing had taken too much out of my tyres – and given Armin Hahne a bit of a clout to get there! There was only one way to go now and that was backwards, quite literally when Armin decided that he ought to show me two can play at that game. I survived to finish sixth but, like most of the field, I had a rather battle-scarred Jaguar to show for it.

While the cars were insured for the racing they had something like a £10,000 excess on the policy – and, until you read the small print, you didn't realise that that wasn't for each race but for each 'accident'! So if the reports mentioned that I'd touched a car that was one excess, then another, then another – and a few bits of bodywork at the team's prices soon gobbled up £30,000. Like most owners, mine were finding it a lot more costly than they'd expected. They got their money's worth out of the insurance at the Spa finale, however, because I did a proper job when I lost it big time going through the most famous corner in the world – Eau Rouge.

We'd all learned by now that the cars were so hard on their tyres that their first lap was their best lap and after that it was downhill all the way, especially on a long circuit like Spa. This meant you had to get on it straight away, and for qualifying the big question was how hot to get the tyres on your out lap without taking away any of that precious new-tyre grip. The first corner at Spa is the most crucial of all – the very, very fast left out of Eau Rouge – so a good exit speed here pays dividends all the way up the long, uphill straight to Les Combes.

Having made sure of a clean exit out of La Source Hairpin, the acceleration seemed much more impressive as I blasted down the hill towards Eau Rouge, winding the big V12 up through the gears and shaving the pit wall on my right to help open up the left-handed entry into the corner. Braking as little as I dared, carrying as much momentum as I could, I fired it into the bottom of the valley and then began the long, uphill, right-handed climb...

Whether I was too fast, or the tyres were too cold, I'll never know. All I did know was that the back suddenly stepped out of line half-way up the hill and, while I caught the first slide, I had no chance of catching the one that went the other way. Disappearing over the crest backwards at well over 100mph I'd hoped it would spin up the straight, but the left-handed kink of Raidillion sucked me into its unwelcoming barriers big time. In a series in which I had so hoped to do well, this was the final straw. Patsy had to go into consoling overdrive.

The car was repairable for the next day and I never dared to ask at what cost. I qualified it a chastened 13th in the second practice and was trying at least just to finish the race in one piece, and then John Watson found out how awful these cars were and arrived backwards at Les Combes with me in his path. With bodywork hanging off and a stop for a new wheel, I made it home in 13th – and, yes, I was beginning to think that number gave me bad omens! Still, I was better off than Derek Warwick whose XJR15 spat him into the Blanchimont barriers at high speed, while Armin Hahne was the man with a million dollars at the end of a series most drivers just felt glad to have survived.

It would be a full six months after my return from China before I could find myself another GT ride in 1995, and it came in another Jaguar. This time, though, it was in a much better developed version – a race-prepared XJ220. Once again it would be my friend Richard Piper and his racing partner Patrick Capon who stepped forwards with an offer. First came a drive in a standard aluminium-bodied machine in the Global Endurance series race at Donington and then, to my utter delight, a return to Le Mans to drive a lightweight XJ220C carbon-fibre version that had won the GT class back in '93 – well, at least until it was disqualified!

Unfortunately 1995 was the year that the racing version of the McLaren F1 Supercar hit the tracks – and if you didn't have one you were struggling. At Donington, where the carbon car was ineligible, I qualified the big Jaguar seventh – *four* seconds a lap slower than the nimble McLarens – with the only non-McLaren ahead of me the Porsche 911GT2 of... Bob Wollek! For once the Porsche broke, and we were best non-McLaren for a while, but then the clutch went.

However, Le Mans was the race we most wanted to do, and I was delighted when Richard asked James Weaver to join us and put the team back together. Mind you, even the lightweight XJ220C felt like a cumbersome truck in comparison to all the Group C cars I'd raced, but although I lapped it faster than it had gone two years earlier I could only manage 14th in our class. Ahead of us were no fewer than seven McLarens, three F40 Ferraris, two Porsches and one Venturi.

We actually lined up 22nd overall on the grid, in exactly the same spot as the winning XJ220C of David Coulthard two years earlier, although back then he was fastest in the GT class. Although it started in the dry, the race would be one of the wettest in modern times, made worse by the on-off nature of the rain that would constantly leave you having to make a brave decision as to whether to stay out on the tyres you had or lose time in the pits changing them. With all sorts of dramas, the challenge from the thin field of the new generation of

World Sportscars which were supposed to set the pace almost immediately evaporated, and the fight for the GT class would be the battle for the overall lead from the end of the first hour all the way to the finish.

My first stint coincided with the arrival of the rain and, out on slicks, it wasn't the nicest of feelings. The problem with the GT cars compared to the Group C machinery we'd become used to was that they were both heavier (so wouldn't stop) and lacked downforce (so wouldn't go round corners). Add to that a track with no grip and you can probably begin to understand that hurtling towards a corner at nearly 200mph on treadless tyres, not knowing if the corner ahead is still just 'greasy' or flooded with rain, can cause a slight rise in the nervous tension in the cockpit.

Ultimately it's always the driver's call to make a stop for tyres, but you are very aware that such a stop will lose the best part of a minute and you always want to wait until you are due fuel at the same time. The worst thing is stopping for wet tyres and then going out to find the rain has gone and now you need to go back in again for slicks. By getting our heads down and sticking to the task we avoided making mistakes and, in the middle of the night, with the rain at its worst, James put in a particularly brilliant double stint which helped see us rise to an amazing fourth place overall! Our big Jaguar was beginning to turn a few heads – but then, just short of half-distance, the crankshaft broke. There are times when this sport just drains your spirit...

The fact that that was pretty much the end of my 1995 season also highlighted how low my racing career had gone. Three international races, all ending in retirement, plus a couple of TV outings in a Ford Mustang and a Maserati Biturbo rounded off by a less than successful return to South Africa for their end-of-year touring car fixture does not a great year make!

However, it was while I was at Le Mans that I first met a certain robust character named Laurence Pearce. Laurence was a former mechanic who'd had the brainwave of bringing the iconic Lister brand, which had built great sportscars in the fifties, back together with the Jaguar engines that had so often powered them. He'd set up Lister Cars Ltd at his Leatherhead base in 1986 and started tuning and restyling Jaguar XJSs before adding the Lister badge and a not inconsiderable premium to the price tag. In the Supercar boom of the late eighties and early nineties they were a huge success, and that encouraged Laurence to go ahead with his dream of building his own road car – the Lister Storm. To show off his machine Laurence had also made a race version which made its debut at Le Mans that year, driven by my old mate Geoff Lees, who was another man looking to reinvent his racing career. When Geoff suggested I head over to see Laurence in Leatherhead with a view to a drive for '96, I had nothing to lose.

Laurence is one of those people whose enthusiasm is completely infectious. 'Yes, that first race car was a bit of a dog, but look at this new one!' From the outside it looked like just another small-time operation that was about to bankrupt itself chasing an impossible dream, but I knew that Geoff was impressed and I respected his opinion. Mind you, when Laurence mentioned he was about to conclude a deal to be sponsored by Newcastle United football club I thought we were back in the fantasy league. However, it turned out that one of his XJS Lister Jaguar customers was Douglas Hall – son of the football club's chairman, Sir John Hall – and before I knew it Geoff and I, with another great friend and refugee from the Japanese 'gaijin' racing drivers' club, Kenneth Acheson, were rolling out an immaculate black and white striped Lister Storm in front of the Toon Army faithful before a home match on the hallowed turf of St James' Park!

So began an on-off love affair with Laurence and his monstrous seven-litre V12 Jaguar-powered beast that would keep my passion for being a racing driver very much alive for the next five years. There wouldn't be that many races, as budgets were always tight, but with Laurence there was never a dull moment.

Most of the first two years were spent developing the Storm into a reliable, race-finishing machine. The speed was there from the word go, but the reliability quite definitely was not. From a driver's point of view the first concern was simply to insulate the engine bay from the cockpit as much as possible, as cockpit temperatures were soaring towards 60° centigrade. With the front-mounted V12 shoved right back under the windscreen, to shift as much weight to the rear as possible, the only thing between the driver's left side and glowing red-hot exhaust pipes was a thin sheet of aluminium honeycomb. You could quite easily fry an egg on the centre console.

The biggest Achilles heel, though, was the gearbox. These were the early days of the pump-action sequential-shift manual gearboxes, and with nearly 600 horsepower being transmitted through them they needed to be strong. Add to that engines supplied by TWR that demonstrated their own fair share of faults and just getting to the finish of a race was an achievement.

With Geoff as the striker, Kenny the midfield dynamo and me cast as the central defender, the Newcastle United team's first fixture was the 1996 Daytona 24 Hours. With the cockpit temperature issue yet to be resolved, it was certainly one of the hottest 24 Hours I had ever driven. Starting 17th on the massive 76-car grid we were pretty much on the GT pace from the word go, but driveshaft problems and a gearbox change gradually dropped us way down – but at least I was back racing in the big time. Thundering round that daunting banking once again, I was still living the dream!

However, with the sports prototype field beginning to grow stronger, for the first time in my career I had to accept that, while busy overtaking cars myself, I had to be constantly aware of the quicker cars coming up behind me. Having always raced cars from the fastest class I now began to appreciate the problems of all those poor drivers I'd cursed on so many previous occasions.

One of the wildest aspects of Daytona were the restarts after pace-car periods – especially at night. The huge crocodile of cars would be formed up in a long snake around the infield section of the circuit and the pace car would pull off and release the pack as it rejoined the banked NASCAR track at Turn 1 – but in America, as soon as the pace car pulls off, you can all start racing! If you were towards the back of the pack you might have 50 cars and four corners between you and that wide open banking, but as soon as you heard 'Green Green Green' over the radio the gloves were off...

Despite all our problems we were determined to make it to the finish, but with just one hour to go a slow Mazda RX-7 came off the Turn 2 banking and began wandering out towards the wall – directly into the gap that Kenny had been aiming for as he approached at something like 50mph faster. With a 76-car grid putting over 300 drivers out on the track, not all are seasoned professionals – and coming across a dopey amateur is one of the greatest hazards of endurance racing. Trying to squeeze through an ever-diminishing gap Kenny just clipped the Mazda with his rear wheel, but at that speed it was enough to tear it off the car. Turning around across the front of the Mazda it looked like the Lister would just take a long 150mph spin across the infield but, without the wheel, the floor dug into the turf and spat the Lister high into the air. Landing on its roof and then back on its wheels, the car was destroyed but mercifully Kenny walked away.

However, the force of the impact had caused slight damage to his vision. While it wasn't bad enough to prevent him from racing again, with the cosmetics company Acheson & Acheson that he'd started up with his wife a few years earlier really beginning to take off, Kenny decided that if he couldn't be 100 per cent committed to his racing it was time to call it a day – so we had to look to the transfer market and find a replacement.

Another happy reunion saw Anthony Reid join us for Le Mans that year, and we qualified ninth in the 25-car GT1 class and 21st overall, right in among a pack of McLaren F1s and Ferrari F40s. Unfortunately Porsche had produced a 911 GT1 homologation special that was about to upset what had been a very healthy GT scene and lead first to the ugly long-tail McLaren versions and then the Mercedes-Benz CLK-GTR which would ultimately be so dominant it killed off the resurgent GT category.

With the Porsches heading for a 1-2 finish in the GT class and second and third overall, the battle was on to be best of the rest, and for the first 14 hours we were right in the mix, hovering just outside the top ten overall. And then the gearbox broke! A disintegrating brake master cylinder didn't help our recovery and nor did an off-song engine, but we made it to the finish, classified 19th overall and 11th in class.

For the rest of the year Geoff and I contested the remaining rounds of the BPR Global GT series run over races of between three and six hours' duration, and we were on course for a podium finish in all of them before problems intervened...

At the Nürburgring we were heading for third when a mounting point on the steering rack broke, leaving me to try and limp the final 20 laps home with decidedly erratic handling. When a second mounting point broke it was game over.

Delighted to be back in Japan for the first time in five years, the six-hour Suzuka sauna bath event was about three hours too long: the gearbox broke yet again while we were in second place. Then, back home at Brands Hatch, we were fighting the fastest McLaren for the honour of being second best to the dominant 911 GT1 and this time it was the engine's turn to fail.

Yet another engine failure early on for Geoff, at Spa, before I'd even had a chance to drive it in the race, was the last straw. It finally persuaded Laurence that if he was going to get anywhere, he was going to have to set up his own engine shop at his Leatherhead base and do the preparation himself. He also realised that, with the rules being stretched by the big manufacturers, he was going to have to build himself a new car.

There was nothing wrong with the old one, though, when we took it back to Daytona for the start of the 1997 season, where the new Porsches were yet to be eligible. We qualified second in class and 15th overall and were firmly in the class lead and up to fourth overall after eight hours when... the gearbox broke. With the gearbox being buried in the middle of the car it was a 90-minute job to change it and, once completed, we ran strongly almost all the way to the finish to be classified, just as at Le Mans, 19th overall but this time a better fourth in class.

A year later we'd return to Daytona for one more time, but now with the new GTL version of the Storm. It was a struggle from the word go with gear-selection and throttle-response problems in qualifying and then, just an hour into the race, a chronic misfire that no amount of rewiring or engine-management alterations could fix. We gave up the struggle!

Mind you, every trip to Daytona was fun with the Newcastle United team because Douglas Hall and Freddy Shepherd – one of the club's key shareholders who, by the last visit in 1998, was the new chairman of the club – would bring out some guests and members of the football press for a bit of February sunshine – and when these boys entertained they did so in style. Everywhere we went we travelled in a pair of huge stretch limos, escorted by police outriders on their bikes, and with lights flashing and sirens wailing. Daytona Beach may be a bit of a sleepy town at that time of year, but they certainly did their best to wake it up a little.

Unfortunately, just a month after that last trip to Daytona, Douglas and Freddy were subjected to a *News of the World* exposé that alleged they had been mocking their own club – even if, to us, they seemed immensely proud of what they had achieved. When it all hit the press I was convinced that at any moment one of the journalists would spot that 'that bloke on Top Gear' was one of their racing drivers and there'd be someone inquisitive on the other end of the phone line, asking all sorts of awkward questions. Fortunately that never happened.

The new GTL model had made its debut at Le Mans the previous year but it hadn't been particularly successful. Not fully sorted, we struggled for both reliability and pace. This time Geoff and I were joined by another star of the Japanese Group C scene, South African George Fouché – and he stuck it off the road with terminal damage on his first race lap. It was hard to know whether to punch him or put an arm round him, because we've all been there at one time or another, and he was a driver renowned for his car control, so we had a few beers and reminisced about the good times back in Japan. Of course at the time I didn't know that that would be my last Le Mans. It was hardly the way I wanted my 15th and final visit to end.

Back home Laurence decided to lick his wounds for a while and concentrate more on the domestic scene. He'd sold a car to American amateur Jake Ulrich to run in the British Championship, and when he was short of a co-driver for a race on the Brands Hatch Indy Circuit I was the man for the job. With races lasting less than an hour, at least the lack of reliability was less of a problem. Putting the car on pole position I'd set the first ever GT lap to average over 100mph and, from the start, stormed off into the lead, set a new lap record and handed over to Jake to cruise to the finish... then the prop shaft broke!

And that was that for 1997. Yes, I'd had some fun doing a bit of rallycross and racing a Vauxhall Vectra and a Formula Vee for the TV cameras, but the Lister frustration was beginning to wear me down. The potential was obvious, but with two 19th-place finishes and eight retirements to show for our efforts, we were hardly packing the shelves with silverware. However, although it was hard to see, there *was* a plus side to our deplorably bad reliability record. No-one, but no-one, would back us to win a season-long championship so to put a bet on such a thing would surely be madness – but that's exactly what we did!

'Prize indemnity' insurance is probably best known for its coverage of hole-in-one prizes at golf tournaments. Insurers will work out the odds of it happening and then offer a premium for the organisers, to insure against them having to pay out the prize. That way, the premium is written into the cost of staging the event and there will be no nasty shocks if a golfer just happens to get lucky. Now a few racing teams seeking to attract young drivers with budgets had seen this and realised it was a way to promise a driver that, if they won a championship driving for their team, they would run them for free the following season – and then insure *against* that happening! So when Laurence found the odds against us winning the 1998 British GT Championship were 50:1 he suggested that if I drove for him for free, he'd pay me £600,000 if we did just that. This would be life-changing money for Patsy and me...

Just to make life a little harder, Laurence decided to build a new one-piece carbon-fibre monocoque version of the GTL for us to race – and he only finished it the day before the first round. Former Lotus

Grand Prix driver Julian Bailey had replaced Geoff Lees as the team's 'striker'. Although he managed to qualify the car third, a damp track allied to a shock-absorber problem combined to pitch him sharp right into the Silverstone pit wall as the field accelerated across the line for the rolling start. One round down, eight to go.

Things weren't that much better at Oulton Park for round two, where the car was an evil beast over the humps and hollows of this great natural racing track. Add in a typical bit of English drizzle and I was elected to start the race from our second position on the grid, with wet tyres like the rest of the front few rows. With nothing to lose, way back in 15th, my old friend Steve O'Rourke, contesting the series in his McLaren F1, opted for slicks. Partnered by his latest hotshot protégé, Tim Sugden, his team had missed the dry first practice, having been away at the Le Mans test session, so they'd had to set their time in the wet. But slicks turned out to be the right choice on the day and the McLaren soon cruised to the front of the field to add a win to their second place at Silverstone while we only salvaged third. The bookies' odds were already looking about right...

An oil leak put us out before we'd even started the third round at Croft, but at Snetterton I put the car on pole position, stormed into the lead, set the fastest lap, handed over to Julian – and we won! It's so nice to have days like that, not just because of the relief of finally winning after all that trauma, but because the answer to the question 'How did you get on?' becomes a simple 'We won!' instead of the usual 'Well, if it hadn't been for...'

We'd turned the corner, but my £600,000 was still a long way off and another horrible wet/dry race at Silverstone saw us robbed of a victory the lap after Julian had brilliantly regained the lead in the dying minutes of the race. Out of our control, an accident had then brought out the red flags and, as the rules dictate, the results were declared from the positions at the end of the previous lap, when we were still second. With O'Rourke having a big off through the gravel yet still managing to escape and finish fourth we were closing – but not closing fast enough!

After a fourth at Donington, where some modifications had only made the handling worse, our hopes for great riches were beginning to fade. Only at the end of the year would Laurence discover a major problem with the construction of the car that had caused all our woes – but there were still three races to go and, if things went our way, the title could still be ours.

We won the two races at Silverstone, but the penultimate round at Spa sealed our fate. Julian had pulled out a big lead while Steve O'Rourke's steady pace had seen the McLaren dropping back into the pack, but then another accident brought out the safety car and closed everyone back up. To make matters worse, Julian's radio had gone dead and he didn't know if the pit-stop window for making driver changes had been reached, so he stayed out. Steve swooped in to hand over to Tim Sugden and it was game over.

If... It's the worst word in motor racing but, apart from our own self-inflicted dramas, if I just pick out one: *if* those two other drivers, whose Voodoo dolls I regularly revisit, had not had those crashes at Silverstone and Spa I would have been £600,000 richer – yes, six hundred thousand pounds richer. Once again I had been so close to pulling off something really big and had just fallen short. The fact that it was my friend Steve O'Rourke, a multi-multi-millionaire thanks to his managing of Pink Floyd, and simply racing for fun, that had come between me and the money somehow made it even more painful.

With the gearboxes now no longer a problem, the engines built in-house and whatever was wrong with our GTL sorted, for the next three years the Lister Storm was the car to beat in the world of GT racing. The only problem was that I was no longer a regular driver of it. When the talented Jamie Campbell-Walter turned up on Laurence's doorstep seeking a drive *and* bringing some sponsorship with him, I quickly found myself back in the reserves and sitting on the subs bench.

While the team stormed to both the British GT1 and GT2 titles in 1999 and then carried Julian and Jamie to the World Drivers' title a year later, I sat on the bench fiddling with my Voodoo dolls! Laurence even got to take his Lister Storm to Monaco and shared the stage with Ferrari at the grand FIA Awards, having claimed the GT Constructors' crown in 2000.

I did get a few rides in international events, but a broken gearbox at Monza – no, it wasn't perfect yet – brake dramas at Zolder and, worst of all, a simple driveshaft failure while dicing for the lead of the 500-mile World Championship round at Silverstone in 1999 were more frustration than satisfaction. At least my life with Lister would have a happy ending.

Brought off the subs bench for a round of the 2000 British GT Championship at Donington I was to share the Lister Storm of David Warnock – my former Jaguar XJR15 owner. In treacherously wet conditions I was more aware than ever that I neither wanted to dent David's Lister nor his chances of adding the GT championship to his 1999 GT2 crown. Fortunately I got the job done – and hopefully the small repair bill from Spa could now be forgotten...

Yet it would be the magnificent Spa-Francorchamps circuit, winding its way up and down the hills of the Ardennes forest, that would be the location for my next call to action in this overseas round of the British Championship. This time I was to partner Dave Clark, who was fed up with being beaten by the Lister in his Chrysler Viper. He'd done a deal to drive one for the last two races and kindly invited me to share the driving.

While we didn't quite have the pace of Warnock's car in Jamie Campbell-Walter's hands, we weren't far short – and with David doing the first stint I was able to pull out a reasonable lead before he handed his car over to Jamie. Out front I was simply revelling in the joys of once again driving a 600 horsepower car round such a demanding racetrack.

There are times when the actual race almost becomes insignificant compared to the sheer pleasure of the challenge of driving such a machine right to its limit, for lap after lap. Diving into Eau Rouge with a minimum of braking, punching down one gear and then firing it up the hill and over the blind crest of Raidillion, blowing away the demons of nine years earlier... magic! Unfortunately it wasn't such a happy return for David Warnock. Although Jamie took the lead from me when I stopped to hand over to Dave, they were soon out of the race when the Jaguar engine in their Lister simply stopped. Again it was my turn for a bit of good fortune and Dave duly drove our Lister to victory on one of the world's greatest circuits.

For the season's finale around the Silverstone Grand Prix Circuit, Laurence had installed his main striker, Julian Bailey, as Warnock's co-driver – and with an outside shot at the title still a possibility, the pressure was on. Niggling problems in practice had left Dave and me down in sixth on the grid and, yet again, it was to be a very wet race. By the end of the third lap I'd deprived Warnock of his second place and was heading off after the leader. There were no team orders in play here! A lap later I was in the lead, and getting my head down to hand over as big an advantage as I could to Dave. In the end I needn't have worried because, matching Bailey's lap times in ever worsening conditions, David held on for another brilliant win.

The result didn't deprive Warnock of the title as he needed his rivals to fall by the wayside and they didn't. It might not have been the perfect day for Lister, but it was the perfect end to what would turn out to be my last race in one of these brutal machines. To end with a hat-trick of victories around three Grand Prix circuits could hardly be better. The only disappointment was that Laurence wouldn't let me keep the car!

With my 49th birthday now only three weeks away I could hardly complain that my professional driving career looked to be all over. However, not being one ever to talk about retirement, I was delighted to make a brief return to the international scene some six years later, sharing Virgin Mobile supremo Tom Alexander's Aston Martin DBRS9 in three of the rounds of the 2006 FIA GT3 European Championship at Silverstone, Oschersleben and, once again, back at Spa.

Having met Tom at a telephone awards presentation where I had been the compere, I'd discovered he was a complete car fanatic and had been a very promising member of the British karting team when he was younger. Faced with the decision of whether to chase his racing dream or go into business he'd probably made the right decision, as he had turned out to be one of the great innovators in the telecoms industry.

By now my brother Chris had become the commercial director of

Barwell Motorsport, which was run by successful racing driver Mark Lemmer. Chris's own racing aspirations had quickly run out of money and he'd spent some time as a motor racing journalist and then a Ford PR man before joining Barwell. When the new Formula BMW single-seater championship was introduced in 2004 they had run two cars in the series and Tom had seen a good opportunity to promote the Virgin Mobile brand in this exciting new series. Tom himself was already campaigning one of his much-loved Aston Martin DB4s in the Heritage GT series and he asked me to share the driving with him. The few outings we did brought a lot of fun plus a win and a second to show for our efforts, but Tom was now keen to move into something more contemporary and asked Barwell to run the DBRS9 for him. In effect, I was now driving for my younger brother!

With Tom a few seconds off the pace our joint efforts combined to produce a best result of ninth in the first race at Spa. The newly launched championship had proved a huge success, and with up to 42 cars on the grid representing eight different supercar manufacturers it was incredibly competitive. Unfortunately our best result had come, as the red flags flew at Spa when torrential rain flooded the circuit and I found myself a passenger heading for the tyre wall. With the count-back system in operation we remained in the results, but the damage was too much for me to take my hard-earned third place on the grid for the second race – fastest of the six Aston Martins.

My only other international race that year was an invitation to the Pro-Celebrity event supporting the Bahrain Grand Prix where I was to partner Status Quo superstar Rick Parfitt in one of the 16 identical V8 Holden Luminas imported from Australia especially for the occasion.

Pretty pleased to qualify fourth behind two factory Holden drivers and Martin Brundle, I would enjoy lining up ahead of the likes of Johnny Herbert and Bruno Senna. Getting to know not just the very personable young Brazilian, en route to following his illustrious uncle into Formula One, but also sports stars like Michael Jordan and Steve Redgrave made for a most enjoyable trip – even if I had to accept that the most exciting thing my new rock legend mate now ingested were copious cups of tea. The fact that we managed to finish fourth at least showed that Rick's talent wasn't just limited to the Quo's famous three-chord trick!

But that, really, was that. I had eased past my 55th birthday and offers to race on the international stage had eventually stopped coming – not that I would ever be heard to use the 'retire' word. Fortunately there still remained one annual fix to feed my continuing desire to race – the Goodwood Revival Meeting.

CHAPTER 20

OUT OF TOP GEAR...

While the 'Top Gear' boom of the mid-nineties had seen my role expand into presenting the 'Motorsport' and 'Waterworld' offshoots, Jeremy Clarkson was fast becoming a major star in his own right. Between 'Top Gear' commitments, he had created his own 'Motorworld' and 'Extreme Machines' series and then, at the end of 1998, he began his own chat show simply called 'Clarkson'. With so much going on, he decided he'd had enough of driving around in cars talking to cameras and waved goodbye to 'Top Gear'. It was obviously a big blow to the show and, with viewing numbers already on a gentle downward trend from our peak figures as our novelty wore off, the ratings unsurprisingly sagged even faster.

The producer's first move was to poach motoring journalist James May from Channel 4's new motoring programme 'Driven' and install him in Jeremy's place, but after just one series they changed their minds and dropped him – and James would have to wait five years before he could be 'discovered' again! The drop in ratings was creating all sorts of uncertainties, even though it was entirely understandable, and in any case we were still one of the most viewed of BBC Two programmes.

But it was the spring of 1999 that brought in sweeping changes. Jane Root had been appointed as the new Controller of BBC Two, the first woman to be a channel controller for the BBC, and it soon became clear that her vision for programmes didn't include 'Top Gear' in its current guise. Neither 'Motorsport' nor 'Waterworld' would be recommissioned and 'Top Gear' itself was going to have a serious overhaul. We were told that the magazine format of the programme was no longer acceptable and that our shows would need to have 'strands' running through them. They would need to start with a challenge, survive with a bit of drama and then end with a conclusion. The well-proven formula of just providing four or five different items appealing to a broad range of motoring interests had to go.

To manage our makeover Jane persuaded Julie Clive, one of her former colleagues from the private sector, out of her Californian retirement, and installed her in the 'Top Gear' office of Birmingham's Pebble Mill television studios to produce the programme. The lovely Kate Humble was brought in to front the new look alongside Quentin Willson, with Vicki being told the move had been made to 'bring a bit of glamour into the show'! The rumour was that I was lucky to be there at all and only some strong support from the *Top Gear* magazine team had kept me in the frame. Brendan – brother of Steve – Coogan was another new face, and they even employed a comedy scriptwriter to try and inject more humour into our items.

While Kate and Quentin were tasked with guiding our viewers through whatever 'strand' each programme demanded, in as light and fluffy a manner as they could, I was at least left to get on and do my segment of the show pretty much as I had always done. I was told, though, to untuck my shirt, put 'product' in my hair and try to use a lot less of those confusing numbers relating to power and speed!

Unfortunately a new habit started to creep in where the item you thought you'd finished wasn't quite the same as the one you saw when the programme went out – last-minute cuts were being made. The normal process was that you would create your script and film an item in collaboration with your director. He would then return to Pebble Mill and cut the item with an editor to the length of time the producer allotted him, using the words spoken to camera and adding the music but leaving 'spaces' where extra words would be added in the final dubbing session.

I'd then head up to Birmingham, look at the final item, perhaps agree some small changes and then record the extra words that completed the story. As the presenter of the item, I've always felt it was 'my' opinion that was being broadcast and not the 'programme's' and that's a very important journalistic standpoint. But now when I watched 'my' items go out there would sometimes be bits missing which hadn't been discussed with me and which could often change the whole balance of my report...

But, doing my best to ignore the politics, I was still making a lot of fun items – even if one of them took me closer to killing myself than I'd like to think. The story was to be the 'Top Gear' contribution to the 1999 Red Nose Day in aid of Comic Relief and the theme that year was record breakers. Now some people came up with fun ideas like 'the most naked people on a stage at one time', but our researchers decided on something a little more adventurous – like the 'the fastest lap of a UK circuit in a production car'! According to the *Guinness Book of Records*, the mark I had to beat was the 180.4mph average set around Millbrook's two-mile Bowl by journalist Colin Goodwin in a Jaguar XJ220S, and there was only one thing I wanted to do it in – a McLaren F1! Fortunately McLaren were up for the challenge and armed with their final prototype model we were ready for the task.

As the Bowl is part of the Proving Ground's non-stop, 24-hours-a-day testing facility it's very rare that it is totally empty. While for normal filming at anything up to 150mph they are more or less happy for you to share the five lanes of varying banking with their test traffic, they didn't want to risk it with me going round like a jet fighter, so we were offered the quietest moments of the week: the Saturday and Sunday lunch hours.

Day one – and it was raining! Our hour was a waste of time but I could at least use it to check our timing equipment and I warmed up with an average of 170.8mph. If I could do that in the wet the record should be easily in our grasp. The question was, just how fast could I go in the dry?

Fortunately it was dry on the Sunday, even if it was a very cold 5°C February day with a biting wind that made it feel even colder – and a wind that would cause me problems I hadn't even envisaged! With the production-car rules dictating I must use standard road tyres we knew the rubber would be the limiting factor. And with the outside lane 'hands free' at 100mph, anything over that and the steering would progressively load up as you had to hold the car down and away from the rather rusty-looking guardrail. With such a constant loading the tread of the tyre would just get hotter and hotter until it fell apart, so Michelin had advised us to do only four-lap runs and constantly monitor the tyre pressures and temperatures. The problem was that with the road surface being so cold, the tyres quickly lost whatever temperature they had on the slowing-down lap so it was hard to check them accurately...

Setting out to build up to speed slowly, not even using full throttle and 'cruising' at a steady 6,000rpm in sixth gear, I breezed to a new record of 183mph on my first run. The speedometer was set in kilometres and there were so many numbers on it I couldn't take my eyes off the road for long enough to read what they were. All I knew was that 6,700rpm in sixth was 200mph, and in my mind that was the target!

A run at 6,300rpm, still not quite holding the throttle wide open, produced a figure of 191.5mph, but the wind was now gusting at 20mph and causing me plenty of problems. The sheer speed was now feeling incredibly fast – I was covering 100 metres every second and my eyes were staring as far ahead as possible out of the top of the screen. The jump from 170 to 180mph seemed like nothing, but every extra 5mph now began to feel like a huge step – and the wind was exaggerating it!

For the first half of the lap the wind was behind me and to my left, pushing me up towards that guardrail and adding yet more load to the steering which, with no power assistance, was now trying to pull my arms out of their sockets. But, as I rounded the Bowl, the nose of the car gradually turned directly into the wind and then, in a flash, it was on my right and pushing the nose of the car down the banking. The transition from one to the other was over in a fraction, but the car was darting up and down and I was now very busy with the steering, trying to hang on to it.

Our hour was almost over and, for the first time, I reached full throttle in sixth. The extra acceleration was astounding. Crossing the line the rev counter eased round to 6,800rpm, but as I came round into the headwind the car was now buffeting around so dramatically that I had to ease off to get through the transition. Once settled, the throttle was back to full and I headed for the line – but suddenly the rear of the car was moving around and, as I lifted to try and control it, it only got worse: the tail was quite definitely wagging the dog! At 200mph the heat build-up had caused the tyres to blister and I had to wrestle the speed off with my heart in my mouth. Millbrook wasn't designed for 200mph accidents and nor was the McLaren. I'd nearly killed myself in the name of Comic Relief but the day was done, with 195.3mph the new record and 200.8mph the registered top speed.

Another couple of highlights that year were two rare, far-away expeditions to bring something a bit different to the 'Top Gear' screens. The only way the tight budgets allowed us to justify a long-haul flight anywhere was if we went for, say, three days and came back with three stories. With budget airline tickets and basic accommodation they were exhausting trips – but a lot of fun.

In October '99, five of us headed for the Malaysian Peninsula – me, director, camera, sound and, this time, the luxury of a researcher – with the first stop being Singapore to do a story about their very advanced integrated traffic system. After a day's travel and two days chasing through the hustle and bustle of Singapore, filming in oppressive heat and humidity, we then needed to work until way past midnight on the second day to grab a quick extra story on their 'Car Park' rally scene – yes, that is a serious motorsport out there.

Next morning it was back to the airport for a flight to Kuala Lumpur and a trip to the old Shah Alam racetrack. This venue used to hold a non-championship Malaysian Grand Prix and, since its closure, I will forever hold the lap record after my Formula Pacific forays there in the early 1980s.

Day five and we visited the brand-new Sepang International Circuit which, just two weeks later, was to host the first World Championship Malaysian Grand Prix. While doing a story on the track I also squeezed in a road test of the new, locally built Proton Satria GTi that I was driving. A trip into Kuala Lumpur for a splendid meal – and far too much alcohol – in the revolving restaurant at the top of the KL Tower courtesy of our Proton hosts completed the fun and games, before it was time to get up, exhausted and early, for the flight home... a brilliant trip.

Just a couple of months later and I was back on budget airlines, this time heading west for the bright lights of Las Vegas and an appointment with Carroll Shelby, his new Shelby Series 1, the new Lexus RX300 and a Ford F150 SVT Lightning pick-up truck. Sadly it all started to go wrong from the moment we arrived.

I'd flown direct to Vegas while the director, who shall remain nameless (Graham Sherrington), had gone via Los Angeles to pick up the pick-up! By the time we all gathered at the far from glamorous 'Howard Johnson Inn Las Vegas Strip' we had our first problem: we would only be able to film the Ford from one side because the other had been driven into by a Hollywood blonde! Well, that was Graham's story anyway.

Over the next few days we would film the Shelby on the Las Vegas Speedway Outfield Road Course, drive to Boulder City to do a piece on the Lexus with the Hoover Dam as a backdrop for a bit of drama, and then it was back to Vegas to try and do something with the one-sided Ford. We obviously cruised the Strip, constantly worried we'd get pulled over for not having some sort of filming permit or other, and somehow we persuaded the front-of-door staff at Circus Circus to allow us to film my arrival there by telling them we were making a corporate video for Ford – with just a three-man crew and a dented pick-up!

We then decided that the rugged image of this very American trend ought to be put to the test in the surrounding desert so, ignoring road signs peppered with bullet holes, we headed off up some tracks to start filming.

First word of warning: if you want to try this, keep to the tracks because if you attempt to turn round off them your rear wheels will collapse into burrow holes made by who-knows-what and it'll take you two hours to dig yourselves out with the odd twig or two lying around...

Second word of warning: don't try jumping over any crests at speed because, rugged though these all-terrain 'veehickles' might look, the sump of the engine is surprisingly low and unprotected. Of course you won't know that you've cracked your sump and all your oil has drained out until the oil light comes on and your engine makes a nasty rattling sound! So now you have to leave the car alone in a bullet-riddled desert and head back to civilisation to buy copious amounts of oil, chewing gum (to seal the crack), tape (to hold the chewing gum in place) and bottles of STP oil treatment (to try and minimise the engine damage).

By some miracle the engine sort of survived and we managed to get the few extra shots we needed – from the right side, of course, and with the 'ticking' noise of the damaged bearing just about audible on the soundtrack. With it now being a weekend there was no-one from Ford to contact about our predicament – and on the Sunday we were scheduled to drive it 250 miles back to Los Angeles to catch our flights home!

As I had broken it, I was elected to do the driving. With the dented door taped up to keep the wind noise down, and with the radio off, I would drive in sympathy with the tune of the ticking sound from the engine. Up hills, as the load increased, it would get louder and louder and I would have to ease back off the throttle to quieten it, while it would almost disappear as we cruised down the other side and I could gently build up speed again. Somehow we made it without the con rod detaching itself from the crankshaft and parked it, as agreed, in the airport car park with the key in a magnetic box under the chassis – and a long letter of apology! Quite what the driver who had delivered this pristine, top-of-the-range pick-up truck just five days earlier thought when he came to collect it we'll never know. More letters of apology were dispatched upon our return, but the reaction was simply one of stunned silence...

Unfortunately, while I was having fun making my own items for the show, the 'Top Gear' ratings were still dropping. The impression we had from above was that this was demonstrating that perhaps there was no longer much enthusiasm for a car show on television; the impression I got from everyone in the car industry was that the new format was just too lightweight for our core audience.

The show rolled into the new century with a very uncertain future. Kate was doing great work, but the new-born theory that a good presenter could present anything was wearing a bit thin when she was given words to describe the handling of a car and yet it was clear from her driving style that they weren't her words. Meanwhile I was dispatched on a shopping trip to Selfridges with a stylist to help buy me new clothes – but still the ratings dropped! By now we were under the three-million mark, still matching other specialist programmes for gardeners, DIY addicts and makeover fanatics but nowhere near the numbers of the good old days. On the plus side, at least my Grand Prix experience was on the up as I got to blast around Barcelona in one of Jaguar's brand-new R1 Formula One cars.

In the middle of 2000 it was all change again. Julie Clive had gone, and so had Kate Humble, as Jane Root moved to poach another 'Driven' presenter, Jason Barlow, and promote him to be our new front man, with his smooth Northern Irish brogue. Unsurprisingly, this ruffled a few feathers of the existing team. Richard Pearson and John Wilcox were the new producers, while Quentin had already decided to jump from the leaking ship to concentrate on trying to make a million or two selling cars on the internet. The team therefore now consisted of just me, Vicki, Jason and new recruit Adrian Simpson – after a young Granada TV 'Men and Motors' presenter called Richard Hammond had been turned down for the second time...

I did manage to hop on another mission to America to cheer myself up, filming on the set of the film *Swordfish*, although sadly neither John Travolta nor Halle Berry were anywhere to seen. The 'other' star of the film was a TVR Tuscan and it was thanks to the company's PR man, Ben Samuelson, that we enjoyed the nightlife of Hollywood. Ben's sister is 'Dynasty' star Emma Samms so he knew where to go, and he booked us into the Mondrian Hotel with its famous Sky Bar. We then went for a beer at the infamous Viper Room, failing to see any of the trendy young Hollywood set that frequent it, and the House of Blues, where we did see the legendary John Lee Hooker playing live at the age of 88, just seven months before he died.

I also managed to squeeze in filming my own video for the Christmas stocking market. Jeremy Clarkson seemed to be making a fortune every year so I thought I might as well give it a bash too. Produced by 'Banana Split Productions' it was *subtly* entitled *Burning Rubber*! Showing the world how to do handbrake turns, reverse flicks and 360-degree spins interspersed by some Russ Swift stunt driving and a blast in a Lister Storm, I was quite proud with what we came up with on a tight budget. Mind you, I soon discovered that if you haven't got the big name and resources to stack every store with well-displayed copies you're not going to sell as many as you hoped. While it failed to become a big seller I was still happy I'd done it – and particularly pleased with a complete roll in a Reliant Robin while talking to the camera...

With all the chopping and changing of the 'Top Gear' line-up the viewing figures were now down in the low two millions and even dropped below that mark on the odd occasion. By the time we reached the end of 2000 and the finish of the 44th series of 'Top Gear' we all knew the days of the programme were numbered. The rumour was that after the next series, that would be it.

We were being told that the falling figures proved there was simply no longer enough of a demand for a car show on television – a show that some perhaps didn't want at all. We'd suggested that with a little bit more money and the very occasional use of a helicopter we could make some much more dramatic items, but we were told quite firmly that there was no way there was any more money available for the show.

For over 20 years there had been two series of 'Top Gear' every year, one in the spring and one in the autumn, so little did we expect the 45th series to run and run all the way through the next year. The story was that even though we were on the way out, not enough new programmes were on the way in. However, with far less interference, we were now pretty much left to make the show the way we wanted to make it.

With the four of us concentrating on our journalistic and driving strengths we began to make programmes that *we* were once again proud of, and for the week ending 22 July we were the most-watched programme on BBC Two, with an audience of 3.2 million. However, we all knew it was to no avail. By now the rumours were in full swing that it was all going to come to an end and neither *Top Gear* magazine nor BBC Worldwide, who were spreading our fame across the globe, seemed to be able to do anything about it. I wrote a letter to Jane Root addressing our concerns but didn't even receive the courtesy of a reply. It was time to start planning for life after 'Top Gear'!

By now Richard Pearson had been lured away from the BBC to set up Chrysalis Entertainment (Midlands) as a regional offshoot of the London TV group and he'd brought with him former 'Top Gear' researcher Emma Shaw. Chrysalis also happened to be where Jeremy had produced his chat show with his old friend Andy Wilman who, just to complete the circle, had also been an occasional 'Top Gear' presenter in the mid-nineties. So a lunch with Richard seemed to be a good first step. For a while we tried desperately to invent a completely new format of motoring programme to offer to other channels before realising that we already had one that was pretty good.

Now we were both good friends with the team that made the shows out of the BBC Pebble Mill studios and we knew they would be more than pleased to follow us wherever we went. Richard presented our idea to his London superiors, they made a presentation to Channel Five and, before even we could believe it, 'Fifth Gear' was ready for take-off.

With a spring back in my step and some sort of future assured it was an early 50th birthday present for me. Having worked out the cost of a party to celebrate with my friends I did exactly what they expected of me: I booked Patsy and myself into the luxurious care of the Four Seasons in the Maldives for ten days!

With the 'Fifth Gear' plans being formulated in Birmingham's Chrysalis office by Richard and Emma, Jon Bentley – who had both produced and presented 'Top Gear' – and the young talents of Graham Sherrington, James Woodroffe and Phil Churchward were tempted away from their BBC Midlands posts as the 'Top Gear' team continued its move to Channel Five. Jason Barlow was tied to the BBC on a two-year contract so wasn't available, and the decision was made to ask Quentin to come back and complete the four-presenter line-up alongside Vicki, Adrian and me. Best faces on, and we're ready for a secret photo shoot on 11 November – with 'Top Gear' still having a month to run.

Of course, keeping any of this secret with so many people involved was never going to be possible, and the rumours were soon doing the rounds to the extent that the press started running stories about the move – so much so that Jane Root issued an internal email to all BBC staff on 16 November stating quite categorically that 'Top Gear' was not moving to Channel Five. It went on to claim that 'the BBC remains committed to the programme which still pulls in big audiences for the channel' and that a 'new series will go out next year' – but quite what that was going to be no-one seemed to know!

In fact, with Richard also working on future programme ideas with Jeremy and Andy down at Chrysalis in London, we already knew that, having been embarrassed by the 'Fifth Gear' publicity, Jane Root – realising he was the BBC's only hope – had approached Jeremy to see if he would be interested in returning to 'Top Gear' – and Channel Five was also trying to tempt him to join us. All of a sudden money for 'Top Gear' didn't seem to be such a problem. Jeremy wasn't sure if he wanted to do it, in any case, but to be fair his final decision wasn't based so much on the money being offered as the extra opportunities that working for the BBC could offer him... so, having said he never would, he was now on his way back! I honestly believe, though, that if we hadn't created 'Fifth Gear', 'Top Gear' would have quietly disappeared from our screens for all time.

I filmed my last item for 'Top Gear' on 16 November, driving the new Mini Cooper, and provided my final voiceover for the item on 3 December 2001. Leaving the Pebble Mill studios with a very heavy heart, I felt both frustrated and sad that it had come to this. Always one keen to wave the flag, I'd loved working for the BBC and was very proud of its reputation all over the world. I'd also been presenting the World Rally Championship from London's BBC Television Centre, but that too had been dropped. After 15 years of making 'Top Gear' at Pebble Mill, to leave it all behind was a big wrench – and I would have felt even sadder if I had known then that after all those years of loyal service there would be no gold watch, no champagne send-off, not even a simple letter of thanks...

CHAPTER 21

AND INTO FIFTH GEAR!

The breath of fresh air that greeted us at Channel Five was like a warm tropical breeze welcoming us to a new world! Dan Chambers was the man in charge of our programme and his was a confidence-inspiring manner that made you feel wanted. As with my motor racing career, where I performed best with a supportive team manager, this was something I'd been missing lately.

After a flashy London hotel launch on 25 March the first programme of 'Fifth Gear' went out on 8 April 2001 and my first item was a road test of a new breed of Supercar – the Pagani Zonda. We were up and running in style. Where the McLaren F1 would define my nineties 'Top Gear' days, the Zonda was definitely *my* car for the noughties of 'Fifth Gear'. Of course we were never going to get the size of audience we could reach on the BBC because, for some reason that defies logic, most viewers rarely seem to get past channels one, two and three but, with a weekly repeat, we would soon start attracting nearly two million viewers and that seemed to make everyone happy enough. How you quantify a good audience still bemuses me. After all, that's the same sort of viewing *total* that the two main channels spend millions upon millions of pounds fighting over with their breakfast-time shows!

I wasn't just a car-show presenter now, either, as Dan put me forward for presenting series such as 'World's Greatest', 'Extreme Engineering' and 'Superships', while I also voiced a history of aviation series called 'Flight Fantastic' that took me back to my Fairey days. And then Vicki and I joined Jenson Button in a 'Be a Grand Prix Driver' series where three hundred contestants were whittled down to just one – Mark Johnston – who got to race a Grand Prix Tyrrell at Monza.

In the first year of 'Fifth Gear' I not only drove the Zonda but also a Lamborghini Murciélago. I still distinctly remember the Italian PR lady insisting I pronounce it 'Mercy-el-igo' – even though none of us ever do – and then I upset more Italians at Ferrari by turning off the traction-control system when I tested their Ferrari Enzo Ferrari – to give it its full name.

The Enzo story does have a bit of background to it because it was yet another typically Italian trip to Ferrari's own Fiorano test track where, with ten or so fellow-journalists queuing up, you are strictly rationed by the number of laps you are allowed. There are definite rules to be obeyed if you ever want to be asked back! Understandable, I guess, when a manufacturer is letting a bunch of unknown quantities loose in their extremely expensive motor cars.

If, however, you do want to discover the full performance of the car, then on hand to demonstrate it to you is their legendary test driver, Dario Benuzzi. Treated by the Italians with the same respect as if he were one of Ferrari's Grand Prix drivers, Dario has been responsible for the testing and development of every production Ferrari since the 246 Dino. He has the most divine amount of car control and feel, yet he's never turned his hand to any serious racing.

I'd first met Dario at the launch of the F50 in the mid-nineties where, as with the Enzo, the test ration was just three laps. Speaking very little English, he'd used an interpreter to talk us through driving the F50 round Fiorano, with specific mention as to which gear you should be in where. Now, having run driving days myself, it was pretty obvious he was doing what I would do by suggesting corners be taken in a higher gear wherever possible to keep the engine out of the higher power band – and us journalists out of the barriers!

Of course when I came to drive the car I was a gear lower almost everywhere, winding the rev counter round to 8,000rpm where the wailing V12 gave its full 520 horsepower whenever I could. No-one seemed either to notice or care that I'd been having a little play, happy that their car was simply back in one piece, but at the end-of-the-day debrief, when questions were called for, I thought I might just open a 'driving style' debate. I ventured to suggest to Dario that it would surely be quicker to use the lower gears. Well, I'm not sure exactly how well the translation went, but from the look that Dario gave me I got the distinct impression that he thought I was suggesting I knew better than him how to drive *his* Ferrari round *his* test track, and the answer was a very short 'No'! Ever since then, on my occasional return, I'd got that look that seemed to say 'There's that idiot of an Englishman again' and, unlike the normal me, somehow I was never tempted to try and reopen the debate and inevitably dig myself a deeper hole.

I'd explained all this to James Woodroffe, who had now worked his way up from being the 'Top Gear' tea boy to a full-blown director on 'Fifth Gear', and the storyline for the item was very much his creation. It is one that is still much talked about. We spent most of the day waiting for our slot and, as the tension of the day built up, I was very much aware of Dario's briefing – where he had stressed that in no way should we turn off the traction control on the Enzo – that was for him to do and for us to watch. Well, you can't get a real feel for the car without turning it off and, encouraged by James, that's exactly what I did. Once again, having not crashed, nothing was said, but this time I headed straight for Dario and thanked him personally for creating such a wonderful machine – and I *think* we are friends now!

Like James, who would go on to produce the show, Emma Shaw and Phil Churchward had also become enthusiastic directors, and would soon be joined by the likes of Ian Bayliss, Mark McQueen, Ben Mann and James Redgate – all tasked with making me look good.

With Chrysalis now running our show we were much more masters of our own budget, able to penny-pinch here and there and then splash out for a big item. On one occasion we used former BBC presenter Mike Smith to get some memorable shots of me powersliding the Ferrari F430 Spider round Snetterton from his specially rigged helicopter camera. There was some equally spectacular stuff when I raced a Porsche 911GT3 against a Gazelle helicopter round Croft.

In trying slowly to evolve the shape of the show – instead of knee-jerking here and there – we also started doing a series of accident simulations and, for those who saw them, they did far more for road safety than any number of speed cameras stuck on poles. Our first, and I still think our best, was simply to drive two cars into each other, both travelling at 60mph. I say 'simply', but it actually entailed some very clever work by a team of radio-control boffins to make them hit head on but with an overlap of half a car.

With two not so old executive saloons from BMW and Volvo you might think you would really be able to survive just such a country-lane accident, especially when you see the clinical tests of cars hitting concrete blocks at 30mph that leave the passenger cells relatively unaffected – but how wrong you would be. Standing level with the impact point, the violence of the crash left us all shocked in disbelief. The damage done to the cars left none of us with any thoughts other than that the results would have been fatal. Just reach for those sweets in the glove box, look down to install a CD, pull the steering wheel down slightly as you do so and, in an instant, that could be any of us. The memory still haunts me now.

To reduce road fatalities we need to spend a lot less time fussing over petty speeding offences and a lot more time persuading people simply to concentrate much, much more on what they are supposed to be doing... driving the car.

I went on another wonderfully exhausting mission to Los Angeles to test drive the new Nissan 350Z and the H2 Hummer, as well as filling in with stories about illegal street racing and some skydiving lunatics who were exiting planes sitting in cars! Once again, the hotel left a fair amount to be desired and there were dramas from the word go. Before we'd even filmed anything our rented minivan woke up with two mysteriously flat tyres in the hotel car park, and then the crew got T-boned by a drunk at an intersection. By the time we'd acquired a new van half a precious day was gone, but at least it gave us plenty of time to play the 'name your breakfast' game.

You can play this anywhere in America. The challenge is to order your entire breakfast without the waitress needing to ask a single supplementary question. Now, if you've never been there this might sound quite simple, but if you have you'll know there are about five ways to cook your eggs, five types of coffee, five types of bread and a series of different combinations that can go together within a single order. One of the crew *almost* got it right once but then, right at the end, after a small pause, made the fatal mistake of saying, 'Oh, and an orange juice please.' 'Large or small, sir?' Doh!

Back to the filming and we headed for Steve McQueen's favourite road, through the Malibu Creek State Park, where I unfortunately had a small puncture problem of my own. With a strong overhead sun, while driving the Nissan and talking to my onboard camera, it had been necessary to mount quite a bright light on the bonnet shining into my face to stop my beautiful features becoming just a black shadow. Now I'd done this many times before and, while it does very slightly restrict your vision, it really isn't a problem – unless there's a huge pothole right in the middle of the white line that's guiding you down the edge of the very narrow road. Boom, boom... two bent rims and *two* flat tyres! I drove slowly back to our temporary base at a deserted tourist hut and we tried to make a plan.

Inevitably, there was no phone signal, and we desperately needed to get on with filming the story. We'd not done the walk round the car yet, to introduce it, so while the soundman headed off to call the cavalry, we made that the next job. Starting on the side with the two good tyres I told one half of the story and then, labouring away in the boiling sun, swapped the wheels from one side to the other before completing this simple, 40-second piece to camera. Then, in the middle of it all, a park ranger arrived and demanded to see our filming permit – which of course we didn't have!

A day trip to the Grand Canyon National Park provided us with some dramatic shots of the Hummer flying across the desert landscape, and then it was back to LA to spend the evening *and* the early hours of the next morning unsuccessfully trying to track down the street racers. The story about the sky 'drivers', as they like to call themselves, was a simple interview and we were ready for a relaxed night out before an early trip to the airport and home the next morning.

The dramas weren't over, however, because we woke up to find the Hummer sitting like a circus elephant on its bottom, with both its two huge rear tyres as flat as flat can be, slashed through the sidewalls with a knife. The director blamed the hotel car park phantom while I blamed the director for not tipping the waitress enough the night before. No, I'm not going to name him here – but the Graham Sherrington jinx had struck again!

I had to forgive Graham, though, when he directed a 'James Bond Special' for me to present. He created a brilliant programme that saw me driving the road-going versions of many of the famous film cars, in locations that re-created their Bond roles – including getting a Lotus Esprit stuck on a beach near Brighton. I even got to drive the Aston Martin Vanquish, complete with all its gadgets, on the RAF Little Rissington set of the latest *Die Another Day* film; sadly my suggestion that I was made for the role fell on deaf ears...

By now 'Top Gear' was back on air, Jeremy and Andy Wilman having come up with a brilliant new format, and while their presenter line-up still needed a bit of tinkering, they were obviously on to a good thing. Richard Hammond's dream of being a 'Top Gear' presenter had finally come true and I often muse at the thought that if the close decision between Adrian Simpson and Richard had gone the latter's way he would most probably have been with us on 'Fifth Gear' – and the whole future of crashing jet cars and the evolution of 'Top Gear' would have taken a completely different path. Such are the mysterious ways of the world.

I also like to think there's a little bit of me in the Stig – indeed, for a long time many thought it *was* me, and some people *still* think I am doing a bit of moonlighting from 'Fifth Gear'! I knew the BBC had been thinking about who would play the part of the tame racing driver for the new programme, to cover some of the items I used to do, and I'd heard that they'd auditioned a few female racing drivers to see if they could find one who fitted the bill. So, when I first saw Jeremy, Richard and Jason Dawe as the presenters, I was a bit confused about who was going to do the fast driving – and then they revealed the Stig. Brilliant!

Like 'Top Gear', we also began to involve celebrities from other fields of entertainment in some of our items and, among a variety of missions, I had the pleasure of rolling one of Jamiroquai front man Jay Kay's off-road buggy racers while chasing him round a field at his home. Jay is completely car mad and has one of the most fabulous collections, and he's also reasonably handy behind the wheel. He was another of the celebs in that Bahrain Holden race and he's always been one of the fastest round a test track – and, as he's quick to point out, it wasn't him driving when his Lamborghini got stuffed…

I also taught Heston Blumenthal how to slice cucumbers – with a knife sticking out of the front of a BMW M5 and the cucumber standing up on top of a post – refereed for the unbeaten, undisputed champion of the world of boxing, Joe Calzaghe, as he lost his crown in a head to head with his girlfriend Jo-Emma, driving off-road Bowler Wildcats, and got rolled in the hay by John Barrowman! Teaching celebrities to drive is always a fairly nerve-racking experience, partly because they all want to impress, but also because to get where they are in their own worlds they all have huge amounts of self-confidence. In a car, though, the difference between confidence and overconfidence can be quite dramatic.

The hay-rolling scene took place on one of the stages used by the World Rally Championship in the Sweet Lamb complex of South Wales. The challenge was for John to set a competitive time in a 270 horsepower full rally spec Group N Subaru Impreza – and he was fully up for the task. Bubbling with enthusiasm, like a kid with a new toy, I sat alongside him and did my best to teach him the basics in an open area, with a course marked out of cones, before we headed for the narrow tracks of the rally stage. From the word go it was obvious that he had a lot of natural driving ability and his sense of balance was good, but his approach was fairly gung-ho to say the least.

As is so often the way, we'd survived a couple of laps of our test stage and probably done sufficient to complete the item for the programme, and John had certainly been quick enough, but of course he wanted to do more. The excitement, the adrenaline… I could see by the concentration he was putting into it that he was revelling in the occasion. Then came those fatal words, 'Okay, you can have one more run!'

We made it all the way to the very final corner – but we didn't make it *round* the corner. It was the trickiest section of the lap because the corner was preceded by a jump, and you had to brake as soon as you landed. Of course, if you took the jump a bit faster you needed to brake even harder as soon as you landed… We made it half-way round, but by then we were already sliding wide towards the edge of the narrow loose track – and over the edge it was downhill across the lumpy grassland all the way to a stream below. Once off the road the wheels quickly dug into the soft earth and over we went. Two quick rolls accompanied by expensive crunching sounds and then silence – soon to be broken by John's expletive-filled reaction. Thanks to all the modern safety devices we were completely unharmed, and by rally standards it was a fairly ordinary accident, but inevitably it would make front-page news the next day, with all the usual 'Barrowman narrowly escapes death' headlines!

'Fifth Gear' had soon become one of the success stories of Channel Five, as their overall audience share steadily grew. By the end of 2005 we were producing a one-hour show hosted from our new Birmingham offices, where Chrysalis Entertainment (Midlands) had now become North One Television Midlands. Quentin Willson and Adrian Simpson had moved on, to be replaced by motoring journalist Tom Ford and racing driver Jason Plato. Jason had been part of the 'Driven' programme which was taken off air by Channel 4 at the end of 2002 – also after a drastic makeover had turned the traditional viewers away.

Unfortunately 2006 saw a downturn in Channel Five's overall audience share, which led to Dan Chambers departing his job as director of programmes. Dan was someone who had always made the effort to show his appreciation for the work that we were doing and I, for one, was very sad to see him go. New faces now became involved in dictating the future look of our programme.

While 'Fifth Gear' had been my main focus, I hadn't quite lost touch with my old friends from the BBC who were once again building up a big audience for the 'Top Gear' brand. Now located in the London offices of the BBC, with their airfield base secured for hosting their shows, they quite obviously had a bigger budget than we ever had and were doing brilliant things with it.

As a sideline, in 2003 Jeremy and Richard had been invited by Brand Events exhibition entrepreneur Chris Hughes to host a live motoring show called MPH 03, and I had been asked to join them. Performing around a dozen shows over four days at Earls Court in London, we set up a series of 'Top Gear' versus 'Fifth Gear' challenges that would be weaved in among all sorts of motoring mayhem and petrolhead banter. For Jeremy and me it was pretty much back to the old 'Top Gear' routine we used to do at the motor shows but now, at the same time, we had live action going on all around us. Richard, of course, easily adapted to the game – *and* the game of dropping in song lyrics – and, while we often used to forget what we were supposed to be doing next, we somehow shambled through show after show to riotous applause.

Andy Wilman was the show's director, so with him and Jeremy working together we were never short of new and innovative ways to entertain. For the next two years it evolved in an ever grander way, expanding to an extra four days at the Birmingham NEC for MPH 05. I would duel with the Stig, race 'Half Cars', see how fast I could accelerate across the exhibition hall, aiming straight at a concrete wall, try – and fail – to drive on two wheels and, best of all, play 'Car Football'! But there was also some breathtaking stunt driving, flying cars, dancing diggers, dancing dancers and stunning 3D sequences to wow the audience.

There was much talk of us taking the show on a world tour, but with the 'Top Gear' duo and James May becoming such a strong team on the television, I kind of knew my days were numbered. James would make his debut at MPH 06 and it seemed I would be put on the substitutes' bench as the three were set to take their bow – but then Richard suffered that bang on the head and I was back on the team for one final hurrah.

With the script now very much evolving around the 'Top Gear' theme, James and I would take it in turns to sit in a supermarket trolley and take the place of a ten-pin bowling ball launched off the front of Jeremy's Ford Mustang, while my part in one of their 'home build' specials was to hurtle across the arena in a rocket-propelled mobility scooter. Of course, not long after I left the show it *did* go on its world tour and, rebranded as Top Gear Live, it has entertained audiences in Ireland, South Africa, Australia, New Zealand, Hong Kong, Holland and Norway. It's also matured into a highly slick professional show with well-rehearsed lines, although there's still plenty of room for ad-libbed mischief.

Chris Hughes has always kept me ready and waiting in the wings and we did do a World Rally Show in Wales in 2006. I also presented my own 'Start Up' area in the Earls Court halls of the 2009 and '10 shows and finally got my trip overseas to host the stunt-driving action supporting the 2011 'Top Gear' extravaganza in South Africa. I'd always fancied being part of a rock band on tour and perhaps I was getting closer!

Back at 'Fifth Gear', with Dan's departure, we suddenly had new brooms making sweeping changes at the end of 2006, and I wasn't exactly the biggest fan of them. Sky TV's 'Soccer AM' presenter Tim Lovejoy was parachuted in to front the show, hosting it alongside Vicki, from the Ace Café in North London – hardly ideal for a programme based in Birmingham and something that stretched our limited resources. Once again I was told that the aim was to 'widen the audience' and thoughts of Julie Clive's arrival at 'Top Gear' brought on a bad dose of déjà vu. All I could do was get on with my own items and try to make them as good as I could, especially as I didn't seem to be wanted anywhere near the Café.

When Tim left after just one series, amid universal disapproval from the motoring world, but ostensibly because he had been offered a better job chasing David Beckham around America, Tom Ford took over his role. The channel, however, now seemed to be looking more for his humour than his excellent car knowledge.

It appeared that they were trying to take on 'Top Gear' but on a fraction of the budget, and without the unique talent of someone like Jeremy Clarkson. My view had always been to let 'Top Gear' do the fun and games that they do so well, while 'Fifth Gear' concentrated on being a real car show – with as much fun in it as possible. But what do I know?!

While Tom and Vicki persevered at the Café, I just got on with using up petrol and burning rubber. I'd always been a big motorbike fan and was on the roads as soon as I was 16, starting on a very old and unreliable Francis Barnett with a Villiers engine before graduating to a 125cc Yamaha on which I passed my motorbike test. Like so many, I never graduated to the bigger bikes I was now licensed to ride because, as soon as my 17th birthday had come, cars were the only way to go. However when, some 30 years later, I was asked if I had a bike licence for a 'Top Gear' item I soon found myself leaping on to the latest 900cc Triumph Triple without any sort of refresher course.

With a new taste for two wheels, I would borrow the occasional bike to blast about on for a week or two, and when Honda offered me some track action at Donington on their new CBR600RR for a 'Fifth Gear' item (yes, I know that's a lot of Rs), I jumped at the chance. One of the big things you just have to do if you want to earn any respect as a biker is to 'get your knee down', and this was my opportunity. If you sit still on a bike and try to get your knee anywhere near the road surface it seems like an impossible task. What you need is speed!

Led around the circuit by Aussie superbike star Dean Thomas, we gradually began to corner faster and faster and I started leaning over further and further, sticking my knee out as much as I could, desperate to get even the tiniest of marks on my shiny new knee-sliders! As the speeds began to increase, though, the concentration took over. Rolling into the corners faster and faster and then picking up the throttle to fire it out of them, I could keep to the pace Dean set in most places, but every time he left me behind down the Craner Curves. I'd simply never realised how strong the gyroscopic effect of the bike's wheels is at the higher speeds. The faster you go the more these forces try to make the bike stand upright, so to switch from the long right to the long left in the middle of these curves took a lot more physical effort to make the bike lean over than I had ever imagined.

Then, arcing through the long right of McLean's, what was that hitting my knee? I'd forgotten all about my mission, simply concentrating on lapping faster and faster, and there was my little knee-slider bouncing off the surface of the track. Next time round I made contact again, and this time pushed my knee down into the road, making sure there was more than a little scratch. By the end of the day I was doing it through the ultra-fast Old Hairpin as well, and I was like a Boy Scout with a new badge! Unfortunately I hadn't yet ridden with the camera and sound recorder in a rucksack on my back, to do the words that would go with the story, but now I was ready… and just then it began, ever so slightly, to drizzle with rain…

Well, all the outside shots had been of me going fast in the dry, so the words had to follow suit. I couldn't start by saying 'Oh dear, it's raining' because the viewers would all be watching me go past on a completely dry track. So off I went again, with the intention of re-creating my gradual transition to 'knee down' hero. I started, pretending it was my first few laps, then gradually got quicker – but the track was decidedly greasy! Of course, on a bike in the rain you try to keep it as upright as possible, but I'd now got to pretend I was getting my knee down, so I turned into Redgate Corner and leaned over as much as I dared. It all *felt* fairly stable so I began to say the words I'd rehearsed in my head. I was going to say '…and we have touchdown!' but, before I could even emit the 't' of 'touchdown' I'd got not just my knee down but my hip and my shoulder as well! Following behind, but inaudible to me, Dean had been screaming 'Don't open the throttle, don't open the throttle' – but I did. The back of the bike spun away from under me and I gracefully followed it down the road on my backside, having well and truly touched down!

As well as the extra shows that Channel Five pushed my way, my knowledge of the powerboat world once again dragged me back on to the water when my early motor racing mentor, Chris Witty, asked me to present his 'ProVee Offshore' racing series that FM Television were producing for Sky Sports. When, after a few fun-filled years, that folded due to the internal squabbling of the competitors – something that is a regular occurrence in this sport – I found myself moving on to do the same thing for the new Powerboat P1 series. With solid financial backing this looked like a series that really could prosper as a World Championship, but the financial crisis that began in 2007 took the wind out of its sails – or should that be the power out of its engines – and it is now a much smaller affair.

The Isle of Man production company Greenlight Television had been in charge of manning the cameras for Powerboat P1, which also went out on the Sky Sports package. Among many other things, Greenlight also produced the European coverage of the American Le Mans series, so when Lord Drayson wanted to film a documentary about his campaigning that very series in 2008, driving an Aston Martin run by my brother's company Barwell Motorsport, they were the obvious choice.

Lord Drayson had a long-held dream of racing at Le Mans but he had been born only having sight in one eye. Unfortunately the international rules under which Le Mans was run barred those with such monocular vision from entering. He was determined to prove it was no handicap, however, and get them to change the rule. With the American Le Mans series run to different regulations Drayson was welcomed by their promoters, and he entered his new GT2 Aston Martin Vantage in their championship. He also brought along Greenlight and me to create a 12-part documentary following his season entitled 'Licence to Le Mans' which went out on Sky Sports.

Flying back and forwards to America and hopping hither and thither across Europe for Powerboat P1 at the same time made it a busy year. With producer and director Rob Hurdman acting as soundman and Guy Hicks on camera it was a tight three-man crew that followed the Drayson entourage – but we did have some fun. Chasing a racing team from an early dawn arrival to midnight engine changes makes for a long day, although you are always very aware that your day isn't as long as that of the actual mechanics.

Over the course of the year I stayed on board the great *Queen Mary* liner that now serves as a Long Beach hotel, brought 16-year-old son Jack along on a ten-day road trip that took in the sights of New York, dined with motorbike legend Wayne Rainey at his Californian home, ate far too many chicken wings and drank too much beer. The season also provided us with a very dramatic insight into the life and times behind the scenes of a racing team on the road. With accidents, engine changes, heat, stress, tempers and tantrums it was all there. Lord Drayson coped with the high-speed traffic as well as anyone while his young co-driver, Jonny Cocker, established himself as one of the fastest GT racers on the grid.

The fact that in the middle of the season Lord Drayson was invited to join Gordon Brown's cabinet as Minister of State for Science and Innovation was just one other extra little story to cover. The most important one, though, was whether or not his performances would justify him challenging the FIA to change the rule for Le Mans and let him enter. They were – and they did!

With Le Mans now on his 2009 schedule we followed the Drayson team to both the Sebring 12 Hours and the Le Mans 24 Hour race itself to produce a two-part follow-up called 'Licence to Le Mans 2' – and I got to experience this epic six-day event from the other side of the fence. Well, a motorhome in the middle of one of the massive public campsites to be more exact, and if I ever thought I drank too much, I don't now!

Back at 'Fifth Gear' and, after three more series at the Ace Café, it was all change again. Motoring journalist Jonny Smith had already joined the team, adding his own unique and entertaining view of the motoring world to our mix, and then it was decided to abandon the Café and set up a new studio at the Millbrook Proving Ground where the show would now be fronted by Tom and 'shock jock' radio presenter Tim Shaw. Me? I just kept on driving Ferraris, Porsches, Maseratis, Audis, BMWs, Mercedes, Corvettes, Ford GTs, Aston Martins, Jaguars, Koenigseggs, Zondas and the ultimate appliance of science, the Bugatti Veyron. I also got scared stiff looping the loop in a stunt plane, checking out the Abu Dhabi Aero Grand Prix, and ventured *under* the surface of Lake Zurich in a Lotus Elise – well, a Rinspeed Squba to be more precise.

I did the Ilkley Trial in a sidecar outfit with Tom, and the same event a year later with Jonny in a Golf. I went back to Daytona Beach, boring Jonny with all my old stories, as we went behind the scenes for the 50th running of the Daytona 500, and upset Ferrari once again by ridiculing one of their great Supercar adventures. To show off the reliability of their new 599GTB Fiorano, they were driving two of them from Brazil to New York in a 'Panamerican 20,000 mile' challenge. Journalists and TV crews were invited to drive the cars for some of the legs of this monstrous journey through 16 different countries – and I got to do a bit in Bolivia. Little did I realise that, forced to run in a very controlled convoy, we would take half a day to crawl about 100 miles. As I said in the item, my Mum's Morris 1000 could have done it at that pace. It made for some stunning film and great photo opportunities but, as a driving challenge, it left a lot to be desired.

But the best of all these wonderful opportunities my life on television has brought me just has to have been the chance I was given to get back behind the wheel of a contemporary Grand Prix car – at the age of 53. Quite how James Woodroffe ever wangled it I'll never know but, when asked to head for the Williams Grand Prix headquarters in Grove to have a seat fitting in a Williams BMW FW26, it didn't need a second call!

The loose premise on which he was working was that we wanted to compare the new V10-engined BMW M5 with the V10 BMW-powered Grand Prix car. I guess it was as good an excuse as any, and with BMW very keen to help us make it happen who were we to argue? The challenge was to see if I could do four laps round Rockingham in the Formula One car before Vicki could complete three laps in the M5.

Getting behind the wheel of a current Formula One car is a virtually unheard-of opportunity these days so complex is the machinery. Just 24 very special drivers get to race one in a Grand Prix, while a similar number are allowed to do the odd test here and there, but to the outside world it's virtually a closed shop. Then reality bit. These are cars capable of more than 200mph. The G-forces would make a fighter pilot wince. And, most worrying of all, with a hand clutch and no room to move my right foot across to the left, I'd quickly have to master left-foot braking – something I'd only ever done briefly on rallies and in charity kart races. Would I be up to the job?

The car was started by a swarm of mechanics armed with laptops. The first surprise was that it wasn't the spitting, snarling monster I'd expected. It just sat there in neutral, purring away without a hint of vibration. To move off, though, you had to use the delicate little hand clutch and, with 800 horsepower to feed in with nerve-jangling fingers, I was convinced I was going to stall. But the second surprise was that the car hooked up benignly, and with the merest stroke of throttle I was cruising smoothly down the pit lane. Maybe this wasn't going to be so bad after all?

The nervous TV presenter worrying about looking daft vanished. The racing driver barged in. Full throttle... and then, quite literally, it was a blur. I don't actually remember what happened between the first blast of acceleration and thinking 'Brake now or it's all over!' I have no idea if it was at 16, 17 or 18,000rpm that I tugged the right paddle to change up. Grand Prix cars don't bother with rev counters any more. You just watch the lights on the steering wheel flash from yellow to red and then change. No clutch, no lifting of the throttle, no dead spots, just more violent acceleration. It was endless. It was magnificent... but the corners started rushing towards me at a frightening pace.

But how would I find the limit? On the slow stuff I could floor the throttle on the exit and the traction control would crackle into life to save me, while at medium speeds there were satisfying moments of opposite lock as the rear end wriggled under all that power. In the high-speed corners, however, as the aerodynamics drilled me into the ground, I was cornering at speeds I'd previously thought impossible, thinking 'What happens when it comes unstuck?'

Three laps done and I was beginning to get used to the sheer speed and acceleration, but the G-force had destroyed my neck muscles. It was an effort to keep my head up, I could feel my heart throbbing, I was finding it difficult even to blink. You simply cannot believe the forces put on your body, when you sit in your armchair thinking how easy it all looks. Gradually I found a groove and got to grips with the stunning brakes. At first I thought they weren't stopping me quickly enough, but a lifetime of pressing soft clutch pedals hadn't prepared my left leg for the effort demanded to get maximum braking – with discs glowing at up to 1,000° centigrade.

The long, fast, left-banked Turn 4 of the oval Rockingham Circuit was the big one. Pushing hard out of a second-gear hairpin that feeds you on to the oval track, the car feasted on gears: third, fourth, fifth, sixth, seventh! The corner that looked a long way off was suddenly on top of me. With the concrete walls right at the edge of the track there were few reference points to judge where to lift and where to turn. I found my left foot beginning to 'lean' on the brake pedal while the right foot was urging the car to go ever faster. Momentarily the left won the battle, but then the exit loomed and the right took back control… vision was still slightly blurred as my eyes tried to adapt to the speed… worse mid-corner as I could no longer stop my helmet falling on to the cockpit edge and picking up its vibrations.

Right up against the wall before braking for the chicane, the wailing engine was even louder as the sound bounced back off the concrete… I later found out I was doing 176mph! Up came the right foot and down went the left. Two tugs on the left paddle and the 'auto blip' eased me down a couple of gears. The car felt light and agile through the left-right-left complex. Full throttle again… lights… change gear… braking points becoming clearer… the brakes were now like hitting a wall… once again I was fully alive… all my life had been spent waiting for moments like this…

When Vicki's M5 suddenly loomed in front of me I'd almost forgotten about the challenge and was past her a good few corners before the end of our little race. We'd started by cruising side by side at 70mph and then flooring it as we crossed the line. With a helicopter catching the action, the visual difference between the performance of the fastest saloon car on the road and a Grand Prix machine was stunning.

Indeed, it had been so impressive that, the day after the item went out, one of my sons took a call from 'someone called Frank Williams' who asked me to ring him back. Convinced it was a wind-up from one of my mates, and not wanting to call on a mobile phone, I was going to wait till I got home. Before I could get there, however, Frank had found my mobile number. He'd been so impressed he'd simply wanted to thank me for making such a great piece of television that so well portrayed the awesome speed of a Grand Prix car. It's easy to understand why Sir Frank Williams is a much-loved man.

With the recession still biting hard and television revenues suffering as a result, our studio presentation at Millbrook lasted for just three series before budget restrictions not only moved us out but returned us to the half-hour format that we'd had for the first four years of 'Fifth Gear'. Tim and Tom departed for other projects, and for the spring of 2010 we were once again back to just four presenters. Somehow, I was still there, about to start my 25th consecutive year of hooning around in the name of entertainment – and I was still loving every minute of it!

CHAPTER 22

SO WHAT NEXT?

As you can probably imagine, 'retire' is not exactly a word that I'm particularly fond of – and not just because too many of my races ended with that classification! No, it's simply that I want to go on and on, doing more and more of what I already do. In fact, I promise 'retire' is a word I shall never use...

Hopefully there is still plenty more television work to come. 'Fifth Gear' is still going strong and recently I even made a couple of cameo appearances back on 'Top Gear'. Of course, I'm always well aware that, as fashions come and go, my face suddenly just might not fit any more – especially as it now has the odd wrinkle or two! Then there are the live events, where I love to get involved: the Autosport Show, MPH and Top Gear Live, which I have just returned from in South Africa. Then there are the corporate jobs hosting events and doing after-dinner talks to keep me busy the rest of the time.

I'm also now having a lot of fun blasting people round Thruxton in a BMW M3 with a DVD to record the experience. I've had passengers varying in age from 7 to 77 sitting alongside me, either in stony silence, or emitting hoots of laughter or screams of terror. My favourite comment so far was from a young boy who, as I flicked the car sideways at the first corner, yelled: 'Stuff Clarkson, you're the man!'

I had always rather fancied ending up inheriting Murray Walker's job behind the microphone, having been groomed as his protégé by the BBC in the early eighties, and I did commentate on the first three Grands Prix of 1991 for BSkyB before they lost the rights to cover it. However, the Grand Prix coverage then switched to ITV so I rather fell out of the loop.

When it comes to racing, it's been quite a while since I could classify myself as a professional driver – actually being paid to do what I most wanted to do! I know now, and probably knew way back then, that I was never anywhere near good enough to be a Moss, Clark, Senna or Schumacher, but trawling back through my career to write this book has reminded me that I wasn't that bad either. In fact, if you've read this far, you'll probably understand why I wanted to call it *So Nearly*, but I was told it would come across as being too negative. Yet I did come so close to so many things that could have completely changed my life. I hate the modern sporting mentality which dictates that 'finishing second you are the first loser'. I've had a brilliant life, despite more often than not just missing out on the top spot, whether it be in a race or in the chase for a drive, and I always like to remind myself that, while I might have been unluckier than a few, I've been luckier than millions.

Motivational speakers love to try and pump you up with stories like those of Olympic gold medallists dreaming of winning their race every day for four years, so that when they stand on the starting blocks they know they are going to win. What do they think the rest of the runners are dreaming about – coming second? Telling people that if you work hard and dedicate yourself to something then you'll get there in the end is the worst advice of all. There simply isn't enough room at the top for everyone who wants to get there. You not only need the hard work and dedication, you also need the natural talent *and* a large dose of good fortune!

And when I say good fortune, in motor racing I mean that in a financial way as well, because nowadays someone is going to have to pay out at least three or four million pounds on their protégé's racing before they are going to get anywhere near racing a Grand Prix car. I'd certainly never have made it in the modern world. Added to that is the stark fact that with motor racing getting ever safer, Grand Prix drivers are holding on to those prized 24 slots for longer and longer. As our sport reaches out to more countries, more brilliant young talents are being discovered, but very few will get that *big* chance.

While I look back and reflect on how I was one of those very fortunate few, and how I would have loved to have gone further and established myself as a full-time Grand Prix driver, I can console myself by the fact that the variety of racing I discovered outside that Formula One bubble gave me a greater wealth of experiences, although not, of course, the same financial wealth! And with the commercial pressures on the modern Formula One drivers preventing them from racing anything else, they can never hope to display their all-round talents in the way that Stirling Moss and Jim Clark did. By the time today's GP racers come to retire with their millions, races like Le Mans look far too dangerous to risk.

When I talk to my former team-mate Derek Bell, and friends of his like Brian Redman and David Hobbs, who all had brief Grand Prix careers but never drove for a full season, I am more envious of them than of any modern Grand Prix driver. They can recount tales of racing all over the world in Formula Two, Sportscars, CanAm cars, Indycars, Formula 5000 and even, in Hobbs's case, NASCAR. Theirs was never the monotonous tour of the same tracks every year. They raced at Montjuïc Park in Barcelona, the Targa Florio, the old Nürburgring and Spa circuits, frequent Le Mans and Daytona 24 Hour races, and other weird and wonderful racetracks the world over. They never had the fame and fortune of our Grand Prix heroes, but they enjoyed themselves immensely. I know I did some of the same, but I wanted more.

Of course, the other side of the coin is that by not going to those sorts of places means we are now racing in much safer times. Yet our sport will never be completely safe. I went through the pain of losing five of my team-mates in racing accidents. As well as Leigh Gaydos, Jo Gartner and Keith O'dor, my Japanese Toyota co-driver Hitoshi Ogawa was killed in a Formula 3000 race at Suzuka in 1992, while the very same year my great friend Ian Taylor, racing a Rover 216GTi for a bit of fun, was killed at Spa in an accident very similar to Keith's.

Just a year earlier, driving the 'celebrity' car, I had beaten Ian to win the round of the Rover Championship held at Thruxton. Ahead of a full grid of battling Rover 216s we had had as fierce a fight as any we'd ever had in Formula Ford or Formula Three, and I won by the thickness of the paint on my bumper. At least that time we were both able to laugh together afterwards! The days when I drive the BMW M3 are run by the racing school Ian created, and every time I go there, I spare a thought for my old mate...

Of course, while I might not want to retire, the day may eventually come when the sport retires me, so I am hugely grateful to Lord March for creating his awesome Goodwood Revival Meeting. It's the only racing I've done for the last three years, but it's some of the best racing I've ever enjoyed. As long as Lord March keeps inviting me, I'll keep going!

Having grown up clinging to the Goodwood railings my life has turned full circle, and I'm now able to visit something that's akin to a 'Star Trek' episode I once saw where a 'vacation planet' offered to re-create your dreams and allow you to live in them. When I walked into the very first meeting, back in 1998, lumps filled my throat and tears welled in my eyes. Here I was, about to drive the very cars that I had watched flashing past as a young boy, and everything inside the circuit looked just as it had done when I was there, back in the fifties and sixties.

To add to the nostalgic atmosphere there are Spitfires either looping the loop in the skies or parked up surrounded by actors waiting to 'Scramble'. There are spivs mingling with the crowd, offering dubious watches and ration books for sale. Dad's Army is on parade and Marilyn Monroe is always somewhere to be seen. The extent to which Lord March has succeeded is reflected by the many thousands of spectators who line the circuit and also join in with the nostalgic dress code, even though it is not a requirement for them.

For the first eight Revivals I was delighted to be asked to drive Chris Lunn's yellow Lister Jaguar, a 1958 sportscar that I'd watched the likes of Archie Scott-Brown hustle through the famous chicane. At that first meeting I raced it against a certain Stirling Moss, who was driving the actual Aston Martin DBR1 that I'd watched him win the Tourist Trophy in that same year. I really was now living in some sort of amazing time warp!

Although the Lister had become 'my' Goodwood car – after two thirds, one second and 'so nearly' a win – Chris then decided I was having too much fun and got behind the wheel himself. But, as well as the Lister, I've also been extremely fortunate to have raced in a variety of other saloons and sportscars, often sharing with their owners in the two-driver races – Jaguars of all shapes and sizes, an AC Cobra, a Chevrolet Corvette, the three-million-pound Project 212 Aston Martin, a Mini and even an ex-Jim Clark Lotus Cortina.

Even if the racing cars don't particularly excite you, you can take a wander back into post-war Britain at its finest. Linger at the champagne tent, marvel at the period funfair or wander the second-hand car lots and try to find your first family car. There's rock 'n' roll music filling the air and everybody, but everybody, is walking around with a smile on their faces.

In the drivers' lounge Stirling Moss now greets me like an old friend and, of course, Bell, Hobbs and Redman are all there, as well as many, many more heroes from the past. I'm still not really convinced I'm worthy enough even to be there! Stirling is just the nicest of men, and one of the most wonderful things I've found about being a 'face' on television is that many of *my* heroes still surprise me by actually knowing who I am.

Of all such occasions the one I will treasure the most is seeing George Harrison walking towards me at Goodwood – 'Hi Tiff, how are you?' – then turning to his wife, Olivia – 'Here, take a picture of me and Tiff!' We'd never met before and here was the nicest of all the Beatles greeting me like a long-lost friend and wanting a picture of *me*! How I would love a copy of that photo.

I've mixed and mingled with many other stars by becoming involved in both SPARKS and Variety Club events, mainly helping them to raise funds by playing in their golf days, and again it's great to discover how pleasant and down to earth so many of our sporting stars and entertainment icons can be. At a time when the word 'celebrity' is beginning to earn itself a bad reputation, I'm pleased there are still plenty with their feet firmly on the ground. Mind you, I do find it a bit surreal to wander into a golf club and nod a casual 'hello' to great actors like Robert Powell and Kevin Whately, sporting superstars like Steve Redgrave and Matthew Pinsent, and comedians of the calibre of

Jimmy Tarbuck and Tim Brooke-Taylor, who all give so much time to these great causes.

Helping these two charities is something that I find really rewarding. Patsy and I have been blessed with three very healthy boys and the joy that parenthood has given us is immeasurable. Anything we can do to help others have healthy children or ease the burden on those who have been less fortunate than us seems the very least we can do.

Indeed, while my life has been filled with what is, I readily admit, a very selfish Peter Pan style of existence, never wanting to grow up at all, rearing children for the next generation is the most important thing we're here to do. Fortunately for me, while I've been gallivanting around the world, Patsy has done all the hard work and played the major role in bringing up three sons of whom we are very proud. Without Patsy's support and encouragement I would never have gone on to achieve many of the things I did. When tricky decisions had to be made I knew she would always give me her honest opinion – even if sometimes it wasn't the one I wanted to hear! Worse still, her ideas more often than not turned out to be right in the end...

Bringing up children means making so many important decisions. I well remember the first time we started discussing what school Jack should go to and I suddenly realised that, for what felt like the first time in my life, I was having to be responsible for something terribly important: making a decision that would affect someone else's future.

About seven years ago we upped sticks again and moved into the countryside near Salisbury. Jack's now at university, and having gone from English to art to drama, film and animation is still not sure where he is heading. Harry and George have done us proud by earning places at a great grammar school, and who knows what they will end up doing. Harry does a bit of karting at the local track, but they all know that they're not going to be racing drivers. I mean, what are their chances of being 'unluckier than a few but luckier than millions'!

PHOTO APPENDIX

One of the hardest aspects of putting together this book was to source various photos from all corners of the world and then decide which ones to use. Having raced nearly 100 different cars and tested dozens more, it wasn't easy, but the final selection best represents the broad cross-section of machinery I have driven during my 41 seasons of racing to date.

As there were so many photos to squeeze into the four pictorial sections, I decided that best use of precious space required the captions to be brief – hence this appendix of further information. Wherever possible the narrative that follows gives credit to the photographers concerned, but sometimes it has been impossible to locate a source. So may I thank all the photographers who persevere, whatever the weather, to record the images we so enjoy – especially if they discover one of their great works in this book.

Page 65 – Chapter 3

- Great Uncle Sir Richard Fairey's Swordfish Biplane swoops in to cripple the *Bismarck*. Launched from the HMS *Ark Royal* aircraft carrier, two squadrons of Fairey Swordfish attacked the *Bismarck* on 26 May 1941 and one of their torpedoes crippled the great battleship's steering gear, thus rendering it immobile and making it a sitting target for the Royal Navy fleet. *Painting by Wes Lowe*
- Mum spent the war on the London stage dancing in productions like this one with Arthur Askey in 'Follow the Girls'. Just 16 when the Second World War started, she spent the duration living there and never once used an air-raid shelter. She met Dad during the

VE Day celebrations in London on 8 May 1945 and they married two years later.

- War over, Goodwood is the place to be and Dad is there competing in the first Members' Meeting, 13 August 1949. Having done a few sprints at Brooklands before the war in his Mum's Fiat, Dad finally got to race in his road-going Ford V8 Coupé and finished eighth – but by then the pressure of becoming a parent led to an early retirement from the sport.

Page 66 – Chapter 3

- Cool cowboy. No 'Play Station', no 'Toy Story', not even a television, so playtime was left to your imagination – and whatever fancy dress you could lay your hands on.
- With Mum and brother Michael – dressed smartly for Goodwood. The Brooklands tradition of 'the right crowd and no crowding' was still in evidence at Goodwood and dressing up to watch the great heroes of the day remained very much in vogue.
- On Tommy Sopwith's winning boat at the *Daily Express* Cowes Torquay race in 1961. Having driven her Morris 1000 as fast as she could, Mum and I made it to Torquay after the winners arrived – and she seems more than a little stressed as she looks on from the dockside steps as I join Dad and brother Michael on the boats.

Page 67 – Chapter 3

- A taste for four wheels – go-karting at Mallory Park in 1961. We only went to Mallory because Dad was running some powerboat races on the lake in another of John Webb's novel ideas. The go-karts were there just as a pay-as-you-go ride in the car park but they were all I wanted to do.
- Dad's *News of the World* powerboat in 1966. Along with Colin Mudie, Dad was commissioned to design this stunning offshore powerboat, which was powered by four massive Foden diesel engines. Built in Cowes using a fairly radical 'cold-moulded' wooden hull that created a type of monocoque construction, it was much admired but sadly caught fire and sank in only its second race.

- On the test bed! Having converted one of Dad's little water scooter designs to a sit-on-the-floor racing boat, my first job was to run-in the outboard engine. As it was water-cooled, we lowered the engine into a dustbin tied to a tree and kept filling it with cold water.
- The euphoria of the first test in 1968. Having run-in the engine, the next step was to get the boat on the water at a Chertsey gravel pit. Buzzing across the waves at only 40mph feels pretty fast, but more speed was now all I'd want for the rest of my life.

Page 68 – Chapters 3 and 4

- 'The Summer of '69' – learning to slide in Mum's Morris 1000! The only problem was trying to make her believe that it was perfectly normal for tyres to wear out within 2,000 miles.
- My first Formula Ford drive at Brands Hatch. A Lotus 51 was pretty outdated by this time but that's what the Motor Racing Stables racing school used and it felt like a Formula One Ferrari to me.
- In its 24 December 1970 issue, *Autosport* launched a competition to win a Lotus 69F – but what are the chances of actually winning a competition like that?
- *Autosport* magazine 1 April 1971, and this passport photo was the only one of me I could find when they wanted to announce the winner of their Lotus 69F.
- Ready for my public racing debut at Snetterton on 2 May 1971 with Jim Russell racing school mentor John Paine giving some last-minute advice. Having qualified ninth, I finished fifth and was in complete awe of the whole experience. *Mike Dixon photo*

Page 69 – Chapter 4

- My third race, 18 May 1971, and for the first time I'm ahead of Jim Russell's Belgian protégé Patrick Neve, but he beat me to the finish by half a second. I was still wearing my open-face helmet and goggles as the Les Leston emporium had yet to supply my new full-face helmet.

- Hair-raising to say the least – well 'big' hair was all the rage back then and once you took off your helmet it never looked quite right!
- Crashing down to earth – 25 July 1971. Having achieved a front-row grid position for the first time, my ninth race, at Snetterton, ended in the worst possible fashion. Having to avoid a car spinning in front of me at the high-speed Russell Corner, I was directed head-on into the earth bank on the exit at around 100mph...

Page 70 – Chapter 4
- Victory at last. A garland, a girl and the Cona Coffee trophy make it a great day to remember at Thruxton, 28 May 1972.
- DIY racing with Roy and the Anglia van, parked in the grassy Mallory paddock where we used to pitch the tent. No trucks, awnings, motorhomes and teams of mechanics back then. Where are you now, Roy?
- Changing gear ratios – again! Every week and often between practice and racing the Hewland gearbox would have to be pulled apart to change the ratios to seek that extra tenth or two. I can still smell the distinctive Hypoid 90 oil in my hands – and remember the gear ratios for each track.
- 'Sponsor needed'! Desperate for money, as far as I know I was the first to go for this direct approach.

Page 71 – Chapter 5
- Durex debut with the Elden Mk 10C in the televised Thruxton meeting of 16 November 1974. With Richard Morgan disappearing in his Crosslé 25F, the cameras stayed focused on this epic multi-car battle for second – which I won! Anyone got a tape of it?
- The awful Elden Mk 17. Using all of the track and a lot of the scenery, doing my utmost to stay on the pace, regularly shedding bits and pieces here and there in a car that just didn't want to know.
- Classic Formula Ford action. Leading in the Crosslé 25F at Mallory Park with Rad Dougall and Geoff Lees right in my wheel tracks. The date is 24 August 1975.

Page 72 – Chapter 5

- First race – first win! The Crosslé 25F at Brands Hatch on 13 July 1975. Leading all the way from pole position to chequered flag. Finally I had the car to truly show my talent.
- The 'High School of Hang Gliding' prepares for take-off! Having 'bought' but not actually paid for the car of my dreams, thanks to Chris Hiatt-Baker's generosity, I agreed to run the Crosslé with the name of Chris's latest Bristol-based venture emblazoned down the side.
- Champion at last – Brands Hatch 12 October 1975. The Townsend Thoresen Formula Ford Champion takes his lap of honour.

Page 137 – Chapter 5

- I move up to slicks and wings with the Formula Ford 2000 Hawke DL14 and big brother Michael takes over the magical Crosslé 25F at Thruxton, 4 April 1976.
- On the ragged edge in the Safir RJ05 Formula 3 through Snetterton's infamous Russell Corner, 19 September 1976. Taken just about flat-out in top gear, this used to be one of the most challenging corners in the country.
- The most promising young British driver of 1976 meets the 1976 British World Champion. Receiving the premier Grovewood Award from James Hunt.

Page 138 – Chapter 7

- Unipart Formula 3 debut on 6 March 1977 in the Dolomite-engined March 773. Fighting to hold off Geoff Lees in his Chevron B38 for third place – and failing!
- Formula 2 debut at Donington on 30 October 1977 in the Chevron-Hart B40; 13th place on the 13th lap of the 13th round of the European Championship – and my engine blows!
- Leaping over the Mountain at Cadwell Park, 25 June 1978, in the March 783 while chasing after the Ralt RT1 of Nelson Piquet, setting fastest lap and getting very close to spoiling his record-breaking run of consecutive wins. *Mike Dixon photo*

PHOTO APPENDIX   319

- The wins, however, would come to an end when, like me, Piquet was involved in the huge crash at the start of the British Grand Prix support race at Brands on 15 July 1978. We both made the re-start but he would be fourth with me, once again, right behind him in fifth. *LAT photo*

Page 139 – Chapters 7 and 8
- Sharing a row of the grid with Alain Prost at Dijon for a round of the European Championship, 4 June 1978 – but it wasn't the front row! As I struggled with the under-powered Dolomite engine, so did Prost with his Renault engine as the Toyota units dominated. We finished 10th and 11th.
- Formula 2 sensation in the Toleman March-BMW 782 at Hockenheim on 24 September 1978, heading for third in only my second Formula 2 drive – until the engine exploded in a ball of flame, allowing Manfred Winkelhock to take 'my' place. *LAT photo*
- Time to say goodbye to a Unipart Triumph TR7 and hello to my trusty Ford Capri. Leaving Unipart meant handing over my cherished company car to my replacement – a young Nigel Mansell. Having only earned just over £2,000 that year – when the UK average was more like £5,000 – splashing out £1,500 on a four-year-old Capri 1600 was a big investment.

Page 140 – Chapter 8
- Dream Formula One debut in the Durex Chevron B41 at Zolder – 1 April 1979. Exactly eight years after *Autosport* announced I'd won the Lotus, here I was in a Grand Prix car, finishing second on my first outing. *LAT photo*
- My first visit to Japan was to drive a Formula 2 March-BMW 792 for the Tokyo-based Le Mans Company. This was the first year of sliding-skirt ground effects and March had sent me out to help sort the new car. The race at Suzuka, on 14 May 1979, was only my third in Formula 2 and I finished fourth. *Photo by i-dea co., ltd (courtesy Ryuji Hirano)*
- Heading for the first corner of the Macau Grand Prix, 18 November

1979, chasing the Ralt RT4s of Kevin Cogan and Bob Earl in my outdated March 76B with Grand Prix drivers Riccardo Patrese, Derek Daly, Rupert Keegan and eventual race winner Geoff Lees all behind me. *Philip Newsome photo*

• Leading the last ever BMW County Championship race at Thruxton, 7 September 1980, ahead of eventual winner Andy Rouse and Martin Brundle. Having fought my way to the front I then dropped it exiting the 'complex' trying to make a break and fell back to sixth – the only consolation was a new lap record. *Chris Davies photo*

Page 141 – Chapter 1

• A Grand Prix driver at last! Making my debut at Zolder at the Belgian Grand Prix driving my Unipart Ensign N180 – 4 May 1980. *LAT photo*

• Qualifying 19th in the rain at Monte Carlo on the Thursday. *LAT photo*

• But failing to qualify in the dry on Saturday – 17 May 1980. *LAT photo*

Page 142 – Chapters 9 and 10

• Trying to impress Rory Byrne with my feedback while testing the Toleman TG280 at Silverstone on 26 February 1980. Struggling to get used to the Pirelli radial tyres, it was as tough a test as I'd ever had. Having learned his trade designing Royale Formula Ford cars, Rory would go into Formula One with Toleman and then Benetton, where he created Michael Schumacher's first World Championship car before following him to Ferrari.

• Le Mans debut driving the Ibec P6, 13 June 1981. I shared the car with Tony Trimmer and owner Ian Bracey, but gearbox failure would see us retire before the night was over. *LAT photo*

• The Aston Martin Nimrod at Spa on 5 September 1982. Having survived my 200mph accident at Le Mans, the Nimrod was repaired but engine failure soon put us out on our comeback. *LAT photo*

Page 143 – Chapters 10 and 11

- Daytona debut for the 24 Hour race in the Pepsi Challenger –
  5 February 1983. I partnered American superstars A.J. Foyt and
  Darrell Waltrip in the renamed Aston Martin Nimrod, but more
  engine woes soon put us out. *LAT photo*
- Turning Japanese in 1983 and making the headlines – if only I
  could read them. Keeping fit with Geoff Lees running round a
  Tokyo park in 30-degree plus temperatures and 80 per cent
  humidity certainly made for a good workout – after which Geoff's
  trainer recommended a cold beer!
- The Dome 83C with its 3.9-litre Ford-Cosworth DFV engine was a
  rough-and-ready device and no match for the Porsche 956 I should
  have been driving in Japan that year.

Page 144 – Chapters 9 and 11

- I finished second in the Selangor Grand Prix driving the Team
  Rothmans March-Toyota 79B – 30 November 1980. In a car entered by
  the Japanese Le Mans Company, I had a great scrap for the lead with
  Kiwi Steve Millen in his Marlboro Ralt but a clash of wheels allowed
  my Rothmans team-mate Graeme Lawrence through to win.
- Waiting for the start of the Macau Grand Prix in my Le Mans
  Company-entered Ralt-Toyota RT4, 21 November 1982. The race
  was a case of 'so near yet so far' as I chased Roberto Guerrero for
  the lead until a gut-wrenching gearbox failure ruined my hopes of
  victory. *Philip Newsome photo*
- In Japan in 1984 I drove Team Ikuzawa's JPS Ralt-Honda RT4 at
  Fuji on 12 August and Suzuka on 23 September, finishing sixth
  and eighth respectively. *Photo by i-dea co., ltd (courtesy Ryuji Hirano)*
- Again in 1984, sharing the Team Ikuzawa Dome 84C with James
  Weaver in the Japanese Endurance Championship. *LAT photo*

Page 177 – Chapters 1 to 22

- Patsy Rowles the young model in 1979, the perfect partner, and the
  beautiful bride; our wedding was on 17 December 1988 at St
  Andrew's Church, Cobham, Surrey.

Page 178 – Chapter 13

- My first Le Mans finish – EMKA Aston Martin with Steve O'Rourke and Nick Faure in 1983. *LAT photo*
- First top-ten finish at Le Mans – Kremer Porsche 956 with David Sutherland and Rusty French in 1984. *LAT photo*
- First laps leading Le Mans – EMKA Aston Martin with Steve O'Rourke and Nick Faure in 1985. *LAT photo*

Page 179 – Chapter 14

- Being chased by Jim Crawford as 'the two speedfiends' entertain in India driving Bob Fearnley's Formula Atlantic Chevron B45s in February 1985. I won the Bangalore Grand Prix and Jim won in Madras – and, sponsored by Vijay Mallya's United Breweries, fun was had by all! *LAT photo*
- Thundersports in South Africa in a Chevron B26, on the front row at the Cape Town track of Killarney in South Africa on 8 December 1985. I was racing at brother Michael's adopted home circuit just days after he succumbed to the dreaded cancer – a weekend of mixed emotions but retirement and no Hollywood finish.
- Thundersports in Britain, sharing Richard Piper's Texas Chevron B26 to win at Brands Hatch on 7 April 1985. *LAT photo*
- And I won again in his Texas CanAm March Chevrolet 847 at Thruxton on 31 August 1987, although this shot is actually at Brands where this beast of a machine made its debut on 28 June 1987.

Page 180 – Chapters 11, 12, 13 and 14

- Pressing on towards a podium finish with Austrian Jo Gartner in the Kremer Porsche 962 at Silverstone on 4 May 1986. Another last-minute one-off drive that brought a great result, but tragically it would be Jo's last race before he was killed at Le Mans just four weeks later. *LAT photo*
- Brother Chris about to make his racing debut in 1987 in his Formula First car – for which I had somehow become the guarantor for the hire-purchase deal. This is the type of car in

which I'd made my 'Top Gear' debut in the spring of that year. Despite showing plenty of promise, Chris's racing career wouldn't last long before he ran out of money.

- The Toyota boys at Le Mans – with my mate Eje Elgh. Swede Eje was Ronnie Peterson's protégé who I befriended when he contested the British Formula 3 Championship in 1977 and we would go on to be founder members of the Japanese 'gaijin' drivers club when we shared the Dome 83C in 1983. Great friends for many fun-filled days in Tokyo, we were both at Le Mans in 1987 for the Toyota factory team. *LAT photo*

- The Toyota crew get busy with the Dome 87C in the crowded Le Mans pit-lane, June 1987. *LAT photo*

Page 181 – Chapters 12 and 17

- Anything goes! My one and only run in a Dragster for an *Autosport* story at Long Marston, where my 9.23sec, 154mph run earned me the 'Best Time of the Day' award at the 'Run What Ya Brung' event on 30 October 1982. *LAT photo*

- TV stardom for 'Top Gear' driving one of Will Gollop's Metro 6R4s in the Rallycross Grand Prix at Brands Hatch on 11 December 1988. I made it through to fourth in the 10-car 'B Final' in what was surely the heyday of this dramatic form of motorsport. *LAT photo*

- Back on the water in a Formula One Powerboat for 'Top Gear Waterworld' driving Andy Elliot's boat at the Rother Valley Country Park on 21 June 1998. I'd sold my Junior Runabout to Andy 20 years earlier and he'd been the champion in it for the next four years! He went on to race on the international circuit and won two Formula One Grands Prix.

- I made it onto the 'chair' of four-times World Sidecar Champion Steve Webster's outfit both for *Autosport* in December 1989 at Brands Hatch, where this photo shows us rounding Druids Corner, and then again for the 'Top Gear' cameras at Cadwell Park the following spring. Exhilarating and scary are the two words that come to mind! *Jeff Bloxham photo*

Page 182 – Chapters 14 and 15

- Saab racing in 1987, driving for the Butler family's Kentish Saab dealership. This was the most unlikely car I would ever race but there was money to be earned, a road car on loan to me, a lot of fun, six wins *and* Damon Hill as a one-off team-mate!
- Employed by Porsche to demonstrate the competitiveness of its new 944 Turbo against the ever-popular 911s in 1988 – a much tougher task than I had imagined. Four wins came my way but, more importantly, so did a Porsche 962 drive. *John Colley photo*
- It was an honour to join forces with Le Mans legend Derek Bell for Porsche Cars Great Britain. Derek is just two days short of being ten years older than me and I have always followed his career with great interest – and while he's still racing I keep thinking I still have at least ten years to go! *LAT photo*
- Derek and I made our Porsche 962 debut at Silverstone on 8 May 1988 and took an encouraging fourth place – the best Porsche placing but we were beaten by two Mercedes and a Jaguar. *LAT photo*

Page 183 – Chapter 15

- Having finally made it into a top Porsche drive, my constant nemesis was the brilliant Bob Wollek, who was one of the fastest of all Porsche drivers over three decades of endurance racing. The French star won Daytona four times but frustratingly never won Le Mans in 30 attempts. Tragically he was killed cycling to his hotel from Sebring in 2001. Doubtless James Weaver is about to embarrass me yet again with one of our tales of trouble sharing the Team Ikuzawa Dome 84C in Japan. *LAT photo*
- The Richard Lloyd Racing Porsche 962 was the car that Derek Bell and I would share for the full 1989 World Sports Prototype Championship. Built in-house by the team with aerodynamics by Peter Stevens, it looked fast but failed to live up to our expectations. *LAT photo*
- At Le Mans we dragged the Porsche from a lowly 21st on the grid up to seventh with just two hours to go when a fuel leak turned it into a ball of fire. Fortunately I hopped out unscathed.

Page 184 – Chapter 16

- The Alpha boys – Anthony Reid, David Sears and me – on parade at Le Mans on 16 June 1990. Despite our pensive expressions, the drivers' parade on the Saturday morning is generally a lot of fun and something to take your mind off the task ahead.
- Pressing on in our Porsche 962. *LAT photo*
- David, Anthony and me on the podium, after we'd finished third in the Le Mans 24 Hour race, 17 June 1990, still trying to take in just what we had achieved with such a small team – and simply loving the occasion. This would be the last time the famous balcony would be used before the evocative pits complex would be bulldozed to make way for the modern world – Patsy is at far right.

Page 249 – Chapters 12 and 17

- Is it me or is it Nigel Mansell? Renault France decided they wanted to make a television commercial recreating the famous Mansell versus Senna duel down the straight at Estoril during the 1991 Portuguese Grand Prix. With my racing and filming background Williams put me forward for the job and thus I became a Grand Prix driver again!
- 'Top Gear' makes the cover of *Radio Times*, 8–14 May 1993. As the programme soared in the ratings we became front-page news. Jeremy Clarkson, Chris Goffey, Michele Newman, me, Quentin Willson, Tony Mason and Janet Trewin all try to squeeze into the smallest of cars.
- Driving in my dreams. Filming stories for 'Top Gear' gave me opportunities that very few are privileged to experience, such as driving Stirling Moss's 1955 Mille Miglia-winning Mercedes-Benz 300SLR (seen with my silver-haired producer Ken Pollock, holding clipboard) and Graham Hill's 1967 Lotus 49 (producer Chris Richards looks on).

Page 250 – Chapters 17, 18 and 19

- Forza Ferrari! On the cover of the June 1996 edition of *Top Gear* magazine, driving Alain Prost's 1990 Ferrari 641/2 alongside

Jeremy Clarkson in the new F50. Another dream world experience! *Simon Childs photo*

- The wildest car I ever raced: the Jaguar XJR15 at Monaco on 12 May 1991. These 450bhp, 6-litre beasts had little aerodynamic downforce and were hard to handle – and quickly wore out both their tyres and their drivers. The three-race Jaguar Sport Intercontinental Challenge must have been the most expensive one-make series ever!

- Last Le Mans in the legendary Porsche 962 with Derek Bell and his son Justin, 20–21 June 1992. The ADA-prepared machine was no longer a front-running proposition but the three of us nevertheless soaked up the simple joy of racing such an iconic machine just one more time. *LAT photo*

- It's all about to kick off at Donington! Nigel Mansell looms large in my mirrors while Steve Soper keeps a watching brief – 31 October 1993. *LAT photo*

Page 251 – Chapter 18

- Splashing through the Lombard RAC Rally with Tina Thörner in a Group N Ford Sierra Cosworth, November 1992. Trying to adapt to the whole new world of rallying by entering this World Championship event proved a steep learning curve but we finished a respectable 30th overall and seventh in class. *LAT photo*

- Sideways in a Mini! Ian Bond hangs on in the passenger seat as I sort things out on the Charringtons RAC Historic Rally, 28 March 1993. Having a complete blast in consistent dry conditions, playing at being Paddy Hopkirk in a 1960s Mini Cooper. *Chris Harvey photo*

- Surviving in the snow with Brian Hardie in our Skoda Felicia on the treacherous Network Q RAC Rally, November 1996. This was the most terrifying event of my career: sheet ice, no studs, no 'winter' tyres. Even the regulars didn't like this one but we made it to the finish – a magnificent 53rd out of 182 starters. *Tony Large photo*

Page 252 – Chapter 19

- Presenting the Lister Storm to the Toon Army at Newcastle United's St James's Park stadium, January 1996. Kenneth Acheson, me and Geoff Lees wave to the fans. Meeting chairman Sir John Hall and manager Kevin Keegan was all part of a fun trip to present ourselves to the footballing world.
- Pit stop action at Brands Hatch, 8 September 1996, as I take over the Lister Storm from Geoff Lees. By now the car was right on the pace and we were battling for second with the fastest of the McLaren F1s but trailing the new GT1 Porsche, a car that would change the face of GT racing. *LAT photo*
- My last Le Mans. Driving the GTL Lister Storm, 14 June 1997. Having taken over from Geoff Lees, sadly all I got was just a single stint in the race before George Fouché took over and stuck it in the wall! *LAT photo*

Page 253 – Chapters 19 and 21

- Flame-throwing towards a hat-trick of British GT wins in a Lister Storm in 2000. Having won at Donington on 2 June partnering David Warnock in his Lister Storm, I switched over to Dave Clark's car to win at Spa-Francorchamps on 24 September and then win again at Silverstone on 8 October – when this photo was taken. *LAT photo (Kevin Wood)*
- Spraying the champagne on the podium with Dave Clark, Silverstone, 8 October 2000. Normally I keep the bottle to drink it but with the hat-trick of wins there was cause for a little extra celebration! *LAT photo*
- 'Fifth Gear' is go! Vicki Butler-Henderson, Adrian Simpson, Quentin Willson and me – April 2002.

Page 254 – Chapter 21

- Back in a Grand Prix car! Blasting a Williams-BMW FW26 past the Rockingham walls at 176mph for the 'Fifth Gear' cameras, 22 May 2005. Very, very few get such an opportunity – and even fewer 53-year-olds!

- Hamming it up on stage with James May and Jeremy Clarkson at MPH 06 – November 2006. Having linked up with Jeremy and Richard Hammond to appear in MPHs 03, 04 and 05, I thought my fun was over when the inevitable joining of the 'Top Gear' trio threatened – but then Richard had a 'small' accident and I was back for one more time.
- Taking my rocket-powered mobility scooter for a test drive at MPH 06. They do get to drive some odd things on 'Top Gear' nowadays – on 'Fifth Gear' we stick to cars!

Page 255 – Chapters 19, 21 and 22

- Back at Spa driving Tom Alexander's GT3 Aston Martin DBRS9, on 29 July 2006. Three races back in the thick of European racing action showed the pace was still there as I qualified third on the 42-car grid. Unfortunately we were unable to start after I aquaplaned off the circuit in pouring rain during the earlier race and had a sizeable accident.
- Having fun in a Subaru with John Barrowman for 'Fifth Gear' – before he crashed. Putting celebrities behind the wheel has become a popular theme in recent years but with it comes the ever-present risk of over-confidence. Barrowman displayed a great deal of talent behind the wheel of the Group N Subaru Impreza but, unfortunately, the talent ran out...
- Glorious Goodwood! Leading the Sussex Trophy field into Madgwick, driving Chris Lunn's 1958 Lister-Jaguar. I raced this very original and very beautiful car, resplendent in its original Ecurie Belge colours, in the first Goodwood Revival in 1998 and the following nine meetings, but then Chris decided I was having too much fun and wanted to have a go himself. *John Colley photo*
- Taking a guest for a ride at Thruxton in a BMW M3 – what a way to earn a living. Starting in 2010, I now offer the 'Tiff Experience' at my local track and it has proved to be popular. *Pete Gibson photo*

Page 256
- With Patsy, dressed up for the Goodwood Ball, 1 September 2007.
- Happy days – the family having fun on holiday at Sharm el Sheikh, July 2005, without a shark in sight.
- Jack, Harry and George, growing up fast! From 2000 to 2009 the time simply flew by – and haven't they grown?

INDEX